The Powerful Women
of Outremer

The Powerful Women of Outremer

Forgotten Heroines of the Crusader States

Helena P Schrader

PEN & SWORD
HISTORY

First published in Great Britain in 2024 by
Pen & Sword History
An imprint of Pen & Sword Books Limited
Yorkshire – Philadelphia

Copyright © Helena P Schrader 2024

ISBN 978 1 52678 755 2

The right of Helena P Schrader to be identified as
Author of this Work has been asserted by him in accordance
with the Copyright, Designs and Patents Act 1988.

A CIP catalogue record for this book is
available from the British Library

Typeset by Mac Style
Printed in the UK by CPI Group (UK) Ltd, Croydon, CR0 4YY.

Pen & Sword Books Limited incorporates the imprints of After
the Battle, Atlas, Archaeology, Aviation, Discovery, Family History,
Fiction, History, Maritime, Military, Military Classics, Politics,
Select, Transport, True Crime, Air World, Frontline Publishing, Leo
Cooper, Remember When, Seaforth Publishing, The Praetorian Press,
Wharncliffe Local History, Wharncliffe Transport, Wharncliffe True
Crime and White Owl.

For a complete list of Pen & Sword titles please contact

PEN & SWORD BOOKS LIMITED
47 Church Street, Barnsley, South Yorkshire, S70 2AS, England
E-mail: enquiries@pen-and-sword.co.uk
Website: www.pen-and-sword.co.uk
or
PEN AND SWORD BOOKS
1950 Lawrence Rd, Havertown, PA 19083, USA
E-mail: Uspen-and-sword@casematepublishers.com
Website: www.penandswordbooks.com

Table of Contents

Introduction

The *Powerful Women of Outremer* challenges two of the most persistent – and egregious – myths about the Middle Ages. First, that the crusader states were fragile, apartheid-like colonial societies established by barbarous warriors intent on genocide and destroying the cultures around them. Second, that women in the Middle Ages were mere chattels without power or self-determination and subject to pervasive misogyny. As a rigorous examination of the historical record demonstrates persuasively, neither myth is true.

The crusader states, known collectively as 'Outremer' (i.e., 'Beyond the Sea'), were political entities established in the Levant in the wake of the First and Third crusades. They were multicultural societies in which different ethnic and religious groups lived harmoniously together for nearly 200 years, despite periodic violent clashes with the neighbouring Islamic world that we have come to call 'the crusades'.

The native population in these states, composed predominantly of Orthodox Christians, experienced an economic boom and religious renaissance for almost 200 years following the re-establishment of Christian control over the region in 1099. The affluence and power of the native inhabitants found expression in the restoration and establishment of multiple Orthodox monasteries, the construction of hundreds of Orthodox churches and the widespread building of commercial and domestic structures for the native population. Native Christians were landowners, officeholders and patrons of the arts and formed the backbone of the bureaucracy as well as the bulk of the fighting forces in the crusader states. Meanwhile, Jews fleeing rising anti-Semitism in Western Europe, immigrated to the Latin states in the Holy Land, where they experienced no persecution. As a result, Acre developed into a thriving centre of Talmudic study. At the same time, the minority Muslim population remained free to practise their religion in public, build mosques and make pilgrimages to Mecca (Hajj).

The entire population (Latin, Orthodox, Jewish, Samaritan, Shia and Sunni) profited from the intensive investment in infrastructure undertaken by the ruling Latin elites. Crusader-era aqueducts, urban sewage systems, rural irrigation, terracing and road networks have all been identified by archaeological surveys. Irrigation reversed the encroaching desertification of the previous centuries, and under the 'Franks' (as the Latin Christians were collectively called, regardless of their country of origin), trade skyrocketed. Goods from China, Ethiopia, Arabia and India passed through the ports of the crusader states on their way to London, Paris, Cologne, Lisbon, Barcelona and the trading centres of the Italian peninsula such as Genoa, Pisa and Venice. Meanwhile, under Frankish rule, domestic industries such as industrial-scale sugar manufacturing and the mass production of manuscripts and icons developed in the Christian states of the Levant.

Sitting at the interface of the Byzantine, Turkish, Arab and Western European spheres of influence, Outremer became a hotbed of cross-cultural and technological exchange. A hybrid culture drawn from these diverse traditions and reflected in the art, architecture, institutions and military tactics evolved. The inhabitants of these unique multicultural, highly urbanised political entities were diverse and mostly polyglot and tolerant. At the apex of this society, a feudal elite notorious for its wealth and love of luxury ruled. It was composed of politically savvy, diplomatically adept, well-educated and multilingual men – and women.

Western European women from the tenth to thirteenth centuries, throughout the era of the crusades, enjoyed a period of exceptional power and self-determination. It proved to be short-lived. By the fourteenth and fifteenth centuries, women's status and opportunities had already begun to deteriorate. In subsequent eras – the Renaissance, Enlightenment, and Industrial Revolution – women became disenfranchised, increasingly demeaned, restricted and discounted. Women would not again attain a level of empowerment comparable to that of the eleventh and twelfth centuries until the early twentieth century.

This is not to say that women in the era of the crusades enjoyed full equality with men; they did not. Nor does it mean that no one in mediaeval society expressed misogynous sentiments; many did. The same, however, is true for the early twenty-first century. Unfortunately, there is a tendency among feminist historians to focus on the limitations and restrictions faced by women rather than the possibilities open to them. In contrast, *The Powerful Women of Outremer* emphasises what women in this time and place are known to have *done*. Against this record of action and influence, the misogynous commentary of individual mediaeval clerics is as irrelevant as the Facebook whining and tweets of early twenty-first century 'incels'.

That said, when writing about people who lived some 700 to 900 years ago, we depend on the contemporary chronicles, histories, charters, deeds, letters, literary works and other objects from the historical record combined with the evidence of art and archaeology to reconstruct events. We know little about the people who did not find their way into the historical record. Inevitably, this work has an unavoidable bias in favour of the fate of women from the literate, ruling class.

Fortunately, precisely because women played a prominent role in Outremer, their deeds commanded a place in the contemporary Latin, Old French, Greek, Syriac and Armenian sources. Only one source of information is eloquently silent about them: the Arab chronicles, which depict the crusades from the Muslim perspective. While Arab documents usually enrich our understanding of the people and events in the Near East of this era, they conspicuously slight the women rulers and powerbrokers of Outremer, drawing a literary veil across their faces. As one of the leading crusades historians put it: 'The Moslem world was clearly shocked by the degree of social freedom which Western women enjoyed and reacted to women with political power much as misogynist dons did to the first generation of women undergraduates, by affecting not to notice them'.[1]

Yet, while contemporary Christian sources were not reluctant to record and discuss noteworthy actions taken by women in the crusader states, modern historians have tended to neglect them. This is largely due to the modern obsession with the military expeditions to the Holy Land, i.e., the crusades, at the expense of the political, social and economic history of the crusader states. While it is true that women in this era rarely took an active part on the battlefield, that does not mean they did not contribute to the defence, survival and prosperity of the states in which they lived.

On the contrary, militarised states and states in dangerous geopolitical situations generally delegate a larger share of the non-military burden to women precisely because the men are called to arms and absent much of the time. This was as true in ancient Sparta as it was in WWII Britain. The crusader states were no exception. The laws that evolved reflected a need to ensure the maximum number of fighting men were available to defend the realm; a by-product of that concern was a willingness to allow women to fulfil other functions.

The Powerful Women of Outremer has not been written for experts, who will find little new here, but rather for hobby historians and students still in the early stages of exploring the exceptional world of the Middle Ages. The book does not pretend to uncover new evidence or contribute to scholarly debates but instead pulls together information scattered throughout other works. It seeks to highlight the position and deeds of women that have been detailed in primary sources yet obscured by the prevailing contemporary emphasis on the era's military history. Rather than put forth new, revolutionary theses on the status of women, it attempts simply to collect in a single volume a summary of the many known contributions of women to the establishment, prosperity and defence of the Christian states in the Eastern Mediterranean in the twelfth and thirteenth centuries.

In doing so, it nevertheless breaks new ground since no comparable book has been published on the topic to date. Existing literature is overwhelmingly skewed towards discussions of women's relationships to and participation in the military expeditions of the crusades rather than their position in the crusader states.

The Powerful Women of Outremer is divided into three sections. First, a narrative history of the crusader states organised around the women at the apogee of society, the queens. It highlights the role of women in the establishment, development, decline and end of the crusader states while inevitably spotlighting the ruling elite who found their way into contemporary accounts. A chronology at the start of the book will, hopefully, help readers unfamiliar with the history of the Latin East to put the events described into a broader context.

Second, the role of women is examined thematically. This section opens with a comparatively lengthy review of women's support for and participation in the various crusades before turning to a description of the women of Outremer proper. The topical description of women in the crusader states starts with an overview of who these women were and where they came from, followed by an examination of their legal status, their political and economic functions, their contributions to the defence of the Latin East, and finally, a look at their fate in defeat and captivity. Throughout this section, an attempt was made to include information about women from the middle and lower classes to the extent we can infer anything relevant about their lives from existing archaeological and historical sources.

Finally, the book concludes with a series of short biographies highlighting the lives of some of the most influential women in the history of the crusader states – not all of whom were queens. A degree of overlap between these biographies and examples used to support the earlier text is unavoidable; I apologise and hope the duplication is not excessive.

Throughout this volume, some anachronistic terms are consciously employed. For example, contemporaries never used the terms 'crusades' or 'crusaders'. Instead, people 'took the cross', embarked on 'armed pilgrimages', 'fought for Christ' and the 'Holy Land', etc. Certainly, no one in the twelfth and thirteenth centuries numbered some – but not all – of the larger military expeditions. Indeed, no one considered military campaigns condemned by the pope (such as the attack on Constantinople in 1203–1204 or Emperor Frederick II's self-serving expedition to Jerusalem in 1228) comparable to the arduous mobile warfare of 1097–1099, which resulted in the restoration of Christian control over Jerusalem. Yet, for the sake of clarity, my text does refer anachronistically to the First, Second, Third, etc., Crusades.

Likewise, although the emperor in Constantinople believed he was a 'Roman' emperor and his subjects called themselves 'Romans', using such terminology today risks confusing modern readers. Therefore, throughout the text, the Empire ruled from Constantinople is referred to as the Byzantine Empire and its inhabitants as Byzantines. On the other hand, the terms 'Saracens' and 'Franks' are convenient contemporary terms that have been adopted, albeit slightly adapted. In the crusader era, the term 'Saracen' referred to all 'Easterners', regardless of race, language or religion. In this book, the term's meaning has been narrowed for clarity to mean only the Muslim elements in the population of the Near East, regardless of whether they were Turkish, Arab, Bedouin, Berber, etc. Similarly, the term 'Franks', widely used by the Saracens and Byzantines of the crusader era to refer to all 'Latin Christians', is used in this volume to refer only to the Latin Christians living in Outremer. The crusaders and other transients in the region are described by their linguistic (e.g., French, English, German, Italian, etc.) or institutional (e.g., Templar, Hospitaller, Franciscan, etc.) identity.

List of Illustrations

Chronology

Year	Month	Event
ca. 33	Passover	Jesus of Nazareth crucified in Jerusalem; start of Christian veneration of the sites of his crucifixion and burial in Jerusalem.
70		Destruction of the Second Temple.
135–136		Expulsion of the Jewish and Christian population from Jerusalem; Jerusalem renamed Aelia Capitolina and paganised; a temple to Venus is built on the site of the crucifixion and resurrection.
326		Empress Helena, mother of Constantine the Great, finds what is believed to be the tomb of Christ.
335		Construction of a great basilica to mark the site of Christ's tomb begins; this church is henceforth known as the Church of the Holy Sepulchre.
613		Muhammed begins teaching his new religion in Mecca on the Arabian Peninsula.
614		A Persian army besieges Jerusalem, which falls after twenty-one days; slaughter of 26,500 Christians and enslavement of ca. 35,000 more; Church of the Holy Sepulchre utterly destroyed.
629		Emperor Herakleios regains control of Jerusalem; resettlement and reconstruction of the Church of the Holy Sepulchre begins; Muhammed, after defeating his enemies in armed conflict, returns on 11 December with his army from Medina where he was in exile.
632	June	Muhammed dies.

Year	Month	Event
634–644		Muslim conquests of Egypt, Libya, Persia and Syria.
637		Muslim forces under Caliph Umar the Great lay siege to Jerusalem; the city falls after a year.
649		First Arab attacks on Cyprus.
655		Muslims destroy the Byzantine fleet in a naval engagement.
656–661		War breaks out between Muslim factions resulting in the split of Islam into Shia and Sunni divisions.
678		First Muslim siege of Constantinople.
688		Muslim troops withdrawn from Cyprus and the island is required to pay tribute to both Constantinople and the caliphate in Baghdad.
698		Christian city of Carthage falls to Muslim forces.
711–713		Muslim conquest of much of the Iberian Peninsula.
713		Corsica falls to Muslim forces.
717		Second Muslim siege of Constantinople.
732	10 October	Invading Muslim forces are defeated by the Franks under Charles Martel at the Battle of Tours.
746		Byzantine forces regain control of Armenia and Syria.
768–814		Reign of Charlemagne in Europe.
ca. 825		Muslim conquest of Crete.
827–902		Muslim conquest of Sicily.
837		Muslim forces raid the Italian peninsula.
846		Muslim raiders sack Rome, including St Peter's Cathedral.
853		Byzantine raids in Egypt.
878		Egyptian forces under Shia leader Ahmad ibn Tulun capture Jerusalem from the Abbasid caliphate.
888		Muslims establish a base in Provence for raiding throughout the region.

Year	Month	Event
904		Sunni Abbasids regain control of Jerusalem.
961		Byzantines regain control of Crete.
969		Fatimids (Shia Muslims) conquer Jerusalem from the Abbasids a second time; establish Fatimid caliphate in Cairo.
965		Byzantines re-establish a presence on Cyprus.
997		Muslim raiders pillage the Cathedral of Santiago de Compostela in Northern Spain.
1009		Fatimid caliph al-Hakim orders the destruction of all churches and synagogues in his realm; destruction includes the Church of the Holy Sepulchre.
1030		Fatimid caliph Ali az-Zahir authorises the rebuilding of a church on the site of Christ's tomb; the second Church of the Holy Sepulchre is built with funding from Byzantium.
1034		Pisans launch a raid against Muslim North Africa.
1061		Norman conquest of Sicily begins.
1066	14 October	Battle of Hastings; Normans establish their rule in England.
1071	26 August	Seljuks, recent converts to Islam, decisively defeat the Byzantines at the Battle of Manzikert; Normans end Byzantine rule in Italy with the capture of Bari.
1073		Seljuks under Emir Atsiz ibn Uvaq capture Jerusalem from the Fatimids.
1074		Pope Gregory VII proposes a campaign to liberate Jerusalem and assist the Eastern Roman Empire against the Turks.
1077		Jerusalem rebels against Emir Atsiz while he is fighting in Egypt; on his return he massacres the population.
1081		Norman invasion of Greece.
1085		Alfonso VI, King of Castile, expels the Muslims from Toledo.

Year	Month	Event
1086		Christian Antioch falls to the Seljuks.
1087		Joint Pisan, Genoese, Roman and Amalfi forces destroy one of the main bases for Arab raiding and piracy in what is now Tunisia.
1095	November	Council of Clermont: Pope Urban II calls for fighting men from the West to go to the assistance of the beleaguered Eastern Roman Empire and liberate Jerusalem from Muslim rule.
1096		Crusading enthusiasm results in massacres of Jews in many cities;
	Spring	The 'Peoples' Crusade' departs from Western Europe;
	August	Main crusade under the papal legate Adhemar departs Western Europe for Constantinople; 'Peoples' Crusade' crosses the Bosphorus and enters Turkish-held territory;
	September–October	Turks obliterate the 'Peoples' Crusade' led by Peter the Hermit;
		Contingents of the main crusade begin arriving in Constantinople.
1097	19 June	Crusaders in cooperation with the Byzantines recapture Nicaea;
	1 July	Crusaders defeat Turks at the Battle of Dorylaeum;
	21 October	Crusaders begin siege of Muslim-controlled Antioch.
1098	March	Baldwin of Boulogne becomes Count of Edessa;
	3 June	Antioch falls to the Crusaders;
	August	The Fatimids recapture Jerusalem.
1099	15 July	Crusaders capture Jerusalem;
	22 July	Godfrey de Bouillon elected 'Protector of the Holy Sepulchre';
	August	Crusaders defeat an Egyptian army at Ascalon.

Year	Month	Event
1100	18 July	Death of Godfrey de Bouillon;
	20 August	Franks capture Haifa with Venetian assistance;
	25 December	Baldwin de Boulogne crowned king of Jerusalem in the Church of the Nativity, Bethlehem.
1101	29 April	Arsuf surrenders to Franks and Genoese; population spared;
	17 May	Franks capture Caesarea with Genoese support; population slaughtered;
	August-7 September	Second wave of crusaders wiped out by Turks in Asia Minor;
		Baldwin I defeats the invading Egyptian army at the Battle of Ramla.
1102	April	Raymond of Toulouse defeats Muslim forces from Damascus and Homs near Tortosa;
	27 May	Baldwin defeats Egyptians at Jaffa;
		Franks capture Tortosa and Jubail with Genoese assistance.
1104	7-8 May	Defeat of combined Frankish army at the Battle of Harran;
	26 May	Capture of Acre by Frankish forces with Genoese assistance.
1105	28 February	Raymond de Toulouse dies while besieging Tripoli;
	27 August	Franks defeat another Egyptian army at the second Battle of Ramla.
1108	September	Prince Bohemond of Antioch acknowledges Byzantine suzerainty over Antioch.
1109	26 June	Tripoli surrenders to the Franks; Genoese and Provencal support decisive; population spared;
		County of Tripoli established.

Year	Month	Event
1110	13 May	Beirut falls to the Franks with Genoese and Pisan support;
	5 December	Sidon surrenders to the Franks, the latter supported by a Norwegian fleet under King Sigurd; population spared.
1113	15 February	The Hospitallers established as an independent order by Pope Paschal II;
		Frankish expansion to the Jordan halted by defeat of Baldwin II at Sinnabra.
1114		Earliest date for the founding of the Knights Templar.
1118	2 April	Death of Baldwin I;
	14 April	Consecration of Baldwin de Bourcq as Baldwin II;
	25 December	Coronation of Baldwin and his Armenian wife Morphia as king and queen of Jerusalem.
1119	28 June	Defeat of Frankish army under the prince of Antioch at the 'Field of Blood'.
1123	18 April	Baldwin II captured by Balak in Edessa;
	May	Venetian fleet (120 strong) destroys the Fatimid navy; Franks defeat Egyptian army assault on Jaffa;
		Venetians then join the siege of Tyre, providing a blockade by sea.
1124	7 July	Surrender of Tyre to the Franks/Venetians, population spared;
	24 August	Release of Baldwin II;
	October	Baldwin lays siege to Aleppo.
1125	January	Siege of Aleppo abandoned;
	11 June	King Baldwin defeats a coalition of Turkish forces at Battle of Azaz.
1127	September	Imad al-Din Zengi appointed governor of Mosul.

Year	Month	Event
1128	June	Zengi takes over Aleppo.
1129	January	Papal recognition of the Templars; Templar rule drawn up at the Council of Troyes (Champagne);
	2 June	Marriage of Fulk d'Anjou to Melisende of Jerusalem;
	November-December	Baldwin II and Fulk besiege but fail to capture Damascus.
1131	21 August	Death of Baldwin II;
		King Fulk and Queen Melisende ascend to the throne, ruling jointly.
1132	11 December	City and castle of Banyas falls to Zengi's forces.
1136	Spring	Princess Constance of Antioch marries Raymond de Poitiers.
1137	July	Louis VII marries Eleanor of Aquitaine;
	1 August	Louis VII becomes king of France;
	August	Zengi defeats Fulk at Montferrand and captures town.
1138	June	Zengi seizes Homs.
1140	12 June	Joint Frankish/Damascene army recaptures Banyas.
1142		Castle of Kerak constructed.
1143	8 April	Manuel I Comnenus becomes Byzantine Emperor;
	10 November	King Fulk dies in a hunting accident;
	23 December	Melisende and her son Baldwin crowned jointly; Baldwin rules as Baldwin III.
1144	23-24 December	Zengi captures Edessa; a massacre of the population ensues; all captive Franks executed.
1145	1 December	Pope Eugenius II proclaims the Second Crusade.
1146	14 September	Bernard of Clairvaux preaches the Second Crusade;
	November-December	Zengi dies; Count of Edessa briefly recaptures Edessa before being driven out by Zengi's son Nur ad-Din.

Year	Month	Event
1147	May	Unsuccessful invasion of Hauran by Baldwin III;
	mid-May	Second Crusade: departure of German crusaders under Conrad III;
	11 June	Second Crusade: departure of French under King Louis VII;
	17 October	Second Crusade: Iberian crusaders capture Almeria;
	24 October	Second Crusade: Portuguese with Flemish/English support capture Lisbon;
	25 October	Second Crusade: Seljuks obliterate most of Conrad's army at the Second Battle of Dorylaeum.
1148	6 January	Second Crusade: Louis VII ambushed and suffers heavy losses;
	March	Second Crusade: Louis VII abandons what is left of his army at Adalia and sails for Antioch with his clergy, household and wife, Eleanor of Aquitaine; quarrels with Raymond of Poitiers and continues to Jerusalem;
	April-June	Second Crusade: arrival of the remnants of the Second Crusade under Conrad III and Louis VII;
	24-28 July	Second Crusade: Unsuccessful siege of Damascus;
1149	29 June	Nur ad-Din defeats and kills Raymond de Poitiers at the Battle of Inab;
	15 July	Consecration of the renovated Church of the Holy Sepulchre;
	by year end	Second Crusade: Iberian crusaders drive the Muslims out of Catalonia.
1150	May	Capture of Joscelin II, Count of Edessa;
		Evacuation of the remaining regions of County of Edessa of all Latins and as many native (mostly Armenian) Christians as wish to join.
1151	March	Temporary division of the Kingdom of Jerusalem due to conflict between Queen Melisende and King Baldwin III.

Year	Month	Event
1152	March	Frederick I ('Barbarossa') elected king of the Germans;
	April	Baldwin III attacks his mother, forcing her to withdraw to Nablus; unity of the kingdom is restored;
	May	Raymond II of Tripoli murdered by assassins.
1153	Spring	Reynald de Chatillon marries Constance, heiress of Antioch and becomes prince of Antioch;
	18 May	Henry Plantagenet marries Eleanor of Aquitaine after the dissolution of her marriage to the French king;
	22 August	Franks capture Ascalon; population spared.
1154	25 April	Nur ad-Din gains full control in Damascus;
	25 October	Death of King Stephen of England; Henry Plantagenet becomes king.
1155	2 January	Frederick Barbarossa crowned Holy Roman Emperor;
		Nur ad-Din captures Ba'albek, unifying all of Muslim Syria;
		Reynald de Chatillon attacks Byzantine Cyprus.
1157	April	Nur ad-Din briefly gains control of Banyas, instituting a massacre among the population and destroying much of the infrastructure.
	19 June	Nur ad-Din defeats Baldwin III at Jacob's Ford;
		Almohads recapture Almeria and open new Muslim offensive in Iberia lasting to 1212.
1158	September	Marriage of Baldwin III to Theodora Comnena, niece of Emperor Manuel I Comnenus;
	December	Chatillon submits to Emperor Manuel.
1159	April	Ceremonial entry of Emperor Manuel in Antioch.
1161	11 September	Death of Queen Melisende;
	November	Reynald de Chatillon captured by Nur ad-Din.

Year	Month	Event
1163	10 February	Death of Baldwin III;
	18 February	Coronation of Amalric;
1163	Spring	Nur ad-Din suffers a resounding defeat at Krak de Chevaliers;
	September	First invasion of Egypt.
1164	April-October	Second invasion of Egypt;
	10 August	Nur ad-Din defeats a combined Frankish-Byzantine army at the Battle of Artah, taking Bohemond III of Antioch, Raymond III of Tripoli, Byzantine dux Coloman and Hugh VIII of Lusignan captive;
	Oct.	Nur ad-Din captures Banyas from a weak garrison, ending Frankish control of the city.
1167	January-August	Third invasion of Egypt; occupation of Alexandria; Nur ad-Din raids into the county of Tripoli, taking advantage of the absence of troops and leaders in Egypt.
	29 August	Marriage of Amalric and Maria Comnena.
1168–1169	October-January	Fourth invasion of Egypt.
1169	March	Saladin becomes vizier of Egypt;
	October-December	Amalric's fifth invasion of Egypt.
1170	December	Saladin's first invasion of the Kingdom of Jerusalem; sack of Darum and siege of Gaza;
	29 December	Murder of Thomas Becket in Canterbury.
1171	Spring	Amalric visits Constantinople;
	10 September	Saladin ends Fatimid caliphate; Egypt submits to Abbasid caliphate.
1174	15 May	Death of Nur ad-Din;
	June	Sicilian fleet besieges Alexandria;

Year	Month	Event
1174 (cont.)	11 July	Death of Amalric;
	15 July	Coronation of Baldwin IV;
	28 October	Saladin seizes control of Damascus.
1176	July	Baldwin IV leads raids in the vicinity of Damascus and defeats Saracen forces under Saladin's brother Turan Shah at Ayn al Jarr; release of Raynald de Chatillon;
	17 September	Seljuk Turks defeat Byzantine army under Emperor Manuel I at the Battle of Myriocephalon;
	October or November	Marriage of Princess Sibylla to William 'Longsword' de Montferrat.
1177	June	Death of William de Montferrat, possibly from malaria;
	August	Arrival of Philip, Count of Flanders, with large crusading force;
	25 November	Baldwin IV decisively defeats Saladin at the Battle of Montgisard following Saladin's first invasion of the Kingdom of Jerusalem.
1178		Baldwin IV orders the construction of a castle at Jacob's Ford.
1179	10 June	Saladin defeats Baldwin IV at the Battle on the Litani/Marj Ayun;
	24-29 August	Saladin destroys the unfinished castle at Jacob's Ford.
1180	April	Marriage of Princess Sibylla to Guy de Lusignan;
	May	Truce between Baldwin IV and Saladin;
	18 September	Philip (Augustus) II becomes king of France;
	24 September	Death of Emperor Manuel I Comnenus.
1181		Maronites unite with the Roman Catholic Church.
1182	May	Outbreak of anti-Latin riots in Constantinople; Andronicus I deposes Alexus II as Byzantine Emperor;

Year	Month	Event
1182 (cont.)	5 July	Baldwin IV defeats Saladin at the Battle of le Forbelet, ending Saladin's second invasion of the Kingdom of Jerusalem;
	August–September	Franks repulse an attempt by Saladin to seize Beirut;
	November	Reynald de Chatillon launches ships in the Red Sea that prey on pilgrims and attack the Red Sea coast.
1183	February	Chatillon's ships are destroyed and his men killed or captured;
	11 June September	Aleppo surrenders to Saladin; Henry the 'Young King', eldest son of Henry II and Eleanor of Aquitaine dies;
		Guy de Lusignan named Baillie of Jerusalem; Baldwin IV retains crown but retires from government;
	29 September–8 October	Saladin's third invasion of the Kingdom of Jerusalem ends in a stalemate;
	1–2 November	Saladin lays siege to the castle of Kerak;
	20 November	Lusignan relieved of his office of baillie; Baldwin V crowned co-king to his uncle Baldwin IV;
	3–4 December	Saladin lifts siege of Kerak because of the approach of a relieving army commanded by Baldwin IV; Nablus and other cities in Galilee are sacked during his withdrawal.
1184	July	Patriarch of Jerusalem and the masters of the Temple and Hospital depart on an embassy to the West;
	August–September	Saladin again lays siege to Kerak and is forced to withdraw.
1185	ca. 15 April	Baldwin IV dies; Raymond de Tripoli named baillie;
		Raymond signs a four-year truce with Saladin;

Year	Month	Event
1185 (cont.)	June	Emperor Andronicus proposes offensive alliance to Saladin, which includes a joint attack on the crusader states;
	Summer	Saladin besieges but fails to take Mosul; alliance negotiated.
1186	August	Death of Baldwin V; Sibylla usurps the throne and crowns Guy king-consort;
	September	Emperor Andronicus murdered by a mob; Isaac II Angelus becomes emperor of Constantinople;
	Autumn	Baldwin de Ramla departs the kingdom; Raymond de Tripoli refuses homage to Guy and signs separate peace with Saladin.
1187	1 May	Saracen reconnaissance-in-force destroys a small force of Templars, Hospitallers and secular knights at the Springs of Cresson;
	May	Tripoli reconciles with Lusignan;
	27 June	Saladin begins his fourth invasion of the Kingdom of Jerusalem;
	3-4 July	Saladin decisively defeats the army of the kingdom at the Battle of Hattin;
	8-10 July	Saladin captures Acre; citizens spared;
	14 July	Arrival of Conrad de Montferrat in Tyre;
	ca. 20 July	Al-Adil captures Jaffa followed by sack, slaughter and enslavement;
	29 July	Sidon surrenders to Saladin; citizens spared;
	6 August	Beirut captured by Saladin; slaughter and plunder follow;
	4 September	Saladin captures Ascalon;
	20 September-2 October	Siege of Jerusalem; surrender on 2 October followed by forty days to pay ransoms;

Year	Month	Event
1187 (cont.)	October	Pope calls for the Third Crusade;
	November–December	Richard of Poitiers, later King Richard I of England, takes the cross;
		Saladin unsuccessfully besieges Tyre.
1188	January	Pope Clement III preaches the Third Crusade;
	July	Timely arrival of the Sicilian fleet prevents the fall of Tripoli; Saladin ends his siege;
	August	Saladin and Byzantine Emperor Isaac Angelus renew alliance against the crusader states; Byzantium promises to prevent crusades crossing its territory;
	August–September	Saladin systematically invades Antioch, taking Tortosa, Jabala and Latakia, as well as major strongholds before signing eight-month truce with Prince Bohemond.
1189	11 May	Third Crusade: Frederick Barbarossa officially sets out on crusade, traveling overland;
	6 July	Death of Henry II; Richard of Poitiers, son of Eleanor of Aquitaine and Henry II becomes king of England, crowned September 3;
	28 August	Guy de Lusignan commences siege of Muslim-held Acre with Pisan crusader fleet.
1190	22 April	Surrender of Beaufort to Saladin;
	18 May	Third Crusade: Frederick Barbarossa defeats the Seljuk Turks at the Battle of Iconium; capital of the Sultanate of Rum falls to the crusaders;
	10 June	Third Crusade: Frederick Barbarossa drowns in the river Saleph; his army starts to disintegrate;
	4 July	Third Crusade: Richard I and Philip II depart jointly on crusade;
	22 September	Third Crusade: Richard arrives in Sicily; prepares to winter there;
	7 October	Third Crusade: arrival of Frederick of Swabia with remnants of German crusade at siege camp of Acre;

Year	Month	Event
1190 (cont.)	ca. 10 October	Queen Sibylla and both her daughters die in siege camp at Acre;
	24 November	Queen Isabella marries Conrad de Montferrat; recognised as queen by barons of Jerusalem.
1191	30 March	Third Crusade: Philip II departs Sicily for Acre;
	10 April	Third Crusade: Richard I departs Sicily; runs into storms; fleet disperses across the Mediterranean;
	20 April	Third Crusade: Philip II's army arrives at Acre;
	6 May-5 June	Third Crusade: Richard I of England captures Cyprus from Isaac Comnenus;
	8 June	Third Crusade: Richard I arrives at Acre with English/Angevin crusaders;
	12 July	Third Crusade: Acre surrenders to the French and English kings; Philip of France leaves for the West via Tyre;
	20 August	Third Crusade: massacre of Muslim hostages by Richard;
	22 August	Third Crusade: crusaders leave Acre and advance down the coast;
	7 September	Third Crusade: crusaders defeat Saladin at the Battle of Arsuf;
	10 September	Third Crusade: crusaders reach Jaffa;
	December	Third Crusade: crusaders approach Jerusalem, but stall.
1192	6 January	Third Crusade: crusaders abandon attempt to take Jerusalem; withdraw to the coast;
	28 April	Conrad de Montferrat killed by assassins in Tyre;
	5 May	Henri de Champagne marries Queen Isabella;

Year	Month	Event
1192 (cont.)	7-11 June	Third Crusade: crusaders make a second attempt to capture Jerusalem and again withdraw without a siege or assault;
	27-30 July	Third Crusade: Saladin attacks and captures the city of Jaffa; citadel holds out;
	1 August	Third Crusade: Richard comes to relief of Jaffa; retakes the city;
	5 August	Third Crusade: Richard defeats Saladin's army outside of Jaffa;
	2 September	Third Crusade: three-year truce signed between Richard and Saladin; Treaty of Ramla;
	September-October	Guy de Lusignan goes to Cyprus;
	9 October	Richard departs the Holy Land.
1193	4 March	Saladin dies.
1194		Unification of the Holy Roman Empire and the Kingdom of Sicily under Henry VI of Hohenstaufen;
		Death of Guy de Lusignan; his brother Aimery becomes lord of Cyprus.
1196	April	Isaac II deposed; Alexius III becomes emperor of Constantinople;
	18 May September	Aimery de Lusignan does homage to the Holy Roman Emperor; Cyprus becomes a kingdom, with Aimery its first king.
1197	September	'German Crusade' arrives in Outremer;
	October	Sultan al-Adil assaults Acre unsuccessfully; Jaffa falls to al-Adil;
	October	Death of Henri de Champagne; Germans recapture Beirut for the Franks;
	December	Marriage of Aimery de Lusignan to Isabella of Jerusalem.

Year	Month	Event
1198	July	King Aimery signs a six-year truce with al-Adil;
		Pope Innocent III calls for another crusade;
		German Hospital of St Mary in Acre transformed into a military order, the Deutsche Orden or Teutonic Knights.
1199	6 April	Richard I dies of wounds in France; succeeded by his brother John as king of England.
1200		Sultan al-Adil, Saladin's brother, wins the succession struggles that have been ongoing since Saladin's death; becomes sultan of Syria and Egypt.
1202		Crusaders, unable to pay Venice for transport already built, are persuaded to become Venetian mercenaries and attack Zara.
1203		Mercenary army (former crusaders) and Venetian fleet successfully restore Alexius IV to the Byzantine throne.
1204	8 February	Alexius IV murdered; succeeded by anti-Latin Alexius V Ducas;
	12 April	Latins capture Constantinople and establish a Latin Empire in Greece;
	Exact date unknown	Al-Adil and Aimery agree on the restoration of Jaffa to Frankish control by diplomatic means.
1205	1 April	King Aimery of Cyprus and Jerusalem dies; Walter de Montbelliard named regent of Cyprus for underaged heir Hugh;
	May	Queen Isabella of Jerusalem dies; John d'Ibelin named regent for underaged heir Marie de Montferrat.
1208	December	Frederick II Hohenstaufen comes of age (14) and takes control of his Kingdom of Sicily.
1210	September	Hugh de Lusignan comes of age; accuses Montbelliard of malfeasance; Maria de Montferrat marries John de Brienne;

Year	Month	Event
1210 (cont.)	October	Maria and John crowned queen and king-consort of Jerusalem.
1212	November	Queen Maria dies giving birth to a daughter, 'Yolanda'; Brienne rules alone.
1213	April	Pope Innocent III calls for a new crusade ('Fifth Crusade').
1215	15 June	Magna Carta signed by King John in England;
	25 July	Frederick II crowned king of the Germans in Aachen.
1217	July	King Andrew II of Hungary is first to embark on the new crusade;
	9 October	In Cyprus, King Andrew joins forces with King Hugh of Cyprus, King John of Jerusalem and Prince Bohemond of Antioch;
	10 November	Crusaders defeat army of al-Adil decisively at Bethsaida.
1218	10 January	Hugh I of Cyprus dies while on crusade; Philip d'Ibelin elected baillie by the High Court of Cyprus;
	February	King Andrew of Hungary, ill, retires back to Hungary;
	July	New wave of crusaders arrives and sets siege to Damietta on the Nile, with John of Jerusalem dominant commander;
	Autumn	Death of Sultan al-Adil; his empire is split between his sons: al-Kamil becoming sultan of Egypt and al-Mu'azzam, sultan of Syria;
		Pope Honorius III sends a legate, Pelagius, to lead Fifth the Crusade, undermining unity of command.
1219	August-September	Principality of Antioch and County of Tripoli come into dynastic union under Bohemond IV;
	4-5 November	St Francis of Assissi arrives and visits the sultan of Cairo;
		Damietta finally surrenders to the crusaders.

Year	Month	Event
1220	March	Al-Muazzam, sultan of Damascus, sacks Caesarea, revealing weakness of Jerusalem's defences during the crusade in Egypt;
	April	John de Brienne abandons Fifth the Crusade and returns to defend his kingdom;
	22 November	Frederick II Hohenstaufen crowned Holy Roman Emperor.
1221	July	Fifth Crusade: attempt to march up the Nile to Cairo meets with defeat;
	September	Fifth Crusade: ends with a treaty swapping Damietta for the release of the captive crusaders and an eight-year truce.
1225	Spring	Henry I (aged 7) crowned King of Cyprus;
	9 November	Frederick II and Yolanda of Jerusalem married in Brindisi.
1226		Frederick II concludes a treaty with sultan of Cairo al-Kamil aimed at his brother al-Mu'assam, Sultan of Damascus; Al-Kamil promises Jerusalem as a reward.
1227	August	Frederick II sets out on crusade but returns due to illness;
	September	Pope Gregory IX excommunicates Frederick II;
	November–December	Philip d'Ibelin dies; John d'Ibelin elected baillie of Cyprus.
1228	25 April	Yolanda gives birth to a son, Conrad, now king of Jerusalem;
	5 May	Yolanda dies;
	25 June	Frederick II sails from Brindisi with a small force;
	21 July	Frederick II arrives in Limassol;
	3 September	Frederick II departs Cyprus for Syria, with King Henry and Cypriot barons now in his army.

Year	Month	Event
1229	18 February	Frederick II signs ten-year truce with al-Kamil partially restoring Christian control of Jerusalem for the duration of the truce;
	18 March	
	April	Frederick II wears the imperial crown in the Church of the Holy Sepulchre;
	1 May	Frederick II lays siege to Templar headquarters in Acre;
	May	Frederick II departs Acre, never to return; Balian de Sidon and Werner von Egesheim named baillies in his absence;
	June	Frederick II leaves Henry de Lusignan on Cyprus; sells his bailliage to five local barons; Henry married by proxy to Alix de Montferrat; baillies begin a reign of terror against Ibelins and their allies;
	14 July	Ibelins and supporters land at Gastria, calling for the restoration of their expropriated lands, due process and an end to intimidation of their families;
		Battle of Nicosia; Ibelin victory; baillies take refuge in mountain castles, which are besieged by the Ibelins; King Henry held captive by the baillies at St Hilarion.
1230	April	Baillies at St Hilarion surrender on the condition of a full pardon.
1231	Summer	John de Brienne, former king of Jerusalem becomes emperor of Constantinople;
	Autumn	Frederick II appoints imperial marshal Riccardo Filangieri his baillie in Jerusalem;
		Filangieri brings a powerful fleet and armed force to Outremer; denied landing at Cyprus;
		Seizes city of Beirut and besieges citadel; presents credentials in Acre, but is met with skepticism;
		Filangieri establishes his base in Tyre;
		Commune of Acre formed to resist imperial breaches of the constitution.

Year	Month	Event
1232	February March	King of Cyprus brings his army to Syria in support of Ibelin; Cypriot/Ibelin army attempts unsuccessfully to relieve Citadel of Beirut;
	April-May	Cypriots loyal to the emperor seize control of Cyprus; imperial forces lift siege of Beirut citadel;
	3 May	Imperial forces surprise Cypriot army at Casal Imbert and deliver a humiliating defeat; Henry of Cyprus comes of age;
	mid-May	Filangieri lands on Cyprus; begins a reign of terror;
	late May	King Henry and Ibelins seize imperial ships and sail for Cyprus;
	15 June	Battle of Agridi; decisive Cypriot/Ibelin victory of the imperial army; Filangieri and other imperial knights seek refuge in Kyrenia; siege of Kyrenia begins.
1233	July-August	Kyrenia surrenders to the royal/Ibelin forces; prisoners exchanged.
1235	July	Isabella Plantagenet, sister of Henry III, marries Frederick II;
	August	Papal legate places Acre under interdict for failing to support the emperor;
	October	Pope rescinds interdict because residents are turning to the Orthodox churches;
	Winter	Combined Bulgarian and Nicaean attack on Latin Constantinople defeated.
1236	ca. March	John d'Ibelin, Lord of Beirut, dies of the effects of a riding accident; succeeded by his son Balian of Beirut.
1237	23 March	Death of John de Brienne in Constantinople.
1238		Death of al-Kamil; Ayyubid empire split between his sons.

Year	Month	Event
1239	1 September	Arrival of king of Navarra with 1,500 knights; start of the 'Barons' Crusade'.
	13 November	A portion of this army badly defeated at Gaza, with many important lords taken captive;
	7 December	Frederick II's truce expires; Jerusalem, being defenceless, surrenders to Muslim forces from Kerak und al-Nasr.
1240	Spring	Taking advantage of infighting between the Ayyubids, Navarra negotiates a treaty that restores Jerusalem, Bethlehem, Nazareth, Galilee and key castles;
	September	Navarre departs from Acre; Simon de Montfort arrives;
	8 October	Richard, Earl of Cornwall and brother of Henry III, arrives in Acre; completes negotiations with Ayyubids;
	6 December	Kiev falls to the Mongols.
1241	8 February	Cornwall signs truce with the sultan of Egypt;
	9 April	Mongols obliterate a German army at Leignitz;
	23 April	Cornwall obtains release of key prisoners;
	3 May	English crusaders under Cornwall depart the Holy Land;
	June	Ibelin faction propose Simon de Montfort as a compromise candidate to Filangieri as baillie of Jerusalem; Frederick II rejects the proposal.
1243	26 June	Mongols crush a Seljuk army at the Battle of Kosedag; establish control of Muslim Anatolia, Armenia and Georgia;
	Summer	Ibelin faction capture the last imperial stronghold, Tyre, ending Hohenstaufen rule in the Kingdom of Jerusalem.

Year	Month	Event
1244	11 July	Khwarazmians seize Jerusalem, slaughtering tens of thousands and desecrating churches; Tower of David falls August 23;
	17 October	Combined Christian/Syrian force crushed at the Battle of La Forbie with heavy losses by an Egyptian/Khwarazmian coalition;
	December	Louis IX vows to recover Jerusalem.
1245	2 October	Al-Salih takes Damascus.
1246	date unknown	Pope Innocent IV absolves the king of Cyprus of all oaths to the Holy Roman Emperor, making Cyprus an independent kingdom;
	March	Khwarazmians turn on al-Salih and besiege Damascus;
	May	Ayyubids destroy the Khwarazmians.
1247		Ascalon falls to the Muslims.
1248	25 August	Louis IX's fleet sets sail from Aigues-Mortes for Cyprus, which has been pre-provisioned.
1249	5 June	Seventh Crusade under Louis IX arrives in Egypt; quickly captures Damietta;
	November	Death of Sultan al-Salih.
1250	8-9 February	Louis IX suffers a devastating defeat at the Battle of Mansourah in Egpyt;
	April	Cut off from supplies and trying to retreat, crusading army disintegrates; Louis himself is taken captive along with the survivors of his host;
	2 May	Mamluks murder the Ayyubid sultan of Egypt and seize control;
	late May	Queen of France negotiates a ransom for King Louis; Louis and leading nobles released; bulk of the army remains in captivity pending payment of more money;
	13 December	Frederick II dies; succeeded by his son Conrad.

Year	Month	Event
1253		Death of Henry I of Cyprus; succeeded by Hugh II.
1254	Spring	King Louis departs the Kingdom of Jerusalem for France;
	May 21	Death of Conrad Hohenstaufen, titular king of Jerusalem;
		Start of the War of St Sabas between the Venetians and Genoese.
1256		Mongols destroy the Assassins;
		End of hostilities between Venetians and Genoese.
1258	10 February	Mongols capture Baghdad, execute Abbasid caliph; end of the Abbasid caliphate;
	10 June	Oxford Provisions adopted in England.
1260	25 January	Mongols capture and sack Aleppo;
	2 March	Mongols capture and sack Damascus;
	3 September	Mamluks defeat the Mongols at the Battle of Ain Jalut;
	24 October	Baybars murders Sultan Qutuz and assumes his place as ruler of the Mamluk empire.
1261	13 June	Baybars re-establishes the Abbasid caliphate at Cairo;
	25 July	Greeks recover Constantinople.
1264	14 May	Battle of Lewes; victory of Simon de Montfort over Henry III.
1265		Mamluks capture Caesarea, Haifa and Arsuf, thus cutting the Kingdom of Jerusalem in half;
	January–March	Simon de Montfort's Parliament held in England;
	4 August	Simon de Montfort defeated and killed at the Battle of Evesham.
1266		Charles d'Anjou, brother of King Louis IX, defeats Manfred of Hohenstaufen and is crowned king of Sicily;
		Mumluks expel Franks from Galilee and capture Templar fortress of Safed.

Year	Month	Event
1267	24 March	Louis IX again takes the cross;
	November	Death of Hugh II of Cyprus; succeeded by Hugh III of Antioch-Lusignan.
1268	7 March	Jaffa falls to Baybars, city is sacked and population slaughtered;
	18 May	Antioch falls to Baybars, population slaughtered; this sack is widely recognised as the worst massacre of the entire crusading era;
	29 October	Death of Conradin Hohenstaufen, last titular king of Jerusalem in the Hohenstaufen line.
1269		Hugh III of Cyprus claims Crown of Jerusalem.
1270	25 August	Louis IX sets out on his second crusade (the eighth of the conventionally numbered crusades); dies at the siege of Tunis.
1271	9 May	Prince Edward of England arrives in Acre.
1272	April	Prince Edward signs ten-year truce with Mamluks.
1277		Charles d'Anjou buys Crown of Jerusalem from Marie d'Antioch; divides the kingdom between supporters of kings of Sicily and Cyprus;
	1 July	Death of Sultan Baybars.
1279	November	Sultan Qalawun emerges victorious from vicious infighting as new Mamluk sultan.
1281	29 October	Qalawun defeats Mongols at Homs.
1285	7 January	Death of Charles d'Anjou; Sicilian claim to crown of Jerusalem extinguished.
1286	15 August	Henry II of Cyprus recognised and crowned king of Jerusalem, uniting the kingdoms of Cyprus and Jerusalem.
1287		Qalawun captures Antiochene port of Latakia.
1289	27 April	Despite truce, Qalawun attacks and captures Tripoli.
1290	10 November	Death of Sultan Qalawun, succeeded by his son al-Ashraf Khalil.

Year	Month	Event
1291	6 April	Mamluk siege of Acre begins;
	18 May	Acre falls;
	June	Sidon falls to Mamluks;
	31 July	Beirut surrenders to the Mamluks;
	3 and 14 August	Templars withdraw from their last holdings in the Levant, Tartus and Athlit (Castle Pilgrim).
1307	13 October	Philip II of France arrests Templars on false charges.
1314		Templars dissolved by papal order.

Part I

A History of the Women of Outremer

Chapter 1

Women in the Era of the Crusades

Women in Western Europe

W omen in the crusades era enjoyed a status and level of empowerment almost unprecedented in Western Europe up to this time. This is best illustrated by a brief review of women's status in earlier eras.

The Ancient World

In most of Ancient Greece, with the exception of Sparta, and throughout most of Roman history, women were seen as inherently inferior to men in both mind and body. Aristotle famously asserted that women were 'infantile males' constitutionally *incapable* of developing the ability to reason and, therefore, 'permanent children' in need of constant 'protection' and guidance. Although Aristotle's views did not go unchallenged, they reflected predominant attitudes and the legal reality of women's status, and much of ancient Greek society reflected these views. Inevitably, something viewed as inferior was less valued than their allegedly superior male companions. A casual remark purporting to state the obvious during an Athenian lawsuit illustrates this. Namely: 'Everybody raises a son even if he is poor, but exposes [i.e., kills] a daughter even if he is rich'.[2]

Free Athenian women (i.e., the wives and daughters of citizens, as opposed to slaves or foreigners) were, from birth onwards, fed less and given inferior food than their brothers, denied exercise and fresh air, excluded from education and intellectual life, and incapable of inheriting anything more valuable than a bushel of wheat. At the first sign of puberty, their father gave them away in marriage to a man, usually twice or three times their age, often an utter stranger. They were often dead by the age of 40, exhausted by giving birth to infants, who (if female) were frequently murdered by their husbands immediately after birth because they were a burden to raise.[3]

Although Roman women enjoyed far greater freedom of movement and took a more active part in the social and commercial life of Rome and its colonies, women did not legally exist under Roman law. From birth, they were viewed not only as inferior but also as dispensable. A Roman father had the right to kill a daughter at birth but not a son. That this right was exercised rather than merely theoretical is suggested by records that chillingly demonstrate that few Roman men chose to raise more than one daughter. The others, like their Athenian sisters, were slaughtered at birth. All Roman women, therefore, lived only by the 'grace' of their father – and were expected to be eternally grateful for being allowed to exist at all.

Furthermore, Roman women, like slaves, could not contest anything before a court of law. Legally, they had no status and required a male guardian in every phase of their life. As children, they were controlled by their fathers (or his closest male relative if he were dead). As wives, they were subjects to their husbands, and as widows, they were controlled and represented by their sons or grandsons. Notably, since a woman's sole value to society was defined by her ability to produce children, a post-menstrual woman was of no worth whatsoever. The fate of widows was desperate unless they had sons and grandsons who honoured them.

In Greece and Rome, marriage was a contract between families in which fathers gave their daughters to the man of their choice without any legal or moral obligation to consult, much less consider, the wishes of their daughter. While men often acted on their own initiative seeking to obtain the girl they wanted from her father, such an option was unthinkable for a young girl or woman. The best she could hope for was that the man she favoured would approach her male guardian. Likewise, men – but not women – could divorce an unwanted spouse without cause. They simply sent the woman back to her father and returned the dowry with her. In these circumstances, divorce disproportionately benefitted men and caused untold misery to women. Men (but not women) could discard partners who had grown old, fat, less attractive or failed to produce children. Indeed, they could discard wives simply because a new marriage would bring commercial or political benefits or a larger dowry. The fate of most repudiated wives, on the other hand, was (and still is in many societies) dismal. Many discarded wives were reviled by their parents and brothers because they were blamed for their 'failed' marriage and seen as an unwanted and extra burden. A rejected wife rarely found a new husband, so she was anathema in a society that viewed childbearing as a woman's only purpose. Finally, while only one wife was recognised as the legal partner to produce citizens, men enjoyed multiple sexual partners without approbation; fidelity to one's spouse was viewed as a virtue in women only.

The Impact of Christianity

The teachings of Christ upended Greco-Roman gender norms with a series of radical doctrines concerning a woman's place in marriage, society and the universe. First, Christ categorically condemned divorce for both men and women. Christianity's insistence on marriage as a life bond dramatically increased women's status and financial security. If a man could not simply toss a woman out and get a new wife, he had no choice but to try to come to terms with the wife he had. His wife was elevated from an interchangeable sexual, commercial and political object to a lifetime partner. While wealthy and powerful men in Christian kingdoms throughout the Middle Ages still found ways to set aside unwanted wives, the Church's stance made it more difficult, time-consuming and expensive. The system wasn't perfect, but it was notably better than what had prevailed before.

Second, the Church introduced the concept of mutual consent into marriage; a voluntary exchange of vows by bride and bridegroom stands at the centre of the Christian rite of marriage. Marriage itself became a sacrament, and the Church attempted (largely unsuccessfully) to argue that it should not be treated as a business contract between families. Despite the best efforts of the Church, however, mediaeval parents continued to dispose of their underage children (male and female) with little regard for their wishes. Yet while respect for the participants' wishes might not have been the norm, women at least had the legal and ethical right to be treated as a consenting partner. We shall see how this right represented the thin edge of a wedge which some women effectively exploited in several spectacular cases.

Last but not least, Christ declared there was no difference between men and women in the eyes of God. Whether man or woman, they were souls created by God and redeemed by Christ. The physical body that enjoyed earthly attributes and pleasures was animal and mortal; the soul, consisting of mind and spirit, was immortal. Bodies are male and female; souls are not. While women's bodies are weaker than men's, making them the 'weaker sex' in the physical world, their souls suffer no comparative weakness in the spiritual realm.

The spirituality of women is signalled in the gospels by Christ's willingness to keep company with women and allow them to hear his teachings (i.e., he treated them as rational beings). Most significantly, however, after his resurrection, he first revealed himself – and thereby the truth of his divinity and eternal life – to women rather than men.

The early Church reaffirmed women's spirituality by canonising many female saints. Most of these saints from the early Christian period were martyrs, and many were women (e.g., St Agnes, St Barbara, St Dorothy, St Juliana, St Lucia, and St Margaret of Antioch) who preferred to die as virgins (and Christians) rather than accept a marriage imposed on them by their pagan fathers.

The large number of virgin saints underlines that women were no longer viewed solely as reproductive instruments whose value disappeared if they were unwilling or unable to bear children. In Christianity, women who devoted their lives to Christ, either as virgins or in later life as widows, were revered as admirable, not rejected as useless. By the era of the crusades, the burgeoning Cult of the Virgin had placed a woman (Mary) almost on a par with Christ himself, a fact reflected in doctrine, art and daily practice.

Furthermore, according to Christian doctrine, reason is not only the characteristic that distinguishes humans from animals but also the means to understand God and his intentions. Christian theology places a burden on people seeking salvation to understand the teachings of Christ in order to follow in his footsteps. Thus, the road to heaven entailed using intellect and reason, something expected of Christian women no less than men.

In their search for divine wisdom, some men and women tried to cut themselves off from the world's temptations. This included rejecting luxury, wealth, comfort, vanity, pride, and all worldly pleasures, including sex. Indeed, the Church increasingly viewed chastity as an ideal for both men and women because it aided them in their quest to come closer to a sexless God. To fulfil these ideals, individuals formed self-sustaining communities removed from mainstream society and the distractions of the worldly sphere. In these new communal institutions, they worked, prayed and lived in poverty; they were called monasteries.

The earliest known monasteries emerged in Egypt in the fourth century. Significantly, they welcomed both men and women. Indeed, the first record of such an institution established in the Byzantine Empire in Cappadocia was founded jointly by a man and a woman, St Basil the Great (329–379) and his sister, Macrina the Younger (327–379). From its inception, it included communities for women as well as men. The monastic movement spread rapidly throughout the Byzantine Empire and reached Western Europe by the end of the fourth century. In the sixth century, St Benedict (480–547) composed a written 'rule' for the members of his community at Monte Cassino in Italy, which greatly influenced Western traditions. He established the three vows of poverty, chastity and obedience for acceptance into the religious community. He too accepted women as well as men from the start. From there, the monastic movement continued to spread to France, the Iberian Peninsula, England and Ireland. By the ninth century, monasteries for both men and women were spreading across the formerly pagan heartland of Germany. The first monastery in Poland was founded in 1044. On the eve of the first crusade, there were thousands of these religious houses across Europe, including hundreds for women.

Nunneries, no less than monasteries, were renowned as places of learning. The inhabitants not only worked and prayed but also copied and illuminated books. Furthermore, they taught others basic literacy and numeracy. Because women were perceived as naturally suited to nurturing children, elementary education was often delegated to nunneries and higher education to monasteries. Some historians argue that literacy and numeracy were more widespread among women than men in the early Middle Ages. They hypothesise that secular men (as opposed to monks and priests) were too busy fighting, doing manual labour and traveling on business to learn to read and write. Instead, they left the business of running estates and keeping the books and correspondence to their wives.

By the crusading era, however, literacy had become widespread among men and women of the upper and middle classes. This was more than functional literacy. We have numerous examples of secular lords and knights who were poets, novelists, philosophers and scholars in the era of the crusades. William, Duke of Aquitaine (1071–1127) is credited with inventing the tradition of poetry in the vernacular and sparking the troubadour movement. Chretien de Troyes (1130–1190), a comparatively humble member of the knightly class, is credited with inventing the modern novel. Walther von der Vogelweide (1170–1230), another writer of romantic and politically critical lyric poetry, was a mere knight.

Yet the emergence of secular men of letters did not (yet) displace women from the realm of learning. Instead, they co-existed with them. The mediaeval theologian and logician Peter Abelard famously was attracted to Heloise, later Abbess of Paraclete, because of her learning; she, too, was and is still viewed as a philosopher. Other examples of learned women in the crusader era include Abbess Hrosvitha of Gandersheim (c.935–973), Mechthild of Magdeburg (c.1207–c.1282), Abbess Herrad of Landsberg (twelfth century), and, of course, St Hildegard, Abbess von Bingen (1098–1179). There were many, many others, and their position in society is documented by the books they wrote and the correspondence they maintained with emperors, kings, popes and saints.[4]

The Impact of Feudalism

In addition to the influence of Christianity, women in the crusader era benefitted from the rise of feudalism. Feudalism elevated the status of women by recognising their right to inherit. Simplified, in feudalism, bloodlines took precedence over gender. This means that although the hierarchy elevated the firstborn son over his brothers and sons before daughters, it nevertheless gave daughters precedence over illegitimate sons, uncles and cousins, much less individuals without a blood relationship to the hereditary lord. Bonds of marriage, furthermore, were considered 'blood-ties', meaning that wives shared status with their husbands and deputised for them. With marriage, a woman effectively obtained control over the vassals, tenants, servants and serfs that went with the titles and properties of her husband whenever he was absent or incapacitated.

In practice, the focus on blood ties and feudal hierarchy meant the closest female relative exercised the same authority in the absence of a male, temporarily or permanently. In other words, class trumped gender. Thus, while women, to a degree, were subject to men of their own class and rank, they had a higher standing and more power than men of any lower class or subordinate position.

At the pinnacle of feudal society, queens were anointed and crowned because they were expected to exercise authority over the entire kingdom; consequently, God's blessings were deemed essential. Their power was neither nominal nor ceremonial. When a king died, leaving a minor child as his heir, it was customary for the child's mother to act as regent. In France, the custom goes back at least to 1060, when, at the death of Henry I, his wife Anna became regent for their son Philip I. Even when a king was not dead, circumstances might hand power to his wife. For example, Eleanor of Aquitaine served as regent in England while her son Richard I left his realm to fight in the Holy Land in 1190–1192. Likewise, when Louis IX of France crusaded from 1249 to 1254, he left his mother as his regent – a function she had fulfilled during his minority as well. Indeed, when Louis IX was taken captive by the Saracens, he negotiated a ransom with the caveat that his queen must confirm the terms of the agreement. This was because, as his consort she automatically reigned in his stead and could command the resources of the kingdom (including those entrusted to his mother who had been left behind as regent in France) during his captivity.

In the crusading era, the right of women to rule as sovereigns – in their own right – was recognised in England, Portugal, Castile, Aragon, Jerusalem and France. The latter may surprise readers familiar with the Hundred Years War. However, it was not until after the crusading era in the early fourteenth century that French jurists invented the so-called 'Salic Law' that excluded women from succession in France. This was a legal ploy to prevent an English king from being crowned king of France, and the invented law was in blatant conflict with legal precedent, namely the Edict of Neustria (c.580). The latter had ruled that daughters could succeed to the hereditary domain (including the kingdom itself) if there were no sons. Notably, the same edict ruled that all other property (acquired by purchase or marriage) must be equally divided between all heirs regardless of gender.

At the next level down, women across Europe could serve as barons because they could give and receive feudal oaths. The importance of this cannot be overstated: feudal oaths were the mortar of feudal society and represented the social contract that made feudalism function. The recognition of a woman as a vassal and lord – not in her capacity as a man's mother or wife – entailed recognising her as a fully independent legal entity. This was unthinkable under Roman or Athenian law and, sadly, was not the case in France, England or the United States from the sixteenth to the twentieth century, either.

Famous examples of independent female barons in the crusader era are Mathilda of Tuscany and Eleanor of Aquitaine. Mathilda of Tuscany was a significant supporter of the papal reform movement and also sponsored a raid against the base of Muslim pirates terrorising the Mediterranean from North Africa. In her own right, Eleanor, Duchess of Aquitaine, retained control of this rich and powerful territory, taking it into both of her successive marriages. She personally led her barons and their knights on the Second Crusade. Yet these two examples represent only the tip of the iceberg; there were many others. An in-depth study of the lordships of Troyes in Champagne, for example, shows that women held 58 of the 160 direct fiefs.[5] In other words, women inherited at a rate of better than one out of three. This is unlikely to have been exceptional, although the exact numbers will vary based on local laws and customs.

When women held feudal titles, they controlled the lands and commanded the men and women that went with them. For example, the Constable of Lincoln in 1217 was Nichola de la Haye, who defended the castle of Lincoln against forces attempting to put the king of France on England's throne during the minority of Henry III. She withstood multiple assaults while commanding the men of the garrison in person. There are countless cases of women holding and defending castles against siege and storm in the story of Outremer.

Not all of feudalism's benefits went to members of the ruling feudal elite. The right of women to be barons and vassals was derived from the principle of female inheritance. This applied not only to the apex of society but also to the bottom. Peasant women could also inherit and transmit hereditary rights, whether for land or buildings like a mill or shop. Because mediaeval women of any class could hold property, they could accumulate and dispose of wealth. Few things empower a person more than money.

Significantly, it was not only heiresses that enjoyed property and the benefits thereof. On the contrary, it was customary for all women to receive property from their husband's estate at marriage; this property was called a 'dower'. A dower is not to be confused with a dowry. A dowry was property a maiden took with her into marriage. Royal brides brought entire lordships into their marriage. Lesser lords might bestow a manor or two, while the daughters of merchants brought ships, houses, jewellery, furnishings, etc.; even peasant girls might call a pasture, orchard or some livestock their dowry. The main thing to remember about dowries, however, is that they were not the property of the bride. They passed from her guardian to her husband.

Dowers, on the other hand, were women's property. In the early Middle Ages, dowers were inalienable land bestowed on a wife at the time of her marriage. A woman owned and controlled her dower property, and she retained complete control of this property after her husband's death, even if her husband were attainted for treason. Thus, while a man might be convicted of treason and forfeit his life, land and titles, his widow would not lose her dower.

Whatever the source of a woman's wealth, in mediaeval France, England and Outremer, women did not need their husband's permission or consent to dispose of their property. Thousands of mediaeval deeds provide evidence of this simple fact. While it was common to include spouses and children in deeds, this was a courtesy that increased the deed's value rather than a necessity. Thus, many deeds issued by kings and lords included wives and children as witnesses to demonstrate that the grant or sale was known to their co-owners/heirs.

Middle-class women could inherit whole businesses, and as widows, they ran these businesses and represented them in the respective guilds. Indeed, most wives were active in their husband's business while he was still alive. More importantly, however, women could learn and engage in trades and business independently. They could do so as widows, unmarried women (femme sole) or married women, running a business separate from their husband's. Furthermore, if qualified in a trade, women took part in the administration of their respective profession, both as guild members and on industrial tribunals that investigated allegations of fraud, malpractice and the like.

The diversity of professions and trades open to mediaeval women was surprisingly large. A survey of registered trades in Frankfurt from 1320 to 1500 (admittedly a little after the era covered by this book) shows that of 154 trades, 35 were reserved for women, and the remainder were practised by both men and women, although men dominated in 81 of these.[6]

The Impact of Chivalry

Finally, the era of the crusades was also the age of chivalry. This immensely powerful secular ethos or code of conduct transformed man's understanding of love and set off a revolution in sexual relations.

Chivalry introduced the notion that a man could become more worthy and 'noble' through love for a lady. Love for a lady became a central – if not *the* central – feature of chivalry, particularly in literature. Other characteristics, as defined in contemporary handbooks on the topic, were nobility of spirit, loyalty, honour, righteousness, prowess (courage), courtesy, diligence, cleanliness, generosity, sobriety and perseverance. Wolfram von Eschenbach in *Parzifal* stresses a strong sense of right and wrong, compassion for the unfortunate, generosity, kindness, humility, mercy, courtesy (particularly to ladies) and cleanliness. In essence, chivalry entailed upholding justice by protecting the weak, particularly widows, orphans and the Church. Yet, regardless of the exact definition, the inspiration for knights striving to fulfil the ideals of chivalry was love for a lady.

Critically, chivalrous love had to be mutual, voluntary and exclusive on both sides. It could occur between husband and wife, and many romances, such as *Erec et Enide* and *Yvain or the Knight with the Lion* (both by Chrétien de Troyes) or Wolfram von Eschenbach's *Parzival*, revolve around the love of a married couple. The popular notion that courtly love or the love vaunted by the troubadours was always adulterous is a fallacy. Nevertheless, mediaeval romance put love for another man's wife on par with love for one's own – provided the lady returned the sentiment. The most famous of all adulterous lovers in the age of chivalry were, of course, Lancelot and Guinevere, closely followed by Tristan and Isolde.

Strikingly, in an otherwise excessively hierarchical and class-conscious world, the ideal chivalrous lovers took no note of status and wealth and loved one another for their virtues alone. A lady was supposed to be loved and respected for her beauty, graces, kindness, and wisdom regardless of her status, and a knight was ideally loved for his manly virtues rather than his lands or titles.

Even more important is that regardless of which of the partners was the social superior, the lady always took the role and status of 'lord' to her lover. In the tradition of chivalry, the term that a lover used to address his lady was 'mi dons' – literally, 'my lord'. The term denoted the knight's subservience to his lady, his position as her 'man' – vassal, subject, servant. In art, knights are frequently shown kneeling before their lady and placing their hands in hers, the gesture of a vassal taking the feudal oath to his lord.

Lastly, courtly or chivalrous love was not a device to obtain sexual favours. For lovers who had the luck to be married, it included physical love, and in many adulterous romances, consummation was sometimes achieved. Yet sexual conquest was not the objective of courtly love. The goal was to become a better person – more courageous, courteous, generous and noble; in short, more chivalrous than before. In this sense, courtly love echoed or reflected religious love because it was first and foremost love of the spirit and character rather than the body. These features set courtly or chivalrous love apart from the erotic love of the ancients and the modern age. These features elevated women above the status of a sexual object and reproductive organ.

In summary, the Catholic Church recognised women in the crusades era as rational and spiritual beings, equal in spirit (if not in body) to men. As rational beings, they were encouraged to seek wisdom through education. Throughout this era, women of the middle and upper classes were largely literate, and exceptionally well-educated women were highly regarded. Furthermore, the Church preached chastity as the ideal for men as well as women, and chaste women, whether virgins or widows, enjoyed respect and even veneration. For those of either sex who chose not to remain chaste, the alternative was a monogamous, indissoluble marriage to which both partners consented freely and forsook all other sexual partners. Sexual relations outside of marriage, for men as well as women, were condemned as sinful. Secular laws in the Middle Ages acknowledged the right of women to inherit, hold and dispose of property and viewed adult women as legal persons without the need for guardians or representatives. Likewise, mediaeval society recognised the right of women to learn trades and engage in business. Chivalry raised women of the upper class to the position of lord over their lovers and enshrined the concept that all love must be free and mutual to be true. Ideally, each partner loved the other for their spirit and character rather than their body, a clear echo of Christianity.

Women in the Muslim World

Like Christianity, Islam views reason as God's most precious gift to man and the key feature that distinguishes humans from beasts. Unlike Christianity, however, mediaeval Islam did not credit women with being capable of reason. This inherently relegated women to the realm of animals. Leading Islamic scholars of the eleventh and twelfth centuries, such as Imam Ghazali (1050–1111), considered women not only outside humanity but a threat to it. Based on Mohammed's writings and experience, Ghazali argued that women's sexuality threatened to distract men from God.

At the same time, Islam placed no value on male chastity. On the contrary, male chastity was considered unhealthy, and men were encouraged to indulge their animal nature after a tiring day in God's service. The key to reconciling these apparent contradictions was the complete control, segregation and imprisonment of women so they would not distract men while they pursued God's business but could service men's 'natural' animal urges when men felt it was time to take a break.

Muslim Professor of Sociology and modern Islamic feminist Fatima Mernisse argues: 'The entire Muslim social structure can be seen as an attack on, and a defence against, the disruptive power of female sexuality'.[7] In consequence, as other scholars point out, an entire century before the first crusaders arrived in the Muslim world, Arab women had 'lost the greater part of their freedom and dignity … [and] the system of total segregation of the sexes and stringent seclusion of women had become general'.[8]

Just as the Christian theory of sexless souls and complete spiritual equality profoundly impacted Christian society, the Islamic notion of women as incapable of reason and more animal than human shaped all aspects of their place in society. Since women were not reasonable beings, there was no point in educating them. Since they were not spiritual beings, their only role was sexual and reproductive. Women in mediaeval Islam were not legal persons; like Athenian and Roman women, they lived perpetually under the guardianship of a man, even if that man was a male child decades younger.

Islamic women had no say over whom they married nor any role in the wedding ceremony, which did not require any form of consent on the bride's part. Women had no right to divorce their husbands, but men could discard wives without cause simply by saying, 'I divorce you' three times. Furthermore, Islam recognised polygamy. The importance of this cannot be overstated. Mernisse argues that: 'Polygamy … is a way for the man to humiliate the woman', quoting a Moroccan saying: 'Debase a woman by bringing in another one in [to the house]'.[9] Nor did the humiliation end with polygamy. Since Islam only recognised four legal wives, Islamic elites of the crusader era generally maintained large numbers of concubines as well.

Under the circumstances, it is hardly surprising that Muslims were offended by the Christian reverence of female saints, particularly the Virgin Mary. Indeed, many Muslims of this period ridiculed Christianity precisely because of the role given to women. The *Bar al-Fava'id*, written between 1159 and 1162, remarks:

[The Christians] believe in this iniquity, that their God came forth from the privates of a woman and was created in a woman's womb, and that a woman was made pregnant by their God and gave birth to him … Anyone who believes that God came out of a woman's privates is quite mad; he should not be spoken to, and he has neither intelligence nor faith.[10]

Then again, Muslims of the era generally had a low opinion of Franks. The geographer Ali ibn al-Husayn al Mas'udi described the Slavs and Franks (in this case, the inhabits of France and Germany) as follows: 'Their bodies have become enormous, their humour dry, their morals crude, their intellect stupid and their tongue sluggish'.[11]

Women in Outremer – A Unique Status?

The crusader states established in the wake of the crusades were inhabited by a diverse population adhering to various faiths. Although most of the population was Christian, both Orthodox and Latin, there was a sizable Muslim minority divided between Sunni and Shia, and there were also Jewish and Samaritan communities. The rulers of the states established in the Levant avoided widespread interference in the social and religious lives of the various ethnic and religious groups living inside their territories. On the contrary, Muslims were allowed to live in accordance with Sharia Law, Jews and Samaritans followed their respective traditions, and the various Christian Orthodox groups continued to conduct their lives as they had always done. Only to settle conflicts between religious groups or regulate relations between the subjects and the crown did the Franks seek to introduce new laws and courts. The Franks wisely recognised that meddling in customs governing marriage and women's social status and roles would only cause resentment, alienation and rebellion. Thus, nothing much changed for many women in the crusader states, particularly Muslim, Jewish and Samaritan women.

However, an estimated 140,000 Latin Christians emigrated from Western Europe to the crusader states in the twelfth century. They intermarried with the local Christian population and, together with their offspring, represented a significant portion of the population. They were, by and large, the subjects of the unique laws and customs that came to characterise the crusader states. It is the status of these Frankish women that represent the focus of this book.

All Frankish women were either Western European in origin or the descendants of Europeans on at least one side of their family tree. That is, the traditions of the Catholic Church, feudalism and chivalry had shaped them or their forefathers. Yet, as a minority in an Eastern environment, surrounded by states that denigrated and segregated women, one might have expected Frankish women to undergo a reduction in status once they were settled in the Near East. This was not the case.

Historian Sylvia Schein argues that Frankish women 'enjoyed more legal rights, held more important positions and carried out more functions than their contemporaries in the West ... [they had] more freedom of action within both state and society than in the West, for instance in England and France'.[12] Historian Sarah Lambert, furthermore, draws attention to the fact that the comprehensive account of the crusades written by a leading cleric of the Kingdom of Jerusalem, William Archbishop of Tyre, lacks the misogyny common among clerical chroniclers of this period writing in the West. According to Lambert, Tyre 'seemed to approve of the involvement of women in the First Crusade ... [and] not to share the horror of active sexuality during pilgrimage ... characteristic of [other] First Crusade chronicles'.[13]

In short, not only were women more powerful and active in Outremer, but Frankish men, including clerics, apparently accepted women on these more equal terms without approbation. In the chapters that follow, this volume seeks to highlight and explain this unique situation.

Chapter 2

The First Crusade and the Establishment of the Crusader States

Casus Belli: Jerusalem

In 326 AD, Empress Helena, the mother of the ruling Roman Emperor Constantine I, made a pilgrimage to the Roman city of Aelia Capitolina in the Roman province of Judaea. She had converted to Christianity roughly fifteen years earlier and, in 313, had convinced her son to issue the Edict of Milan that ended the religious persecution of Christians. Thereafter, she sponsored the construction of many churches, but now she was looking for something more spiritual as she approached 80 years of age.

It was 293 years since Christ had been crucified, 256 years since the destruction of the Second Temple, and 190 years since the expulsion of the Jewish and Christian population from the city that had formerly been called Jerusalem. Although expelled and persecuted, she knew that Christians had never completely abandoned Jerusalem. There were still Christians living in Aelia Capitolina whose grandparents' grandparents had lived in Jerusalem in the time of Christ. She knew or suspected these Christians maintained traditions about the sacred venues associated with Jesus. Furthermore, even if knowledge had not been passed down over the generations, Helena knew the Romans had built a temple to Venus on the site where Christ had been crucified and buried. The Romans had intended to humiliate the Christians by burying the most important physical reminder of their messiah under a temple to the pagan goddess of love. The effect had been to mark with marble the location of Christ's execution and resurrection.

In consultation with the local Christian community and their bishop Marcarius, Helena ordered excavations under the porch of the Roman temple. These revealed ancient quarries or tombs, which according to Rufinius (writing less than a century later), brought to light three crosses lying in one of the chambers. Helena and Marcarius brought pieces of each cross to a sick woman, who recovered miraculously on contact with the third. Thereafter, that cross was revered as the cross on which Christ had been crucified, and the place where it was found was identified as the tomb of Christ.

To mark the site of Christ's tomb and commemorate his sacrifice and resurrection, Emperor Constantine the Great ordered and financed the construction of a great church over the grave discovered by his later sainted mother, Helena. This church was constructed in the style of a monumental Greek basilica, 150 by 75 metres, covering almost precisely the same area as the temple to Venus. Furthermore, the church incorporated both the site of Christ's crucifixion and his grave. The latter could be reached by stairs leading underground. From its consecration onwards, this church became the holiest site in Christendom, more sacred than Agia Sophia in Constantinople or St Peter's in Rome. It was known as the Church of the Holy Sepulchre and instantly became the destination of countless pilgrims across Christendom as Christianity spread across Europe.

For almost 300 years, the Holy Sepulchre sat securely in Jerusalem, surrounded by Christian inhabitants and protected by a mighty Christian empire ruled from Constantinople. Yet slowly the power of Constantinople eroded, and in 614 AD, a Persian army swept across Judea. The Persians captured and sacked Jerusalem, killing an estimated 26,500 men and enslaving roughly 35,000 women and children. The Church of the Holy Sepulchre was burned to the ground. It took fourteen years before armies under Emperor Herakleios expelled the Persians in 628.

Although the reconstruction of a church over the tomb of Christ was undertaken immediately, the population and economic losses of the war with Persia inhibited spending. Only a modest structure replaced Constantine's great basilica. The building was probably temporary, with expectations of later expansion. Instead, just nine years later, Jerusalem was again under siege. This time the enemy at the gates was the Muslim Caliph Umar. After a year-long siege, Jerusalem could no longer resist and fell under Muslim domination.

Under Sharia law, the public practice of any religion other than Islam was prohibited, condemning the Church of the Holy Sepulchre to fall gradually into disrepair. Meanwhile, contrary to popular modern myths, the Christian population was subjected to an annual tribute, extra taxes, forced labour, and land expropriation, as well as systematic persecution and humiliation punctuated by sporadic violent attacks entailing plunder, rape and slaughter.[14] All churches and monasteries suffered during the ensuing centuries of Muslim rule. Symbolic of them all, the Holy Sepulchre was burned by Muslim troops in 969 AD, and although partially and modestly repaired by 984, the church was again demolished by the Caliph al-Hakim in 1009. No new attempt to construct a church on the site of the crucifixion was undertaken until almost fifty years later, in 1048. That anything could be built at all was an act of generosity by the Muslim ruler of the period; Sharia law prohibits the construction of any houses of worship not dedicated to Islam. Nevertheless, given the impoverished state of the Christian community under Muslim rule and the restrictions imposed by Islam, this new church was not a significant architectural monument.

Meanwhile, the armies of Islam had spread across the Near East to the gates of Constantinople. They had also subdued the North African continent and stormed onto the Iberian Peninsula. All these conquests were justified by the Islamic concept of *jihad*, which calls for the elimination of the non-Islamic world. The theory was simple. Islam divides the world into two houses or camps: the Dar al-Islam (usually translated as the Abode of Islam) and the Dar al-Harb (the Abode of War). In the name of peace, all regions still in the Dar al-Harb must be conquered and eliminated until the entire world lives harmoniously together in the house of the Dar al-Islam.

Practical politics interfered with this simplistic world view, and Islamic states found it increasingly convenient to make truces with non-believers. This led to the acknowledgement that there was a grey area between the Dar al-Islam and the Dar al-Harb, namely the Dar al-'Ahd or Dar al-Sulh – the Abode of the Treaty. Throughout the crusader era, however, treaties with non-believers were viewed as temporary conveniences that could not exceed ten years, ten months and ten days. In short, during this period the Islamic world fundamentally rejected the concept of permanent peace between Islam and the Christian powers of Byzantium and the West as contrary to Sharia law.

Despite the successful advance of Muslim armies, the Christian states did not entirely collapse. The Byzantine Empire fought off Muslim sieges of Constantinople in 678 AD and again in 717. In 732, the armies of Islam were halted on the Loire by a Frankish army under Charles Martel at the Battle of Tours. Roughly simultaneously, the reconquest of the Iberian Peninsula commenced and would continue for another 700 years. By 746, the Byzantine Empire had regained control of Armenia and Syria but not Palestine. In the succeeding three centuries, the struggle for control of the Mediterranean basin continued with victories and defeats on both sides, but through it all, the Holy Land remained under Muslim rule.

Sadly, that did not mean it was at peace. On the contrary, the Holy Land was a battleground fought over by competing Shia and Sunni caliphates centred in Cairo and Baghdad, respectively. Jerusalem changed hands violently five times between 637 and 1099. In addition, one rebellion against the Arab occupiers was quashed with a massive loss of life. Meanwhile, the Seljuks swept across Anatolia and defeated a large Byzantine army at the Battle of Manzikert in 1071.

A New Kind of War: The Combination of 'Just War' and Religious Pilgrimage

The victory of Muslim armies did not necessarily signify the victory of the Islamic faith. Sharia law prohibits forced religious conversions, although it advocates the humiliation and punishment of non-believers to encourage them to see the error of their beliefs. Despite the material benefits of adopting Islam, the pace of conversion was slow. Historians now estimate that the majority of the Levant's population remained Christian in 1100. It was the dire circumstances in which these Christians lived and the numerous instances of murder, rape and enslavement involving Christian pilgrims travelling to the Holy Land that ignited a new kind of warfare.

The Byzantines had never forgotten Jerusalem, but their strength had been insufficient to recapture the lost territories of the Levant and Egypt. Western Europe, too, had been on the defensive until the victory at Tours, and after that, the struggle ebbed and flowed. However, the West gradually gained wealth and strength, and thoughts turned towards more ambitious projects to reclaim lost territories. In 1074, Pope Gregory VII proposed a military campaign against the Turks to restore Christian control of the Holy Land, but nothing came of it. Twenty years later, in 1095, Byzantine Emperor Alexios I's urgent appeal to Rome for military aid fell on receptive ears. The new pope, Urban II, decided not only to respond positively but added innovative elements in a dramatic appeal he made to the nobles and knights of France in a rousing recruiting speech at Clermont in November 1095.

First and foremost, he put the liberation of Jerusalem (rather than general help for the beleaguered Byzantines) at the centre of the proposed campaign. In feudal Europe, Christ was seen as the 'king of kings and lord of lords'. Since under feudalism, a vassal was obliged to come to the assistance of his lord if his lord were attacked, Urban reminded the assembled Christian knights that the destruction of churches or their conversion into mosques constituted an insult to their ultimate feudal lord: Christ himself. Urban called upon Christian knights to do their duty to their Lord Christ by rescuing his earthly kingdom (the Holy Land) from occupation.

Second, Urban II invoked the concept of 'Just War'. This theory, propagated by St Augustine in the fifth century, broke with earlier Christian pacifist traditions by designating wars declared by Christian leaders against aggression and oppression (e.g., defensive wars) as legitimate or 'just'. While St Augustine explicitly condemned wars of religious conversion and the use of 'excessive force', most mediaeval Christians viewed all wars against pagans as fundamentally legitimate. By the eleventh century, Western Europe had a tradition that honoured, glorified and even sanctified Christian fighting men, provided they fought non-Christians. In his appeal at Clermont, Pope Urban II stressed the fundamental elements of a just war (fighting oppression and aggression) by drawing attention to the suffering of fellow Christians in the Muslim-occupied Near East and highlighting the threat posed by the pagan Seljuks to the New Rome, Constantinople.

Yet, the most radical feature in the appeal at Clermont was Urban's promise of the remission of sins for those who undertook to liberate Jerusalem. In addition to the assurance they were fighting a just war against aggression and oppression, the participants were offered a route to heaven. This transformed the entire campaign from a military expedition into a pilgrimage, albeit an armed pilgrimage. Possibly Urban had not fully thought through the consequences of his offer. He certainly had not expected the response.

Within a short time, tens of thousands of people had taken vows before their local priest or bishop to go to Jerusalem and pray at the Holy Sepulchre. Notably, the vow was *not* to kill or fight Saracens; but to *pray* in Jerusalem. Since the Holy Sepulchre was under Muslim control, the reconquest of Jerusalem was the implicit prerequisite for fulfilling the vow. Yet the vow itself did not require killing or fighting, so it was a vow that anyone could take, regardless of age, gender or health.

To Urban's dismay, women and children, older people and the disabled— all of no military value – rushed to 'take the cross'. (The symbol of the crusader vow was a cloth cross worn on one's outer garment.) This was not what Emperor Alexios had asked for, nor was it what the pope had intended. Alexios had expected trained fighting men who would serve as mercenaries under his officers. Urban wanted Christian knights and sergeants who could fight effectively against the Muslim enemy. Urban vigorously tried to discourage non-combatants from taking the vow and urged the clergy to absolve unsuitable persons of oaths already taken. His efforts may have slowed or reduced the number of non-combatant participants, but neither he nor the secular rulers of the age had the power to stop free men and women from setting off on a pilgrimage to the Holy Land.

The People's Crusade

Thus, while the pope diligently coordinated with leading secular lords for an armed expedition led by noblemen and composed of well-armed and provisioned fighting men, thousands of people set off for Jerusalem on their own. They clustered around and followed charismatic leaders, the most famous and successful of whom was a preacher known as Peter the Hermit.

Peter first recruited tens of thousands of followers in France and then crossed into Germany, where he was equally successful. Although some knights and isolated nobles joined his improvised host, the preponderance of those who filled his ranks – and numbered in the tens of thousands – came from the lower classes. Most were armed with nothing more than farm and household implements. Many were women.

As they advanced, they felt entitled to food and other necessities. If it was not given to them, they stole it. Some elements in this undisciplined yet fanatical host targeted Jews, plundering and killing them to finance their pilgrimage or as a substitute for the more difficult task of fighting Turks. The problems increased after the hoard passed into Byzantine territory. Clashes with the communities through which this zealous and undisciplined mob passed would have been worse had not the Byzantine Emperor responded by setting up markets along the way.

By 1 August 1096, while the organised military contingents were still marshalling in France, the tens of thousands led by Peter the Hermit reached Constantinople. Here they insisted on continuing into Asia against the emperor's advice. Cynically, the emperor provided boats to transport them across the Bosporus on 6 August. Once east of the Dardanelles, the host split into two contingents based mainly on language. The German component was surrounded and exterminated by the Turks first, and then several weeks later, the French pilgrims suffered the same fate. Those that converted to Islam were sent east as slaves, while those that did not were killed on the spot. There are no reliable estimates of how many were killed and captured or how many were women. Historians suggest that 20,000 people were lost in this ill-considered expedition. Whatever their numbers, women participants shared the fate of the men: capture or death.

The First Crusade

The official armed expedition organised by the pope set out from France in mid-August 1096 and advanced by various routes to avoid overburdening the local markets. The various contingents converged again in Constantinople. Most arrived by the end of 1096, although some troops did not reach the Byzantine capital until April 1097. Even after all elements had united in Constantinople, they did not merge into a disciplined army under a unified command. Instead, as Professor Thomas Madden worded it, they remained 'a loosely organised mob of soldiers, clergy, servants and followers heading in roughly the same direction for roughly the same purposes'[15]

Furthermore, all participants were volunteers. Oaths of fealty that bound vassals to their lords at home were irrelevant in the context of a pilgrimage far beyond the borders of their liege's territory. Indeed, it could be argued that oaths of fealty were temporarily suspended or superseded by the oath before God to fight for Christ. That said, at the core of any band of soldiers was a nobleman surrounded by his household, his dependants (vassals) and his kin. Most lords had brothers, uncles, nephews and cousins who rode with them. They travelled surrounded by these close-knit groups of men who knew each other well and spoke the same language.

The total host assembled is estimated at anywhere between 50,000 to 60,000, of which 10 per cent or 5,000 were knights. The most important secular leaders of this host were ten noblemen:

- Robert, Count of Flanders;
- Raymond, Count of Toulouse;
- Robert, Duke of Normandy (and eldest son of William the Conqueror);
- Stephen, Count of Blois, Robert's brother-in-law;
- Hugh of Vermandois, the brother of the king of France;
- Eustace, Count of Boulogne;
- Baldwin of Boulogne (his brother);
- Godfrey de Bouillon, Duke of Lower Lorraine and brother of both of the above;
- Bohemond, Duke of Taranto, a Sicilian Norman; and
- Tancred, his nephew.

The number of women in this host is unknown, but chronicles and accounts testify to their presence. Two of the leading noblemen of the First Crusade, Raymond of Toulouse and Baldwin of Boulogne, were accompanied by their wives, for example. Furthermore, we know that in later crusades, the female presence amounted to roughly three per cent of participants. All in all, it seems unlikely that women made up more than five per cent of a cohort specifically conceived as a fighting force facing an arduous 2,000-mile, overland armed expedition. What is clear, however, is these female participants were not 'camp followers' in the usual sense. On the contrary, Sabine Geldsetzer's meticulous examination of all known references to crusading women, *Frauen auf Kreuzzuegen 1096–1291*, concludes that the vast majority of female participants in all crusades were motivated by religious devotion. Furthermore, while they were drawn from all classes of society, the majority went on crusades with their husbands, brothers or fathers.[16]

On arrival in Constantinople, the Western leaders were astonished to discover that, although he had requested their support, the emperor had no intention of taking command of an expedition to free Jerusalem. After some debate amongst themselves, the Western leaders decided to continue to Jerusalem to fulfil their vows without Byzantine leadership or participation beyond a few advisors. After wintering in Constantinople, they crossed into Turkish-held territory in late May 1097 and decisively won their first encounter with the Turks on 21 May by defeating forces of the Seljuk Sultan Kilij Arslan. This victory forced the Turkish garrison occupying the Byzantine city of Nicaea to surrender. Nicaea, with its predominantly Christian population, was returned to Byzantine control and the crusaders continued eastward.

At once, conditions deteriorated dramatically. The crusaders found themselves in rugged, arid and hostile territory at the height of summer. Water and food were in extremely short supply, and the sultan's army was still intact. On 1 July, the Turkish army surprised the advance guard with a vastly superior host of light cavalry. The knights and men led by Bohemond of Taranto dug in around the baggage train containing the non-combatants. They fought primarily on foot behind a shield wall until heavy cavalry from the main contingent of crusaders came to their relief and scattered the attacking Turkish mounted archers. The battle is known as Dorylaeum; accounts describe women bringing water to the fighting men holding the perimeter.

Despite the absence of major confrontations over the next four months, the crusader host was decimated by thirst, hunger and exhaustion as it dragged itself across Anatolia in the height of summer without adequate provisions. Four-fifths of the horses died, and an estimated thirty to forty per cent of the humans did as well. Among the dead were women and children. Indeed, mediaeval accounts stress the horrors of this march by reporting that women gave birth by the side of the road to premature infants, who they left to die. While historians are quick to point out that such descriptions are intended to shock readers and may be more symbolic than factual, such stories usually have a core of truth. Tellingly, at this stage of the crusade, Baldwin of Boulogne's wife, Godera, died of unknown causes.

Finally, on 21 October, the crusaders reached the plains around Antioch. Like Nicaea, Antioch was a predominantly Christian city that had been in Byzantine hands until eleven years earlier. It was home to 40,000 inhabitants and one of the four patriarchs of the mediaeval Church. A robust Turkish garrison controlled its massive walls studded with 400 towers. Through attrition, the crusading host now numbered roughly 30,000 men and women. This was too few to completely enclose the sprawling perimeter of the city, much less mount an assault on such a well-defended fighting force, but they had too many to feed as winter closed in. All they could do was encamp before the walls of Antioch in the expectation that the Byzantine Emperor would arrive with supplies and reinforcements.

As the winter dragged on, malnutrition, hunger, cold, disease and despair overwhelmed thousands. Some died, and some simply abandoned the enterprise altogether. The most prominent of the deserters was Stephan of Blois and, conspicuously, the Byzantine advisors that had previously accompanied the crusaders. Yet, new crusaders joined the siege, having arrived by sea, and supplies were sent from Cyprus by the Orthodox patriarch of Jerusalem, who was in exile there. The crusaders also fought off two Seljuk attempts to relieve the city. When they learned that the sultan of Mosul had mobilised a huge host to lift the siege, however, the leaders agreed on a daring attempt to take the city by storm.

On the night of 3 June 1098, Bohemond of Taranto led his troops to a sector of the walls guarded by troops under the command of an Armenian defector. Without resistance, they scaled the walls, climbed over them and entered the city. Bohemond's troops hastened to open the gates from the inside to the remainder of the besieging army, and the crusaders swept into Antioch and drove the Turkish garrison back to the citadel, notably without slaughtering or killing the residents, the majority of whom were Christian.

Yet, the situation of the crusaders improved only marginally because the army of the Atabeg of Mosul Kerbogha was on their heels. The siege had long since depleted stores inside Antioch. Starvation and disease haunted the crusaders and the civilian population alike. When word reached them that the Byzantine Emperor, slowly advancing with an army to their aid, had turned back for Constantinople, many despaired entirely. Desertions became so common that the leaders put guards on the gates to stop fighting men from escaping.

At this juncture, a priest with the crusading host had a dream that led him to a rusty spearhead. According to his dream, he claimed this was the very spear that had pierced Christ's side at the crucifixion. Despite extreme scepticism on the part of the leading clerics, the secular leadership recognised the psychological moment was right for a last-ditch attempt to save themselves from certain failure. On 28 June 1098, with their decimated forces, they attacked the far larger army surrounding them – and scattered it to the winds. The victory was celebrated by a joint procession of crusaders and inhabitants through the streets of Antioch to re-throne the Orthodox patriarch in his cathedral.

However, it was the following year before the crusaders recovered sufficient strength and their leaders found the will to continue. The remaining crusaders advanced peaceably and without bloodshed down the coast of the Levant by negotiating with the respective Fatimid commanders in Beirut, Sidon, Tyre, Acre and Haifa. The local Muslim commanders were quite happy to set up markets and allow the crusaders to re-provision in exchange for not attacking or harming their territory. The crusaders were relieved not to have to fight their way south and delighted to have adequate provisions. They reached Bethlehem on 6 June 1099, where they were welcomed as liberators. The following day they finally saw Jerusalem in the distance before them.

By now, the crusading force was too small to surround even a moderate city like Jerusalem. Furthermore, the Fatimid governor of Jerusalem was fully appraised of the crusaders' advance and their goal. He had already expelled the native Christian population to eliminate the risk of the kind of betrayal that had facilitated the capture of Antioch and reduce the number of mouths he had to feed during the siege. In addition, he poisoned the wells around the city so the besiegers had to drag water from the Jordan River. Finally, the Caliph in Cairo promised to bring relief to Jerusalem within three months. All the governor in Jerusalem had to do was hold off assaults by the small forces before his gates until the Egyptian army arrived.

An attempt by the crusaders to take the city by storm on 13 June failed miserably due to insufficient scaling ladders and the lack of siege engines. Fortunately, six Genoese and English vessels arrived in Jaffa harbour shortly afterwards. These ships were deconstructed to obtain timber to build siege towers. After fasting and walking barefoot around Jerusalem in procession in penance, the army brought their new siege engines against the city's walls on the night of 13–14 July. After fierce fighting throughout 14 July, the knights of Godfrey de Bouillon gained a foothold on the city walls early the next day. They fought their way to the nearest gate and admitted the remaining crusaders.

An estimated 3,000 to 5,000 Muslim and Jewish residents of the city were slaughtered in the fighting that followed. This is hardly comparable to the 26,500 killed when the Persians took the city or the casualties incurred by the suppression of the rebellion in 1077, nor was it the entire population. However, Christian chroniclers glorified and eulogised the victory in apocalyptical terms to stress its significance. Their hyperbolic language has deceived readers ever since, although, ironically, Muslim and Jewish sources make no reference to an excessive or exceptional bloodbath.

In any case, the crusaders soon came to their senses. They stopped the killing and instead indulged briefly in rapturous thanksgiving, walking the streets Christ had walked and praying in the ruins of the remaining churches. Then reality set in. As in Antioch, they possessed a city they had besieged, but a huge relief army was already on its way. The crusading host, meanwhile, had been devastated by the loss of roughly four out of every five men to one-fifth its original size. In short, it was approximately 10,000 strong, of which an estimated 1,200 were knights. If any women had managed to make it this far, it would only have been a handful.

Believing themselves too few to defend the walls of Jerusalem against an assault, the remaining leaders decided to take the offensive. They led their forces out of Jerusalem and, at dawn on 12 August 1099, surprised a still-sleeping Fatimid army at Ascalon and put it to flight.

Rarely has an army fought so long and hard to obtain a goal without any thought to the post-conflict situation. Now that they held Jerusalem and had fulfilled their vows to pray in the Church of the Holy Sepulchre, the majority of the crusaders wanted to go home again. Yet abandoning the Holy City would result in it falling once more into Muslim hands. In short, a means of defending their hard-won prize had to be found. The Byzantine Emperor's conspicuous failure to assist the endeavour, however, made the surviving crusaders reluctant to turn the city over to him. More by default than intent, it was decided that a handful of men – and far fewer, if any, women – would remain behind and retain control of Jerusalem for Christianity. Their position was amorphous, and their future precarious. No one yet dreamed of Christian kingdoms in the Holy Land.

Chapter 3

The Crusader States, 1099–1190

Jerusalem Without a Queen

Godfrey de Bouillon, Protector of the Holy Sepulchre 1099–1100: The Bachelor
Only 300 knights and some 2,000 foot-soldiers chose to remain in the Holy
Land after the capture of Jerusalem in 1099. These men represented roughly
six per cent of the knights and only four per cent of the other troops that are
believed to have set out in 1096. From among the remaining nobleman, the
leaders of the crusade elected Godfrey de Bouillon as the man to command
those willing to stay in the Near East. Although the idea of crowning Godfrey
king was mooted, according to legend, he refused with words to the effect that
it would be inappropriate for any man to wear a crown of gold where Christ
had worn a crown of thorns. He chose to call himself 'Protector of the Holy
Sepulchre' instead.

Regardless of his title, his task remained the same: to ensure that the vast
effort and tremendous sacrifices of the First Crusade had not been in vain. He
and his men had to devise a means of establishing lasting Christian control
of Jerusalem. In other words, they had to create a viable and sustainable
state that was militarily defensible against myriad enemies and economically
robust enough to rebuild and restore neglected and damaged holy shrines and
shattered infrastructure in anticipation of thousands of pilgrims. Such a state
needed ports, agricultural land, a sound tax base and a powerful army. These
goals required expansion beyond Jerusalem and the narrow corridor to the
port of Jaffa that the men of the First Crusade had secured. In short, Godfrey
needed to expand the territory he controlled to fulfil his mission of 'Protector
of the Holy Sepulchre'. Yet the men remaining with him were too few to
defend even what they had.

The situation, however, was not as desperate as it seemed. While only 300
knights and 2,000 fighting men of the crusading host remained with Godfrey,
he could call upon the support of a native population that was overwhelmingly
Christian.[17] These inhabitants had greeted the crusaders as liberators. Godfrey
understood it was essential to retain their loyalty and harness their talents
and energy.

The history of the crusader states shows that the Latin rulers proved extraordinarily adept at doing exactly that. The native Christians were not only free of the tax burdens and humiliations imposed by Muslim rule but also had opportunities to advance and prosper in the expanding crusader states. They played important roles in the administration and military and engaged successfully in trade, industry and agriculture. Over the years, many native Christians obtained wealth and power, while even those less prominent benefitted from the economic boom that Latin control of the Levant triggered. Yet, in 1100, all that was in the future, and the records are silent on what Godfrey did in his one year of rule to gain the support of the native population.

One fact, however, should be neither overlooked nor underestimated: Godfrey's crusaders were mostly, if not exclusively, male. Of the roughly 2,300 men who chose to settle in the Holy Land, some may have chosen a life of clerical celibacy, but it is safe to assume the majority did not. Rather, they decided to 'settle', that is, to take up permanent residency and follow peaceful pursuits.

To foster and encourage this, Godfrey introduced feudalism. As feudal overlord, he gave land to men in exchange for military service (i.e. enfeoffed them). Notably, the majority of the bestowed holdings were not knights' but sergeants' fiefs. The men given land to till were not required to render knight's service with horse, lance and sword in wartime but rather to fight on foot as 'sergeants' armed with a pike or bow. In short, the commoners who had fought their way to Jerusalem beside the noble and knightly crusaders were recognized as brothers-in-arms and grated land to hold in their own right, a striking privilege in the medieval world. As fief-holders they were free men and referred to consistently as 'burghers'.

Whether knights or sergeants, holding a fief entailed working the land, and agriculture in the twelfth century was a family business. In short, these men needed wives. Some may have left wives behind in Europe whom they sent for, but most of the men who chose to remain in the Holy Land were bachelors or widowers. Since the local population was Christian, there was no religious or legal barrier to marriage with a native woman.

Marrying a local woman had advantages. First, it embedded the crusader in an existing family network with brothers-in-law, cousins, uncles, nephews, et al., who might contribute to making the fief viable. Also, the native population was familiar with the region's climate, crops, predators and other hazards. Intermarriage with the local population thus enabled settlers to adjust more rapidly to the unfamiliar environment in which they found themselves. The archaeological record demonstrates that settlers generally chose to locate close to the native population, often sharing churches, wells, mills, bakeries and other communal institutions. Furthermore, legal records prove that the settlers did not displace the existing population but built around or beside existing communities, presumably bringing land under cultivation that had lain fallow due to centuries of creeping depopulation under Muslim rule.[18]

This integration and intermarriage process had just started when Godfrey died on 18 July 1100, barely a year after the crusaders captured Jerusalem. He had not married and left no offspring. This fact encouraged the papal legate, Daibert, to advocate the establishment of a church-state controlled directly by the pope through his representative (namely Daibert). The knights and burghers in the Holy Land at the time of Godfrey's death preferred a secular state and turned to Godfrey's brothers.

According to feudal practice, Godfrey's older brother should have taken precedence. This was Eustace, Count of Boulogne, a man who had taken part in the First Crusade. Eustace, however, had returned to France, so eyes turned towards Godfrey's younger brother Baldwin, who was still in the Near East.

Baldwin I, 1100–1118: The Bigamist

Baldwin of Boulogne had been born in France in c.1065, the youngest and third son of Eustace II, Count of Boulogne. He took the cross along with his elder brothers Eustace and Godfrey and set out on the First Crusade with the main body of troops in 1096. However, in 1098 when the First Crusade reached northern Syria, he and his immediate entourage of sixty knights separated from the main body to aid the Armenian city of Edessa.

Some 200 miles northeast of Antioch, Edessa was an ancient and wealthy city that still rivalled Antioch and Aleppo in importance. In 1098 it was controlled by a Greek Christian warlord, Thoros, who was the most recent strongman in a long line of short-lived warlords. His predecessors had all come to power by murder or popular acclaim, only to lose favour rapidly and be murdered or flee. Fearing this fate if he could not fight off the ever-present Turkish threat, Thoros sought help from the most recent military force to arrive on the scene: the crusaders. Thoros, perhaps understandably, conflated crusaders with Frankish/Norman mercenaries and invited the effective commander Baldwin of Boulogne to fight his battles for him.

Baldwin, whose wife had recently died on the crusade, accepted Thoros' invitation. He withdrew from the First Crusade and made his way to Edessa, accompanied by sixty knights. Baldwin was not, however, a mercenary. He rejected material gifts such as gold, silver and horses in a bid for something more important: lasting power and control. When Thoros refused, Baldwin threatened to leave, and the people insisted Thoros give way. Thoros formally adopted Baldwin in a ceremony using Armenian relics and customs.

Unfortunately for Thoros, this proved insufficient to placate an unruly population. Within a month of Baldwin's adoption, the mob turned on Thoros, murdering him, his wife and his children mercilessly. Once Thoros was dead, the citizens jubilantly proclaimed his 'son' (Baldwin) *doux*, a Greek title that usually implied subordination to the emperor in Constantinople.

Although Baldwin of Boulougne benefitted from Thoros' murder, there is no evidence he was behind it. The fact that he was neither well-connected with local elites nor (yet) conversant with Armenian politics speaks against his complicity. Furthermore, despite the title awarded him, Baldwin of Boulogne was no vassal of Constantinople. Yet he was not a conqueror in control of invaded territory either. He still had only sixty knights and owed his elevation to the local, predominantly Armenian population.

From the point of view of the Edessans, they had not helped establish a Frankish, Latin or crusader state at all; they had (as so often in the past) simply replaced one warlord with another. Furthermore, Baldwin's career would have been as short-lived and forgettable as that of the previous half-dozen rulers of Edessa had he not proved astonishingly adept at building alliances with surrounding warlords, nobles and elites. That process started with the simple method of leaving the Armenian administration of the city undisturbed and adopting Armenian symbols and rituals. He also, notably, rapidly married into the Armenian aristocracy. His wife was a Roupenian princess named Arda.

As soon as Baldwin started to exert his authority, the very citizens who had 'elected' him decided to depose him – just as they had rid themselves of all his predecessors. Fortunately for him, one of the conspirators warned him of what was afoot, and Baldwin struck first. He arrested his opponents, threw them in a dungeon, extracted ransom payments from them and released them – without noses, hands and feet or blinded in the case of the ringleaders. Far from provoking outrage or rebellion, the Armenian Church and population welcomed his behaviour and viewed it as the restoration of law and order. They believed they had finally found a truly strong strongman. They probably also hoped he would prove capable of ending the petty wars and general lawlessness that characterised the region since the defeat of the Byzantine army at Manzikert.

At this juncture, Baldwin was called to Jerusalem to take up his elder brother's burden. Baldwin did not hesitate and had no inhibitions about wearing a crown. He was duly crowned king of Jerusalem in Bethlehem's Church of the Nativity. Notably absent was his wife, Arda. She had not joined him on his journey overland through Muslim territory to Jerusalem. Instead, she followed him (slowly) by sea, not reaching Jaffa until September 1101. Here, news came to her that King Baldwin had been killed at a battle near

Ramla confronting an invading Egyptian army. Yet, she did not panic. Instead, she sent for help from Tancred, one of the most dynamic crusader nobles still in the Holy Land, who was then in Antioch.

The news of Baldwin's death proved premature. In fact, he had just won a spectacular victory over the Egyptians, but his reception of his wife in the aftermath was less than euphoric. According to one account, he discovered or alleged that she had been raped by pirates on her journey south. Therefore, he ordered her into the convent of St Anne's. Most historians consider this account fabricated and believe Baldwin's reasons for setting her aside were more prosaic and political. Namely, her Armenian connections were of little value in Jerusalem, and Baldwin already had his eye on a more advantageous alliance. Whatever the reason, Arda was sent to a convent and then later allowed to retire to Constantinople, while Baldwin set about finding a more 'appropriate' wife.

Perhaps this took longer than he expected, or he was too busy to go courting. He defeated invading armies in 1102 and 1105 and expanded his kingdom with the capture of Haifa (1101), Arsuf (1101), Caesarea (1101), Tortosa (1102), Jubail (1102), Acre (1104), Beirut (1110) and Sidon (1110). In addition, Tripoli fell to forces under the Count of Toulouse, paving the way for establishing the County of Tripoli, the third of the crusader states. Nevertheless, in 1112, with the consent and encouragement of Arnulf, the new patriarch of Jerusalem, Baldwin sought the hand of Adelaide, the dowager queen of Sicily. This was a cynical move since his marriage to Arda had never been formally dissolved.

Adelaide was the widow of Roger I of Sicily, who had died in 1101. She had acted as regent for her son Roger II until he came of age in 1112. Adelaide was now in her late 30s and unemployed. She had a substantial dower and could bring needed financial resources to her new husband. Yet the greatest attraction of this alliance lay in the powerful Sicilian fleet, which would be of great use to the kingdom. Meanwhile, Adelaide's son, Roger II, had his own reasons for the alliance. He insisted that should the union between his mother and Baldwin of Jerusalem prove childless, he, Roger, be recognised as king of Jerusalem. Baldwin agreed.

Adelaide arrived in Jerusalem in August 1113 with a large dowry in gold and allegedly 1,000 fighting men, including a company of Saracen (Muslim) archers. Yet, there is no mention of her being crowned queen. Three years later, the money had run out, and Adelaide was still not pregnant. As she was nearing an age when she would be unable to conceive, the prospect of Roger II of Sicily becoming king of Jerusalem became ever more likely. This did not sit well with the barons of Jerusalem. They suddenly remembered that Baldwin already had a wife, Arda, who was alive and well and living in Constantinople. They attacked the patriarch who had married Baldwin to Adelaide and accused him before the pope of various crimes, including concubinage and simony. Patriarch Arnulf managed to clear himself of all charges except officiating at a patently bigamous marriage. He was allowed to retain his office on the condition that he put an end to the king's marriage to Adelaide.

Having dismissed Arda with no cause, Baldwin appears to have had as little difficulty agreeing to dismiss Adelaide. He agreed to recall Arda, and a Church synod in Acre duly annulled his marriage with Adelaide. Understandably indignant, Adelaide left the kingdom in 1117, but she left a legacy; her son and his successors were very slow to forgive the insult to their former queen. In the succeeding seven decades, they remained aloof from the struggles of the Kingdom of Jerusalem and did not aid or support it until Saladin had almost completely overrun the kingdom.

Roughly a year later, on 2 April 1118, Baldwin I died childless. He had been married three times; in all cases, the marriages appear to have been purely political. Neither Arda nor Adelaide had been crowned queen. They had not left any particular mark on the kingdom other than the hostility of Sicily. That was about to change.

Jerusalem's First Queen: Morphia of Armenia

As Baldwin I left no direct heirs, the High Court of Jerusalem elected his successor. The choice fell on the same man Baldwin I had chosen to succeed him in Edessa, his cousin, Baldwin de Bourcq. This Baldwin had also taken part in the First Crusade. On succeeding his cousin in Edessa, he had extended Frankish power beyond the city of Edessa into the surrounding region, a significant challenge given that various rival warlords, Christian and Muslim, held castles at strategic points. Like his predecessor, he had too few Frankish troops to impose his rule and depended on the goodwill of the ruling class and the loyalty of Armenian soldiers. Strikingly, he never faced a rebellion in Edessa, only in outlying areas.

Baldwin of Bourcq succeeded largely by adopting the same tactics as his predecessor and cousin, Baldwin of Boulogne. He, too, had promptly married an Armenian wife, Morphia. She was the daughter of one of the strongest warlords, Gabriel of Melitene. Other Franks in his entourage, significantly his cousin Jocelyn de Courtenay, also married into the local aristocracy. Equally important, Baldwin continued to depend mainly on local Armenian elites to administer his territory. While a few discontents fled to Constantinople and complained, most local warlords preferred to submit (nominally) to the Franks rather than risk seeing one of their Armenian rivals win greater power and authority. Those willing to recognise Frankish suzerainty were richly rewarded with new lands, titles and revenues, while the Frankish leaders with Armenian wives became increasingly integrated into local society, honouring local saints and adopting local symbols, titles and customs.

Then, after eighteen years of ruling and integrating into Armenian Edessa, Baldwin was asked to accept the crown of Jerusalem. Like his cousin before him, he rushed overland to secure control of the kingdom. Unlike his cousin and predecessor, however, he delayed his coronation for almost eighteen months until his wife could join him. Baldwin and Morphia were crowned jointly on Christmas Day 1119 in Bethlehem's Church of the Nativity. Jerusalem finally had a queen.

Strikingly, Morphia, like Arda, had over time become a political liability rather than an asset. Not only was she Armenian, but Turks had overrun her father's lands, so he could no longer offer Baldwin political support or military aid. As the couple had been married for eighteen years, her dowry had long since been spent, which meant she brought no new financial resources to the kingdom. Most damning of all, after eighteen years of marriage, she had failed to produce a male heir. Instead, she had given her husband four daughters. Yet there was no hint of divorce or separation, and the chroniclers agree that her husband was devoted to her.

And she to him. On 18 April 1123, Baldwin II was captured at Balak in Edessa after coming to the aid of his cousin Joscelyn. Morphia took charge of the negotiations for his ransom and relief, but she also attempted a daring rescue. She hired Armenian mercenaries, who disguised themselves as Turkish traders and penetrated the fortress where Baldwin was held prisoner. They killed the garrison and briefly took control of the fortress, enabling some prisoners to escape before the Turks regrouped and regained control. Baldwin was not among those who got away. Morphia now made the excruciating decision to agree to ransom terms that included the surrender of her 6-year-old daughter Iveta as a hostage to secure her husband's release. On 24 August 1124, Baldwin was set free, and Iveta was turned over to his former captors.

Baldwin was anything but broken. He almost immediately laid siege to Aleppo, where the hostages were held. Although this enterprise soon had to be abandoned, Baldwin defeated a large Turkish army at the Battle of Azaz the following year. Nor had he forgotten his daughter Iveta. Contemporary sources agree he secured her release either with the final payment of his ransom or with an extra payment.

Meanwhile, Baldwin elevated the status of his eldest daughter Melisende to heir apparent. This meant that she, with the consent of the High Court, would inherit the kingdom. There is no indication this was opposed by the Church, barons or burghers. The right of women to inherit was already well established across most of Western Europe by this time.

However, even as a ruling queen, her primary duty was to secure the succession by giving birth to an heir, while the duty of leading the feudal host and carrying on offensive warfare would fall to her husband. Therefore, finding the right husband was a public rather than merely a family concern. Just as the council of nobles from the First Crusade had elected the first king and the High Court had chosen both Baldwin I and Baldwin II, the High Court of Jerusalem asserted its right to approve the husband of an heiress to the kingdom. The High Court had the final word on who would be the king-consort of a ruling queen.

The High Court's choice fell on Fulk, Count of Anjou. Fulk was a 40-year-old widower with grown children. He had been on pilgrimage to Jerusalem from 1119 to 1120. In June 1128, Fulk's eldest son Geoffrey married Empress Mathilda, the daughter of Henry I of England. Fulk agreed to renounce Anjou in favour of his son Geoffrey to go to Jerusalem and marry Melisende. The marriage took place on 2 June 1129. Sadly, Morphia did not live to see her eldest daughter wed; she died of unknown causes in 1127.

From Melisende's marriage onwards, Baldwin II treated Fulk and Melisende as joint heirs to his kingdom. Both were frequently called upon to witness charters. Fulk also accompanied Baldwin on his military campaigns, such as the siege of Damascus in November–December 1129. In 1130, Melisende gave birth to a son, thereby fulfilling her primary duty and securing the dynasty, or so it seemed. In August 1131, Baldwin returned from Antioch in ill health. Recognising he was dying, he reiterated that his heirs were Melisende and Fulk. He then took monastic vows at the Church of the Holy Sepulchre and retired from public life. He died on 21 August 1131. Melisende was 26 years old.

Jerusalem's First Ruling Queen: Melisende

Whatever her father's intentions, almost as soon as she and Fulk were crowned, Melisende was sidelined and ignored by her husband. He no longer included her on official documents, and tensions evidently grew between the king and queen and between the king and the High Court. Historians speculate that Fulk aroused opposition because he was – or was perceived to be – favouring Angevins over local barons in royal patronage. Problems came to a head in 1134 when one of the leading noblemen of the realm, Hugh of Jaffa, rose up in rebellion. Hugh of Jaffa was Melisende's second cousin and, as such, a natural focal point for any faction opposed to the newcomer, Fulk.[19]

The king attempted to discredit his rival and wife simultaneously by accusing Hugh of Jaffa of an affair with Queen Melisende. Had it succeeded, the tactic would have cast doubt on the legitimacy of his son by Melisende and paved the way to bar him from the throne. Perhaps, this is why contemporaries feared Fulk intended to disinherit the heirs of Baldwin II entirely in favour of a son by his first marriage.

Whatever Fulk had intended, his tactic backfired dramatically. Melisende's behaviour had been too irreproachable for the accusations of adultery to stick. And the barons and bishops of Jerusalem saw through Fulk's transparent powerplay and unanimously sided with their queen. Yet, Jaffa also overplayed his hand by seeking assistance from neighbouring Muslim lords to help him defend himself against the king. This was viewed as treason by many of Jaffa's vassals, who abruptly abandoned his cause. King Fulk was able to arrest Jaffa and put him on trial before the High Court. Yet, although Jaffa was found guilty of treason, he was sentenced to a mere three years of exile. The mild sentence underlines the fact that Jaffa still enjoyed considerable support among the feudal elite in the kingdom.

Before he could leave, however, he was struck down by an assassin. Suspicion immediately fell on the king, who was believed to be the assassin's paymaster despite his denials. This turned opinion even more heavily against Fulk and, remarkably, in favour of Melisende.

The most reliable mediaeval historian of Outremer, William Archbishop of Tyre, writing only fifty years after these events, described the situation as follows:

'All who had informed against the count [of Jaffa] and thereby incited the king to wrath fell under the displeasure of Queen Melisende ... It was not safe for these informers to come into her presence; in fact, it was deemed prudent to keep away even from public gatherings. Even the king found that no place was entirely safe among the kindred and partisans of the queen. At length, through mediation ... her wrath was appeased. ... But from that day forward, the king became so uxorious that, whereas he had formerly aroused her wrath, he now calmed it, and not even in unimportant cases did he take any measures without her knowledge and assistance.'[20]

The reconciliation between Fulk and Melisende was sufficient to produce a second child, another son, Amalric. In terms of political power, Melisende now witnessed all official documents, and from 1138 onwards, her firstborn son Baldwin III was also included on charters. This amounted to a complete victory for Melisende. Strikingly, her behaviour is consistently praised, even by clerical chroniclers such as the Archbishop of Tyre. In short, the clergy and the barons of Outremer approved of a woman asserting her authority – as long as it was based on legitimate rights.

In 1143, King Fulk died in a hunting accident. At the time, his eldest son, Baldwin, was only 13 years of age and below the minimum age for male inheritance, which in the Kingdom of Jerusalem was 15. Yet his death did not result in an interruption because Melisende had always been a reigning queen rather than a queen consort. Therefore, her rule continued uninterrupted by her husband's demise. Nevertheless, a coronation ceremony was held in which Melisende was re-crowned alongside her son Baldwin, who became Baldwin III. When Baldwin III turned 15 two years later, nothing changed in the kingdom's government – at least, not at first.

While all was well in Jerusalem, the County of Edessa had fallen to Islam's powerful and resurgent armies led by the powerful Seljuk ruler, Imad al-Din Zengi of Mosul. Antioch was threatened and Europe was aroused. In 1147, a new crusade set out from the West that has gone down in history as the Second Crusade, led by the Holy Roman Emperor Conrad III and King Louis VII of France. The latter was accompanied by his wife, Eleanor, Duchess of Aquitaine.

Poor leadership resulted in the bulk of the crusading host being eliminated during the long overland march. Only the leading elements of the French host and some independent contingents from England and Scandinavia that had opted to travel by sea reached the Holy Land. At a council of war, in which the leaders of the crusade and the barons of Outremer discussed what might be accomplished with the troops available, the decision was made to attack Damascus.

In retrospect, the strategy appears ill-conceived. The forces available to the Christians were insufficient to surround the city, leaving it open to relief. Furthermore, the sultan of Damascus and the Kingdom of Jerusalem had concluded a truce and were technically at peace. The campaign rapidly turned into a farce, with the Christians scuttling back to Jerusalem after five days outside Damascus. They fled before mere rumours of an advancing relief army under the dreaded Sultan Zengi.

Inevitably, everyone was at pains to blame someone else for the disaster. Western accounts of the shameful affair are full of unfounded accusations of 'bad advice' and 'treachery' by the nobles of Outremer. Yet, Queen Melisende can hardly be blamed when she opposed the attack on Damascus in the first place and (as a woman) was not present at the siege. Likewise, Baldwin III, an untried youth of 19, played no role in the fiasco. It is far more likely that the entire attack on Damascus was incited by the crusaders, who consistently failed to appreciate the wisdom of tactical truces with Muslim enemies. The reluctance on the Franks' part to break a perfectly good truce was transformed retroactively into sabotage of the campaign.

Yet the campaign may have made Baldwin long for real power. Thereafter, Baldwin began to chaff, perhaps understandably, at being constantly under the tutelage of his mother. In 1152, at 22, Baldwin III insisted on being crowned again – this time without his mother. The patriarch of Jerusalem refused. So, Baldwin turned to his barons. He summoned the High Court and demanded the kingdom be divided into two. Although such an act weakened the kingdom, the High Court agreed. One can only speculate that the court was too divided between Baldwin and Melisende's adherents to adjudicate an alternative solution.

No sooner had this nominal division been implemented than Baldwin swept down from his base in the north with an army. Taking Melisende's supporters by surprise, he defeated them handily. Within weeks, Melisende found herself barricaded in the Tower of David in Jerusalem along with her 16-year-old younger son and some loyal vassals. The king proceeded to lay siege to the Tower of David, and accounts say the fighting was fierce for several days. Eventually, however, unnamed mediators managed to end this absurd state of affairs before the real enemy could take advantage of the situation. Melisende agreed to retire to Nablus,' a large and powerful royal domain, but she had not abdicated.

Within a very short space of time, Melisende was again active in the affairs of the realm. As the lord of Nablus, she took part in sessions of the High Court. More significantly, she mediated between the crown and the commune of Pisa. She was also instrumental in securing, through a mixture of military action and negotiations, the recovery of the fortress of al-Hablis from the Muslims. In short, while she had acceded to her adult son pride of place, she remained – in retirement – an influential figure in the kingdom.

In late December 1160, she suffered what appears to have been a severe stroke. Bedridden, she was nursed by two of her sisters until her death on 11 September 1161.

The Byzantine Brides

The Beautiful Queen Theodora

Having pushed his mother from centre stage, Baldwin III embarked on an ambitious policy to expand his kingdom. His first target was the last remaining Muslim enclave on the coast of the Levant, Ascalon. Baldwin's army laid siege to Ascalon for eight months, accepting its surrender in August 1153. They spared the population, who were allowed to withdraw with their portable possessions. Yet Baldwin suffered two setbacks when he lost the border fortress of Ba'albek to the Sultan Nur al-Din in 1155 and when the latter surprised his field army near Jacob's Ford in 1157. The latter skirmish resulted in the capture of a number of Frankish noblemen and several Templar officers.

Possibly these defeats, or genuine horror at the rapacious behaviour of the new Prince of Antioch, Reynaud de Châtillon, led Baldwin to make overtures to the Byzantine Emperor Manuel Comnenus I. Baldwin sought greater cooperation between the two Christian states in the Eastern Mediterranean, and the powerful Comnenus Emperor Manuel I was receptive. For the first time since the Byzantine Emperor had failed to aid the crusaders in the liberation of Antioch, an era of cooperation between Constantinople and Jerusalem dawned. This was symbolised and sanctified by the marriage of Baldwin III, now 27 years old, to a niece of Manuel I, Theodora Comnena. In addition, Manuel married Maria, the daughter of the late Prince of Antioch, Raymond of Poitiers.

Theodora departed Constantinople in the summer of 1158 and arrived with a dowry of 100,000 gold pieces and an additional 24,000 gold byzants to defray the costs of her entourage and wardrobe. Although she was only 12 years old, she was reputedly a great beauty. Since Baldwin III was 28, he evidently felt he had time to wait for her to grow up before getting down to the business of founding a dynasty. Meanwhile, Manuel I sent an army to help Baldwin fight Sultan Nur ad-Din. In return, Baldwin pledged to bring the current Prince of Antioch (the infamous Reynaud de Châtillon) to heel and induce him to acknowledge Byzantine suzerainty over Antioch. Châtillon indeed submitted to the emperor, and shortly afterwards he was captured by Nur ad-Din and disappeared into captivity for the next fifteen years.

Alongside these military and diplomatic undertakings, Baldwin presided over a period of prosperity and massive public building. In 1149, the modernised and expanded church of the Holy Sepulchre was re-consecrated. In addition, a royal palace was built south of the Tower of David and numerous other projects across the kingdom were undertaken, such as the construction of a huge church on the site of the Annunciation. The Kingdom of Jerusalem enjoyed a period of agricultural, industrial and trade expansion. Irrigation projects enabled the cultivation of marginalised land. Roads connected the more remote rural areas to markets. Sugar plantations and factories were multiplying across the fertile plains, and industries such as glass and silk manufacturing were taking root and flourishing.

Yet Baldwin had made one serious miscalculation; he did not have as much time as he had assumed. In early 1163, while visiting Antioch, he suddenly became ill. Despite allegations of poison, there was no plausible candidate for the assassin nor motive for an assassination; certainly, no one attempted to exploit the situation. Knowing he was dying, Baldwin asked to be carried back to Jerusalem but did not make it. He died in Beirut on 10 February. He was just 33 years old, and his 18-year-old bride had not yet given him an heir.

Baldwin's most obvious successor was his younger brother Amalric, Count of Jaffa. Amalric was in the prime of life at 26 and was a vigorous and competent fighting man, just what the High Court wanted for its king. Amalric would have been proclaimed king immediately if Jerusalem had been a traditional hereditary monarchy. But Jerusalem's kings were elected by the High Court, and the High Court had a problem with Amalric, or rather, his wife.

Amalric was married to Agnes de Courtenay, the daughter of Joscelyn II of Edessa, the Count who had lost the county to the Muslims in 1146 and died in a Saracen prison six years later. Agnes' brother still titled himself 'Count of Edessa', but the county no longer existed, making the title nominal and its holder impoverished. Agnes had been married to Reynald of Marash, who had been killed in battle in 1149. She was next betrothed to Hugh d'Ibelin, but the marriage had not been celebrated before he fell into Saracen hands. While he was still trying to raise his ransom, Agnes married Hugh's feudal lord, the Count of Jaffa, Amalric of Jerusalem.

Later chronicles concocted a story of abduction that is not mentioned in any serious history. Nor is there any evidence of bad blood between Hugh and Amalric, which surely would have been the case had Hugh's intended bride been taken from him by force. A far more reasonable explanation of what happened is that Agnes preferred a wealthy and present bridegroom over one in captivity, who would soon be impoverished by ransom payments. Amalric may even have agreed to contribute to that ransom to appease any anger on Hugh's part at the loss of his bride.

In any case, by the time of Baldwin III's death, Agnes was Amalric's wife and the mother of his two children, Sibylla (then aged 3 or 4) and Baldwin (who was not yet 2). The High Court flatly refused to recognise Amalric as king unless he set Agnes aside. This was an astonishing demand, given that Amalric was otherwise an ideal candidate and unquestionably the closest legitimate relative of the dead king. The fact that the High Court prevailed conclusively demonstrates its power at this juncture and provides irrefutable evidence that it was not a mere rubber stamp for hereditary succession.

What is unclear, however, are the reasons for the court's objection to Agnes. Officially, it was discovered that Amalric and Agnes were related within the prohibited degrees. This is not credible as many marriages of more closely related couples were recognised, provided they obtained a dispensation from the pope or his representative. Historians speculate that the lords of Jerusalem feared Agnes would favour her impoverished relatives and clients from Edessa over the locals. Yet, the Edessans had already been welcomed to the Court of Jerusalem on at least two previous occasions. Others suggested that the lords of Jerusalem feared a powerful woman. This is equally ridiculous, given how loyal these very lords had been to Melisende. Accounts bitterly hostile to Agnes claim she had a sullied reputation and was not deemed virtuous enough to wear the crown of Jerusalem, which sounds like the usual slander trotted out to discredit any inconvenient woman. The most likely explanation is that, in canonical law, betrothals were treated as the equivalent of marriage. If so, Agnes' relationship with Amalric was bigamous due to her pre-contract with Hugh d'Ibelin, which a papal dispensation could not rectify. This later interpretation appears corroborated by the fact that Agnes was said to 'return' to Hugh after Amalric set her aside. The fact that Baldwin I's marriage with Adelaide of Sicily had also been dissolved because of bigamy set a precedent that was probably followed here.

Strikingly, Amalric showed neither scruples nor reluctance about choosing the crown over his wife. He set Agnes aside in less than a week and was crowned king only eight days after his brother's death. The only concession he wrung from the High Court was that his two children by Agnes be deemed legitimate. They were promptly removed from their mother's keeping and provided with nurses and tutors selected by the crown.

Meanwhile, the dowager Queen Theodora retired to Acre, which had been ceded to her as a very generous dower. Acre was the busiest port in the entire kingdom, although not yet as important as it would be in the following century. (By the mid-thirteenth century, contemporary sources claimed that the taxes generated in Acre alone exceeded the royal income of all of England.) In short, 18-year-old Theodora did not lack money. Furthermore, she was not obligated to marry and could rule in her domain indefinitely. In fact, it suited the crown better if she did not remarry since marriage would have put the military and material resources of Acre into the hands of her husband. For this reason, Theodora needed the king's permission to remarry since the crown reserved the right to veto any marriage that would transform the prospective bridegroom into one of the most powerful lords of the kingdom.

For four years, Theodora appears to have been content, but in 1166, she was visited in Acre by an uncle, Andronicus Comnenus, who has been described as an adventurer. Allegedly, '[h]is early life had been a series of political and amorous scandals, but in 1166, the emperor had appointed him governor of Cilicia'.[21] His nature had not, however, fundamentally changed, and he soon incurred imperial wrath by seducing Princess Philippa of Antioch, Manuel I's sister-in-law. Fleeing Antioch, Andronicus visited Acre, where he promptly seduced Theodora. The emperor decided it was time to teach Andronicus a lesson, so he ordered his agents to seize and blind Andronicus.

Somehow, Theodora got wind of the emperor's plans and warned Andronicus. He, in turn, persuaded her to elope with him to Damascus. The arrival of the emperor of Constantinople's cousin in the company of the dowager queen of Jerusalem was a delight to the entire Islamic world. They now had a source of endless gossip and a new justification for disparaging, ridiculing and belittling the morals of Christian women. But there was no going back. Andronicus and Theodora had burned their bridges. In Damascus, Theodora gave birth to a son, Alexis, and a daughter Irene, but she died there before reaching the age of 28 in 1182.

Aside from some embarrassment, her elopement had no negative consequences for the Kingdom of Jerusalem. Acre and its rich revenues simply reverted to the crown.

The Wise Queen Maria

When King Amalric ascended the throne in 1163, he already had two small children and was in no particular hurry to remarry. It was three years before Amalric began negotiations with Constantinople for a new bride. At the time he was actively pursuing a policy of cooperation with the Byzantines in an effort to expand the influence and control of both Christian states into Egypt. Jerusalem's Egyptian policy, conceived and carried out in alliance with Muslim factions inside Egypt, was complex and fluctuating; a detailed analysis is beyond the scope of this work.[22] Suffice it to say that Amalric's ambitions in Egypt were strictly geopolitical, without religious, racial or ideological overtones. Furthermore, in five incursions into Egypt, Amalric acted with the passive or active support of Constantinople. It is against this background that his second marriage must be considered.

After two years at the Imperial Court, Amalric's ambassadors returned to Jerusalem with a bride selected in consultation with Emperor Manuel I. The girl chosen (for reasons we know not) was Maria Comnena, the granddaughter of Emperor Manuel's brother, John the *Protasebastos*. Since no account refers to her beauty, historians generally assume she was not particularly attractive – although it is difficult to picture ambassadors spending two years selecting an unattractive bride for their king. There is also no reference to her age but given Theodora's age at the time of her marriage to Baldwin III and considering that Maria came from the next generation down, she was probably most likely also 12, the minimum age for consent.

In August 1167, Maria arrived in Tyre in grand style, accompanied by a sizeable imperial entourage and was met with due pomp by the king of Jerusalem. She was crowned and anointed queen prior to her marriage, both ceremonies taking place in Tyre and presided over by the Patriarch of Jerusalem. Unsurprisingly for a child, there is no evidence that Maria exercised exceptional influence in the kingdom during her early years as queen-consort.

However, it was after his marriage to Maria that Amalric undertook a trip to Constantinople in which Byzantine sources allege he paid homage to the emperor as his liege. It was also during Maria's tenure as queen-consort that the magnificent Church of the Nativity in Bethlehem was completed. Distinctive elements of the Byzantine style are particularly noticeable in this architectural monument, believed to have been built partly by craftsmen from Constantinople. Lastly, Maria gave birth to one infant girl who died young and to a second daughter in 1172, Isabella, who survived. Throughout Amalric's reign, the Kingdom of Jerusalem enjoyed widespread economic prosperity and booming trade.

Then, unexpectedly, Amalric died of dysentery while returning from an unsuccessful siege against the city of Banyas. It was 1174, and he was only 38 years old. Yet again, the High Court had to decide the succession. It had two possible candidates: Amalric's 13-year-old son Baldwin, from his first marriage to Agnes, or his 2-year-old daughter Isabella by Maria. Baldwin's legitimacy was besmirched by the annulment of his parent's wedding, and his candidacy was further weakened by the fact that he was suffering from an illness that proved to be leprosy. Isabella's bloodlines were impeccable, and her ties to Constantinople in this period were particularly valuable. Yet, at age 2, ten years would pass before she could marry and give Jerusalem a king-consort capable of leading the feudal armies. In the meantime, a foreign princess (Maria Comnena) would have been regent. That did not sit well with the barons of Jerusalem, so they decided to take their chances with Baldwin. For the two years until Baldwin reached maturity at 15, his nearest male relative, the Count of Tripoli (rather than his disgraced mother Agnes), was named his regent. Not one source suggests that Maria, later so scurrilously accused of 'intrigue', made any effort to influence much less contravene the High Court's decision.

At 19, Maria retired to her dower, the powerful barony of Nablus. Note that Nablus had been Melisende's dower as well. It was located on the border with the Sultanate of Damascus and owed eighty-five knights to the feudal levee. As such, it was one of the most critical baronies in the realm, more powerful than, for example, Transjordan or Acre, although it was less wealthy than the latter. Maria's conditions of retirement were identical to Theodora's. No one could compel her to marry; if she did not, she commanded the resources and men of Nablus unimpeded. If she wished to remarry, however, she would need the king's consent.

Notably, during the Count of Flanders' sojourn in the Holy Land in 1177, he travelled to Nablus to seek out the dowager queen of Jerusalem. The reasons for this visit are obscure, yet appear connected to the impending campaign against Egypt, then planned by Baldwin IV. Flanders probably sought Maria Comnena's opinion about probable Byzantine reactions to his demands and intentions regarding that expedition. The fact that he would seek out the dowager queen strongly suggests that Maria was viewed as capable of providing advice and insight. This indicates she was perceived as intelligent and reasonable.

Her choice of a second husband bears out such an assessment. Rather than eloping with a man old enough to be her father and ending her days as a virtual prisoner in Damascus as her cousin Theodora had, Maria selected the highly respected younger brother of one of Jerusalem's leading barons, Balian d'Ibelin. She did so with the king's explicit consent at roughly the same time as Baldwin IV's spectacular victory over Saladin at the Battle of Montgisard in November 1177. The king's consent may have been given as a reward for Ibelin's exceptional contribution to that victory. Certainly, this marriage elevated the younger Ibelin to a position of significant power since he thereby gained control of the revenues and knights of Nablus.[23] Maria's choice proved wise, and she continued to play an indirect role in the fate of the kingdom almost until she died in 1217. (Details are provided below and in the full biography of Maria.)

The Queen Mother: Agnes de Courtenay

When Baldwin IV ascended the throne, he had already lost the use of his right arm. Although he could ride extraordinarily well and bore no marks of disfigurement at that time, it soon became apparent he was suffering from leprosy. The Latin East followed the Byzantine tradition of treating leprosy not as a sign of sin but as an indication of divine grace. It was called the 'Holy Disease', and legends abounded about Christ taking the form of a leper. Thus, Baldwin IV was not isolated or ostracised; he ruled with his subjects' full consent – and with the active and undivided support of his vassals – for as long as he was physically able.

However, it was equally clear that he could not marry and beget heirs of his body. Thus, his full sister Sibylla and half-sister Isabella became his heirs apparent, and finding suitable husbands for them became one of the High

Court's primary concerns. It was the issue of succession, not support for Baldwin IV himself, which ultimately divided and weakened the kingdom.

Meanwhile, in the absence of a queen consort, Baldwin's mother, Agnes de Courtenay, became the first lady of the land. One can well imagine Agnes' satisfaction in returning to the court. She had been discarded by her husband, denied a crown and separated from her two children thirteen years earlier. Now she was back with a vengeance.

Hostile chronicles allege scandalous sexual behaviour to the queen mother. She was accused of carrying on affairs with both Heraclius, the Archbishop of Caesarea and with the French adventurer Aimery de Lusignan, the younger son of Hugh VIII, Lord de la Marche. While such allegations are probably fabricated, she was married four times (Reynald de Marash, Amalric of Jerusalem, Hugh d'Ibelin and Reynald de Sidon) and never demonstrated any inclination towards modesty, chastity or piety.

A more serious criticism of Agnes is that she misused her influence on her son for personal and dynastic enrichment rather than the benefit of the kingdom, something that will be discussed in more detail in the chapter on political power. Suffice it to say that had Baldwin IV favoured other advisors over his mother, he might have left his kingdom in competent hands at his death. Instead, on Agnes' advice, he allowed his sister Sibylla to marry the unpopular and incompetent Guy de Lusignan. As a result, his significant accomplishments have been overshadowed by the collapse of his kingdom little more than two years after his death.

Yet to Baldwin's great credit, despite the ravages of leprosy and the rise of a powerful opponent in the form of Saladin, he was a surprisingly strong king. Saladin had seized power first in Cairo and then in Damascus the same year King Amalric died. Saladin then spent years fighting his Muslim rivals in Aleppo and Mosul while beating the drum of jihad either from conviction or, as a usurper and a Kurd, to rally his disgruntled and divided subjects around him.

If one includes the two sieges of Kerak (1183 and 1184) and the siege of Beirut (1182), Saladin invaded the Kingdom of Jerusalem no less than six times during Baldwin IV's reign. All his incursions were effectively repelled. Indeed, the so-called 'Leper King' Baldwin IV dramatically destroyed Saladin's army in 1177 at the Battle of Montgisard, soundly defeated the sultan's army at the Battle of Le Fobelet in 1182, broke the three sieges mentioned earlier and suffered only two significant setbacks. The first was at the Battle on the Litani/Marj Ayun (1179), where he allowed his army to become dispersed following the rout of Saladin's advance guard. The second, in the same year, was the destruction of a new castle Baldwin IV had attempted to build on disputed border lands near Jacob's Ford.

Baldwin commanded his forces from horseback in the early years of his reign, starting with raids into Saracen territory shortly after obtaining his majority in 1176, again at Montgisard in 1177, and fatefully at Marj Ayun in 1179, where he was unhorsed and unable to remount because, by then, the paralysis had spread to both arms. After that, however, his physical condition deteriorated. He was forced to command his armies from a litter at Le Fobelet in 1182, and in the following year, he temporarily surrendered command of his army to his brother-in-law Guy de Lusignan. The latter's performance was so disastrous that Baldwin dismissed him and resumed the burden of governance and command. He had himself dragged in a litter to the edge of the Dead Sea to lift Saladin's siege of Kerak, and the sultan retreated at the mere approach of the 'Leper King'.

In the last year of his life and reign, Baldwin tried frantically to reverse the disastrous decision he had made by allowing his sister Sibylla to marry Guy de Lusignan. He sought a pretext to prevent Lusignan's ascension to the throne of Jerusalem. Baldwin first crowned his nephew, Sibylla's son by her first husband William de Montferrat, co-king as Baldwin V and the barons swore oaths of fealty to the little boy. He next asked the Church to find grounds for the annulment of Sibylla's marriage to Guy. When that failed due to Sibylla's intransigence and clerical reluctance, Baldwin IV and the High Court took the more radical step of offering the crown of Jerusalem to a completely new dynasty. A delegation composed of the Patriarch of Jerusalem, and the Masters of both the Knights Templar and Knights Hospitaller offered the keys to the Tower of David (symbol of secular power) and the Church of the Holy Sepulchre (sacred power) to the Holy Roman Emperor, the king of France and the king of England, one after another. Yet none of these monarchs were willing to abdicate their power in the West for the honour of ruling in the Holy Land. Nor did they send their sons or other candidates to the East. The delegation returned only with promises of funds and men, not a new king.

In the end, Baldwin could do no more than make his barons swear that if Baldwin V died before he could sire an heir, the barons would seek the advice of the Holy Roman Emperor, the kings of England and France and the pope in deciding who should succeed Baldwin V. It was an unsatisfactory solution. Given the acute threat posed by Saladin's repeated aggression, Jerusalem needed a vigorous and competent king, not a lengthy and politically fraught appeal to Western powers with conflicting interests and little understanding of the situation in Outremer. Unfortunately, Baldwin IV could achieve no more.

In April 1185, Baldwin IV died, leaving his 8-year-old co-king Baldwin V the sole ruler of Jerusalem. The able and experienced Raymond of Tripoli was elected by the High Court to assume the duties of regent, just as he had for

Baldwin IV eleven years earlier. Tripoli's first act as regent was to sign a four-year truce with Saladin to give the kingdom breathing space and his young king time to grow up. But Baldwin V was not well. He died sixteen months later, in August 1186. Baldwin IV's worst nightmare was about to come true.

Jerusalem's Most Disastrous Queen: Sibylla

By the rules of primogeniture, Baldwin V's successor was his mother, Princess Sibylla. However, the Kingdom of Jerusalem did not strictly follow the laws of primogeniture, instead endowing the High Court with the authority to select a suitable successor to a dead monarch from various candidates. In this case, the barons had already sworn to seek the advice of the pope, the Holy Roman Emperor and the kings of England and France before crowning a successor.

Sibylla was in no doubt about her unpopularity or the reason for it. The barons had never approved of Lusignan; he had been foisted on them by the queen mother, abetted by her protégé, the patriarch. Furthermore, the barons had forced Baldwin IV to rescind his appointment of Guy de Lusignan to the regency three years earlier. Finally, her brother's attempts to force an annulment of her marriage received widespread backing among the barons. In short, the majority of the High Court vehemently opposed her husband, Guy de Lusignan, and were unlikely to elect him king.

However, Sibylla was the heir apparent and had the support of her mother and husband's kin, namely the titular Count of Edessa, Joscelyn de Courtenay, who now enjoyed the Lordship of Toron he had inherited from his sister, the queen mother, and likewise the support of the constable, Guy's older brother, Aimery de Lusignan. Also in Sibylla's camp was the Patriarch of Jerusalem, a man who owed his appointment to her mother. In addition, she enjoyed the fickle support of the unscrupulous baron Reynald de Châtillon. Finally, she obtained the backing of the Master of the Knights Templar, a Flemish knight by the name of Gerard de Ridefort, who was a bitter enemy of the Count of Tripoli for entirely personal reasons. There may have been a scattering of lesser knights who likewise favoured the succession of Sibylla, but if they existed, their names are unknown.

Most of the barons and bishops remained staunchly opposed to Sibylla and her despised husband, Guy de Lusignan. They had, of course, sworn to seek the advice of the pope et al before selecting a new monarch, but this was not a practical solution given the acute threat from Saladin. At a minimum, it entailed a lengthy interregnum during which the advice of the Western powerbrokers was sought and required the election of a regent until a candidate had been selected. In short, the need to discuss the situation was urgent, and the acting regent, the Count of Tripoli, summoned the High Court to Nablus for deliberations.

There was nothing nefarious about such a summons. Tripoli had been legally appointed regent of the kingdom, and no new monarch had been crowned and anointed. It was his duty to summon the High Court. There was no single location where the High Court met. It had met in Acre and Nablus in the past, both lordships being part of the royal domain no less than Jerusalem itself. Other factors influencing the venue were a strong and hostile Templar presence in Jerusalem and the friendly protection offered by the Dowager Queen Maria and her second husband in Nablus.

Whatever the reasons, the High Court met in Nablus to discuss the succession. Anticipating that she would not be selected, Sibylla persuaded her supporters to crown her without the consent of the High Court. This was a blatant usurpation of the throne, and both Sibylla and her supporters knew it. Furthermore, Sibylla only managed to convince her followers to undertake such illegal action by promising to divorce Guy and marry again. However, the accoutrements required for a coronation were locked in the Church of the Holy Sepulchre, and the Masters of the Temple and the Hospital each had a key to the chest containing them. When the Master of the Hospital realised what Sibylla and her supporters planned, he refused to open the chest. A scuffle ensued in which the Templar Master and Châtillon intimidated and nearly overpowered the Hospitaller, who – in desperation – threw the key out of a window. This, of course, only delayed things by a few moments. The key was found, and a hasty coronation ceremony was staged.

No sooner was Sibylla crowned and anointed than she declared that her new husband would be the same as her old husband: Guy de Lusignan. This betrayal of her supporters was too much for even the patriarch to stomach. He refused to crown Guy de Lusignan, and Sibylla crowned him herself. The legitimacy of such a coronation was dubious at best.

The word of Sibylla's coup rapidly reached Nablus, where the High Court hastily agreed that the best course of action was to crown Baldwin's other sister, Isabella, as the legitimate queen. Since the Templars controlled Jerusalem, the barons planned to hold the coronation in Bethlehem, the site of Baldwin I and Baldwin II's coronations.

The idea of two rival queens in a kingdom surrounded by enemies is often ridiculed as foolish or even treasonous, yet it was by no means unreasonable. The barons and bishops opposing Sibylla outnumbered her supporters significantly and commanded the bulk of the feudal troops. Furthermore, since she had deceived her followers by first promising to set Guy aside and then crowning him, it is unclear how many of Sibylla's initial supporters were still with her. With the wisdom of hindsight, regardless of how dangerous it might have been to split the kingdom into warring factions, it would not have been worse than what Sibylla and Guy did – namely lose the entire kingdom to Saladin in less than one year.

The High Court's plans to crown a counter-queen to challenge the usurper Sibylla collapsed when Isabella's husband Toron slipped out of Nablus in the dark of night to go to Jerusalem and swear homage to Sibylla and Guy. This act made the coronation of Isabella impossible, as she needed a king-consort, and her husband had just disqualified himself. Until she rid herself of Toron, Isabella could not wear the crown. So, most of the barons and bishops of Jerusalem reluctantly caved in and came to terms with the situation. They paid homage to Guy de Lusignan, who made it as difficult for them as possible by gloating and exalting in his new status.

Two barons flatly refused to accept the patently illegitimate king: the Baron of Ramla and Mirabel and erstwhile suitor for Sibylla's hand, Baldwin d'Ibelin, and Raymond, Count of Tripoli, the former regent. Instead of doing homage to Guy de Lusignan, Ramla demonstratively left the kingdom to seek his fortune in Antioch, where he was reputedly well-received. The Count of Tripoli, on the other hand, simply refused to recognise Guy as Jerusalem's king. As the County of Tripoli was an independent political entity and not legally subordinate to Jerusalem, this position was perfectly legitimate. However, Tripoli also held the principality of Galilee by right of his wife. This was a component and strategically vital part of the Kingdom of Jerusalem. Tripoli's refusal to do homage to Guy for his wife's barony put him on a collision course with Lusignan and earned him the sobriquet of traitor in some accounts.

The salient point, however, is that by alienating and offending these two powerful noblemen, Sibylla and her husband had put the kingdom at risk. To be sure, Ramla's feudal levees were commanded by his younger brother, Balian of Nablus, who thereby commanded the third largest contingent of troops in the feudal levee. However, Tripoli controlled many more, roughly one-quarter of the knights in the combined armies of Jerusalem and Tripoli. Even more dangerously, his wife's barony of Galilee sat on the kingdom's eastern border, straddling the Jordan River. If it were lost, the kingdom would become indefensible. Sibylla had usurped a crown and made her kingdom more vulnerable than ever in the process.

As if that wasn't bad enough, in his hubris over his coronation, Guy de Lusignan was not content to let Tripoli withdraw to his lands and stew in his dissatisfaction. Instead, Guy declared his intent to bring Tripoli to heel and summoned the feudal army, intending to attack Galilee and force Tripoli into submission. Tripoli responded by concluding a defensive pact with none other than Sultan Saladin. In doing so, Tripoli put himself in the wrong, yet it is important to remember that he was the injured party. Not only was the constitution of Jerusalem on his side concerning Guy's legitimacy, but Tripoli was also being threatened.

Fortunately, wiser heads prevailed, and Guy was persuaded not to attack. Balian d'Ibelin offered to mediate and eventually succeeded, but not before Saladin had taken advantage of the situation to carry out a 'reconnaissance in force' through Galilee into the province of Acre. This was the prelude to a full-scale invasion and retaliation for attacks by Reynald de Châtillon against Saracen convoys that were in blatant violation of a truce King Guy had just signed with Saladin.

Châtillon notoriously denied that King Guy could commit him to any truce, claiming complete independence from the king of Jerusalem as absolute lord in his barony of Transjordan. Châtillon's stand revealed either the reason why he had supported Sibylla in the first place (he considered Guy so insignificant he could ignore him at will) or that he was one of Sibylla's supporters who had expected her to replace Guy with a more competent new husband and now viewed Guy as illegitimate.

Whatever Châtillon's motives for his attacks, Saladin's counter-incursion provoked a response from the Templars and Hospitallers. On 2 May 1187, at the Springs of Cresson, a small force of roughly 110 knights clashed with a Saracen army, allegedly 6,000 strong, that wiped out the Franks. Shaken by the sight of Christian heads spiked on the lances of the withdrawing Saracens, Tripoli agreed to reconcile with Lusignan. Tripoli knelt before Lusignan in homage, and King Guy raised him, embraced him and gave him the kiss of peace.

It was not a moment too soon. Just over a month later, Saladin was back again, this time with his entire army. It was his seventh and largest invasion. Guy called up the feudal army, denuding the cities and castles of their defenders. Notably, all the barons of Jerusalem followed the king's summons, including erstwhile rebels and insubordinate barons such as Tripoli and Châtillon. While the army of Jerusalem gathered at the Springs of Sephorie, Saladin seized the city of Tiberias in Galilee, which was defended by its feudal lord, Lady Eschiva, Tripoli's wife. She sent word to her feudal overlord, King Guy, requesting relief.

As was customary, King Guy called a council of war to seek the advice of his barons. Tripoli advised caution, arguing it was a trap and the Frankish army should stay where it was and force the Saracens to come to them. Such a policy, however, contradicted the traditions of the kingdom; for nearly a century, it had been most successful when on the offensive. Furthermore, Guy had been heavily criticised by the barons of Jerusalem for not going on the offensive in 1183. The decision to advance towards Saladin was, therefore, not inherently foolish. In his detailed analysis of the battle, historian John France suggests that the army's initial advance to the springs at Turan was strategically sound. France argues that at Turan, 'Guy would have been in an unassailable position ... and from there he could threaten to advance and oblige Saladin to keep his forces on the edge of the plateau in readiness. This was a game that Saladin's army could not play indefinitely'.[24]

Guy's mistake was in continuing across the arid plain against the advice of his barons, who nevertheless followed him. France quotes a letter from Saladin to the Caliph in Baghdad in which he says: 'Satan incited Guy to do what ran counter to his purpose'. Namely, he took his army away from the water at Turan. Before the army of Jerusalem could reach the springs of Hattin, it had been surrounded. The Christian forces were forced to camp for the night on the arid plateau without water, mocked by the surrounding Saracens who poured their surplus water on the earth. The Saracens also lit fires upwind of the army of Jerusalem so that the smoke aggravated Frankish thirst. The following day, on 4 July 1187, battle began. After a day-long struggle, the feudal army of Jerusalem was all but obliterated. Only three barons fought their way off the field with a few hundred knights and an estimated 3,000 infantry. These were Raymond de Tripoli, Reginald de Sidon and Balian d'Ibelin. Joscelyn of Edessa also escaped capture, but it is unclear if he took part in the battle or had remained behind in Acre. The rest, including King Guy, were either dead or captured by the enemy.

And Queen Sibylla, who had brought this disaster to the kingdom by refusing to divorce Guy at her brother's or her own followers' urging? Sibylla was in Jerusalem. Yet when the sultan demanded the city's surrender, it was a delegation of burghers, not Sibylla, who offered defiance. Rather than rallying the defenders of the holiest city in Christendom, Sibylla begged to be allowed to join her husband in captivity. That is: the reigning queen of Jerusalem begged to be allowed to desert her kingdom and her subjects to place herself in the hands of her enemies for the sole purpose of being near her husband, who had just led her kingdom to a disastrous defeat.

Saladin naturally obliged. Sibylla was allowed out of Jerusalem to join her husband in captivity in Saracen-held Nablus while his armies swept over the rest of her kingdom. Without defenders, city after city offered terms to spare the citizens rape and slaughter. The few cities that showed defiance – Jaffa and Beirut – were overrun, and the inhabitants were mercilessly put to the sword or dragged away into slavery. By the end of September 1187, only the island city of Tyre and isolated castles such as Kerak and Crak des Chevaliers held out, along with Jerusalem itself. The latter was flooded with tens of thousands of refugees who had fled before the Saracens from other inland cities and the surrounding countryside. After a spirited defence in which non-combatants outnumbered fighting men by fifty to one, the Holy City fell to Saladin. The Kingdom of Jerusalem effectively ceased to exist.

The shock allegedly killed Pope Urban III and set in motion a new crusade that has gone down in history as the Third. This crusade was led by the Holy Roman Emperor Frederick Barbarossa, King Philip II of France and King Richard I of England. Yet before the cumbersome process of finding the finances, volunteers and ships for this great expedition to the east was complete, Saladin released King Guy from captivity on the basis of an oath to never take up arms against Muslims again. It was 1188, and the moment Guy de Lusignan was released, he went to Antioch and raised an army of roughly 700 knights and an unknown number of other volunteers. With this force at his back, Guy resumed the fight against the Muslims in blatant violation of his oath to Saladin. Sibylla rode at his side.

Guy's immediate destination was Tyre, the only city in his wife's former kingdom still in Christian hands. To Guy and Sibylla's surprise, their reception in Tyre was frigid. The nobleman in command of the defences of Tyre was a certain Conrad de Montferrat, the brother of Sibylla's first husband, William de Montferrat. Conrad kept the city gates closed and bluntly told Guy de Lusignan that he had lost his crown when he lost his kingdom; Sibylla did not rate even a mention.

So, Guy continued down the coast until he came to Acre. The inhabitants of Acre, who had surrendered to Saladin in 1187, had been allowed to withdraw with their moveable goods. When Guy and his small army arrived in 1189, Acre was garrisoned by Egyptian troops devoted to Saladin. Guy's decision to lay siege to Acre proved nearly as senseless and costly as his insistence on leaving the springs of Turan to advance towards Hattin. The siege of Acre swallowed tens of thousands of Christian lives in the next two years, including the Patriarch of Jerusalem, 6 archbishops, 12 bishops, 40 counts and 500 barons. As much as seventy-five per cent of the men who took part in the siege, most of them crusaders who arrived from the West ahead of the armies led by the crowned leaders, perished. Most fell victim to disease and malnutrition, even starvation, but many died in the near-constant skirmishing and occasional assaults. Militarily, this siege was senseless. In terms of immobility, filth and misery it was reminiscent of the trench warfare of WWI. Yet, in one way, it proved poetically just; this brainchild of Guy de Lusignan killed his last remnant of royal legitimacy, Queen Sibylla.

In October 1190, while living in a tent in the squalid siege camp before Acre, Queen Sibylla died of fever. So ended the life of one of Jerusalem's most powerful queens. Like Melisende, she ruled in her own right, not as a consort, and throughout her reign was in a position to influence the course of events directly. Had she married the mastermind behind the rout of Saladin at Montgisard, Baldwin of Ramla, for example, Saladin might have been trapped at Turan rather than obliterating the army of Jerusalem at Hattin.

Sibylla had power, and she could be ruthless in exploiting it, as her usurpation of the throne in 1186 demonstrates. Yet she used her power only to elevate her husband and then to slavishly submit to him thereafter. To her last breath, Sibylla appears to have loved Guy de Lusignan more than she loved her kingdom, her subjects or her life. While such love is romantic and admirable in Victorian literature, it is misplaced and ridiculous in a ruling queen. Fortunately for the Kingdom of Jerusalem, her sister was made of much sterner stuff.

Chapter 4

The Crusader States, 1190–1291

A Queen for All Seasons: Isabella I

Isabella was the youngest of King Amalric's children, born to his second wife, the Byzantine Princess Maria Comnena, after his coronation. In the eyes of many contemporary legal scholars, this gave her precedence over her elder half-siblings, born of a dissolved marriage before her father was crowned. She was, however, only 2 years old at the time of her father's sudden death, and the High Court of Jerusalem had elected her half-brother Baldwin as her father's successor. Nevertheless, her unimpeachable legitimacy and close ties to the Byzantine royal house made her a latent threat to Agnes de Courtenay's two children, born of an invalid marriage before Amalric was anointed.

Agnes sought to reduce the risk to her offspring by removing Isabella from her mother and stepfather's care at age 8 to betroth her to a man unlikely to defend Isabella's claims to the crown. The man she chose was Humphrey IV of Toron. Humphrey was a minor under the control of his mother's third husband, the infamous Reynald de Châtillon. Châtillon conducted the marriage negotiations on his ward's behalf, but not necessarily in his interests. Humphrey lost his barony, which reverted to the crown in exchange for a money fief. Three years later, at age 11, Isabella married Humphrey in Châtillon's fortress of Kerak in the midst of a Saracen siege. When Baldwin IV died less than two years later, the majority of the High Court chose Isabella as their queen over her sister Sibylla. Humphrey preferred to do homage to the usurpers Sibylla and Guy rather than wear the crown himself. He loyally fought with King Guy at Hattin and went into captivity with him. On his release from Saracen detention, he joined Guy at the siege of Acre, and Isabella joined him there.

Thus, Isabella was living in his tent in the siege camp outside Acre when in October 1190, her sister Queen Sibylla succumbed to illness and died without heirs. It is worth reviewing this in detail since the most fulsome contemporary account of what happened next has coloured all subsequent histories and warped perceptions of Isabella ever since.

The anonymous *Itinerarium Peregrinorum et Gesta Regis Ricardi*, written by someone close to the English court, describes with blistering outrage how Conrad de Montferrat had long schemed to 'steal' the throne of Jerusalem and, at last, struck upon the idea of abducting Isabella – a crime he compares to the abduction of Helen of Sparta by Paris of Troy, 'only worse'. To realise his plan, the *Itinerarium* claims, Conrad 'surpassed the deceits of Sinon, the eloquence of Ulysses and the forked tongue of Mithridates'. According to this English cleric, who was unlikely to have ever met any of the principals, Conrad set about bribing, flattering and corrupting bishops and barons as never before in recorded history. Throughout, the chronicler says, Conrad was aided and abetted by three barons of the Kingdom of Jerusalem (Sidon, Haifa and Ibelin) who combined 'the treachery of Judas, the cruelty of Nero, and the wickedness of Herod, and everything the present age abhors and ancient times condemned'.[25] The anonymous slanderer then admits that, although Isabella at first resisted the idea of divorcing Humphrey, she was soon persuaded to consent to it because 'a woman's opinion changes very easily' and 'a girl is easily taught to do what is morally wrong'.[26]

It should be clear to modern readers that something is wrong with this account. First, the author notably brings no evidence of a single act of treachery, cruelty or wickedness and, second, completely ignores the High Court of Jerusalem and its constitutional right to elect kings and select husbands for heiresses. Rather than looking at the legitimate interests of the kingdom and the political forces at play, the chronicler wallows in melodrama, slander and prejudice.

The situation looks significantly different if seen through the eyes of the power brokers on the ground in Acre in 1190: the barons of Jerusalem. The hereditary queen was dead. She had been predeceased by all her children, while her husband had been foisted upon the kingdom in a secret marriage that circumvented their legitimate constitutional right to select husbands for heiresses to the crown. Sibylla had then usurped the crown, without obtaining the consent of the High Court for her coronation, and personally crowned the man she had promised to set aside. This man had promptly attacked his most powerful baron, the Count of Tripoli, driving the latter into an alliance with Saladin. When threatened by a Saracen invasion, he arrogantly ignored the military advice of the collective barons. As a result, the army was crushed, thousands of Christians killed and many more enslaved, while Saladin swept over and occupied the entire kingdom, bar only a single city.

In short, Guy had been detested since he married Sibylla ten years earlier, and his popularity had declined ever since. By October 1190, he had not a shred of credibility or support left, and with Sibylla's death, he lost the last lingering whiff of legitimacy. In short, anointed or not, the barons refused to view him as their king and were determined to elect a new monarch.

In the established tradition of seeking a new monarch from among the closest relatives of the deceased monarch, the barons focused on Sibylla's most immediate blood relation, namely her sister Isabella, whose claim to the throne was arguably better than Sibylla's (or Baldwin IV's) claim had ever been. The barons were happy to recognise Isabella as their reigning queen, but in so doing, her husband would automatically become king consort and commander of Jerusalem's armies.

That was the problem. Isabella's husband, Humphrey de Toron, was as unacceptable to the barons as Guy de Lusignan, if for different reasons. Aside from his alleged femininity, he had already betrayed the High Court in 1186, when they offered him the crown only for him to do homage to the very man they were trying to depose. The barons would not have Humphrey as their king, which meant their support for Isabella was contingent upon her setting Humphrey aside and marrying the man of their choice as she should have done in the first place. It will be remembered that the High Court had also required Isabella's father (Amalric I) to separate from his wife, Agnes de Courtenay, before it recognised him as king.

In short, there were legal precedents and rational reasons for the barons' actions that the *Itinerarium* ignores in its effort to explain events as base deeds of 'corruption', 'treachery' and 'cruelty'. Far from being corrupted by a treacherous, greedy and corrupt Montferrat, the barons of Jerusalem chose a man they believed would serve their interests best. In November 1190, the barons and burghers of Jerusalem wanted a militarily competent leader around whom they could rally, and there were not many candidates available after the debacle of Hattin. Conrad de Montferrat, however, seemed to fit the bill.

This Italian nobleman had rescued the only free city in the kingdom when it was on the brink of surrender. He had defended it twice against sieges by Saladin, thereby retaining a bridgehead in the Levant into which massive reinforcements had been poured, first from Sicily and then from farther West. Nor were Montferrat's military successes in the Holy Land his first; he had a distinguished military career fighting in the Holy Roman and Byzantine Empires. As an outsider, he did not raise one local baron above the others. Finally, he was the first cousin of Emperor Frederick Barbarossa and a more distant cousin of Philip II of France. As such, he was a far more suitable spouse for the ruling queen of Jerusalem than the obscure and impoverished Guy de Lusignan had been.

His only flaw was that his second wife, a Byzantine princess, was still alive in Constantinople. Montferrat somehow convinced the barons she was dead or that he was legally separated from her, or perhaps he simply convinced them to close their eyes to this undesirable fact as they had once been willing to ignore Baldwin I's marriage to the Armenian Lady Arda when he married Adelaide of Sicily. What no one could cover up or overlook, however, was the fact that Isabella had been married to Humphrey de Toron since 1183. This marriage needed to be publicly dissolved before marriage to Montferrat could be celebrated.

Four years earlier, Sibylla had promised her supporters she would set Guy aside after she was crowned, only to break her word and place the crown on Guy's head. The surviving members of the High Court remembered that deceit all too well. Determined not to be tricked and trapped a second time, they insisted that Isabella rid herself of Humphrey *before* they would recognise her as queen. This is the context in which Isabella's alleged 'abduction' took place.

As to what happened, all chronicles, including the *Itinerarium*, are in surprising agreement. Shortly after Sibylla's death, knights entered the tent Isabella shared with Humphrey and removed her against her will. She was not, however, taken to Conrad, much less raped by him, but rather put in the care and protection of high-ranking clerics. She was sequestered and protected to prevent harm from coming to her while a clerical court was convened to rule on the validity of her marriage to Humphrey. The case hinged on the critical theological principle of mutual consent. Humphrey claimed that Isabella had consented, but when challenged by a witness to prove his word with his body (i.e., in judicial combat), Humphrey hung his head and refused to take up the thrown gauntlet. Isabella testified that she had *not* consented.

Ultimately, a clerical court headed by the papal legate ruled that Isabella's marriage to Humphrey was invalid because, regardless of consent, she was not of legal age at the time of the marriage. That is, she was not yet 12 years old, the age at which girls were deemed adults and legally capable of giving consent. On 24 November 1190, Isabella married Conrad de Montferrat. Immediately following the marriage, the barons of Jerusalem did homage to her as their queen.

The question that remains is Isabella's role in this affair. There seems little doubt she was taken by surprise when strange knights burst into her tent in the dark of night and dragged her away from the man she had viewed as her husband for the past ten years. When they took her, she could not have known what they intended to do. She may have believed they were Saracens in disguise or simply unscrupulous men intent on rape for the sake of a crown. Resistance was logical and understandable.

Once she had been separated from Humphrey and put under Church protection, however, the situation was explained to her by her mother, the dowager queen of Jerusalem, Maria Comnena. The Lyon Continuation of

William of Tyre's history, which is believed to be based primarily on sources from within the crusader states rather than Western sources states:

> [Queen Maria] remonstrated with [Isabella] repeatedly and explained that she [Isabella] could not become lady of the kingdom unless she left Humphrey. She reminded her of the evil deed that [Humphrey] had done … [when he] had done homage to Queen Sibylla. … So long as Isabella was his wife, she could have neither honour nor her father's kingdom.[27]

This text confirms that Isabella was initially reluctant to take her mother's advice because she presumably loved Humphrey. Yet all sources agree that, in the end, she not only testified she had not legally consented to the marriage with Humphrey but also went willingly into the marriage with Montferrat. The latter is significant. While the clerical court ruled that Isabella's marriage to Toron – when she was only 11 – was invalid, it also explicitly told her she was free to marry whomever she chose now. She could have decided to remarry Humphrey immediately; she did not. The reason seems obvious. Isabella understood that the barons refused categorically to do homage to Humphrey. She could not have both Humphrey and her kingdom. Unlike her sister Sibylla, Isabella chose the crown over the man.

The following spring, the kings of England and France arrived with large armies to reinforce the stalled siege of Acre. Philip II of France recognised his cousin Conrad de Montferrat as king of Jerusalem, but Richard I of England backed Guy de Lusignan. As long as the powerful western monarchs were present in the Holy Land, squabbles over claims to a kingdom that had effectively ceased to exist seemed irrelevant. Guy continued to call himself king yet docilely followed Richard the Lionheart wherever he went. Conrad remained in Tyre and tried to cut a separate peace with Saladin, while the sultan attempted to play Conrad against Richard.

Meanwhile the crusaders forced the garrison of Acre to surrender on 12 July 1191. Immediately afterwards, the French king abandoned the crusade, weakening Conrad's (and Isabella's) position, while the rest of the crusading army continued down the coast under Richard the Lionheart's leadership. Outside Arsuf on 7 September, the joint Frankish/crusader army effectively rebuffed an attempt by Saladin to halt their advance. On 10 September, they recaptured Jaffa and turned towards the ultimate goal: Jerusalem.

Saladin, however, had garrisoned Jerusalem strongly and poisoned the wells around it. By late December, the crusaders were forced to face the fact that they did not have the strength for an assault nor the time to besiege the city. More importantly, as the local barons, Templars and Hospitallers noted, even if they took Jerusalem by storm, they could not retain it for long because the vast majority of the crusaders would return to the West. The forces remaining in the Holy Land were insufficient to defend an isolated outpost such as Jerusalem against the overwhelming might of Saladin. The combined Frankish and crusader host withdrew to the coast.

Here, Richard of England received word that his brother John and the king of France were trying to steal his inheritance. Since he would soon have to return home to defend his empire, Richard finally conceded that he had to leave Jerusalem in the hands of a king capable of protecting the gains he had come so far and fought so hard to achieve. He agreed to let the barons of Jerusalem elect their king, as was their constitutional right, and they unanimously elected Conrad de Montferrat. Richard accepted their decision, dropping his support for Guy de Lusignan. The English king, however, softened the impact of withdrawing his support from Lusignan by allowing him to buy the island of Cyprus.

Richard had captured Cyprus on his way to Acre. While the Mediterranean island was technically a part of the Byzantine empire, an unpopular Greek tyrant, Isaac Comnenus, had seized it several years earlier and declared his independence from Constantinople. The English king captured the island in less than six weeks without incurring significant casualties, largely because he had been welcomed by most of the island's residents as a liberator. He secured their continued cooperation by promising to restore the laws of Manuel I Comnenus, the powerful and highly respected Byzantine Emperor and so ruler of Cyprus from 1143 until 1180.

Yet Richard's interests in Cyprus were not dynastic. He did not need or want another lordship. Richard the Lionheart was a consummate strategist who recognised Cyprus' military and strategic importance in securing the lines of communication between the West and the Holy Land. Cyprus controlled the Eastern Mediterranean and, with it, the coast of the Levant. Richard rightly foresaw that Cyprus would become an important staging ground for future crusades and a breadbasket for the territorially diminished crusader states on the mainland. In other words, although the Third Crusade restored Frankish control over the key coastal cities and the coastal plain between them, this much-reduced kingdom was not self-sufficient in foodstuffs. It was dependent on supplies of many vital materials from Cyprus. By selling Cyprus to Lusignan, Richard replenished his coffers and distracted Guy from losing his former kingdom while ensuring Cyprus remained in Latin Christian hands.

Just when everything appeared settled, however, assassins struck down Conrad de Montferrat in the streets of Tyre on 28 April 1192. Mortally wounded, he was carried to Isabella and died in her arms. At the time, she was carrying his child.

Isabella was now a 20-year-old widowed queen. She was not a pawn; her barons had already paid homage to her. She could legally marry whomever she liked – or choose not to remarry. Yet she was also the queen of a fragile and vulnerable kingdom surrounded by enemies. The powerful crusading armies that had come to restore it were already disintegrating. The king of France had left, and the king of England had declared his intention to leave shortly. With him would go most of the crusaders. If Jerusalem were to survive, it would need a king capable of defending it, a king the barons respected and were willing to obey.

Most narratives of what happened next focus poetically on personalities rather than institutions. Some accounts say King Richard recommended a candidate as Isabella's next husband, while other accounts claim that the 'people of Tyre' spontaneously acclaimed him. Both versions ignore – again – the geopolitical reality in Outremer. The notion of the common people of one city in the kingdom having the right to 'elect' a king by acclamation is ludicrous. By this time, Acre, Caesarea, Arsuf, Jaffa and Ascalon were also in Frankish hands. If the common citizens elected Jerusalem's kings, then the burghers of all these cities would have had a say in his election. But the common people in the Kingdom of Jerusalem did not – and never had – elected their kings any more than the commoners of England or France did.

As for the English king, he had only days earlier acknowledged that the barons of Jerusalem had the sole right to select their king. Therefore, he would not have attempted to impose his candidate on them. The Lyon Continuation of Tyre correctly states that Richard acting 'on the advice of the barons of the kingdom' went to Tyre with their favoured candidate.[28] Yet, it is equally unthinkable that the barons would have made a recommendation (as they had the last time) without first consulting their ruling queen and obtaining her consent. The man they proposed to King Richard was, therefore, most likely Isabella's choice, possibly based on the advice of her barons, but not against her wishes. It was Henri de Champagne.

As the son of Marie de Champagne, Eleanor of Aquitaine's daughter by her first husband, Louis VII of France, Champagne was a nephew of both Philip II of France and Richard I of England. This made Champagne a worthy match for the ruling queen of Jerusalem and a highly diplomatic choice since neither the French nor English crown could object. He was also an ardent crusader who had come out to the Holy Land in advance of the main crusading armies. He was wealthy, young, courageous, courteous, educated and pious – in short, the personification of chivalry – and single. He was also just 26 years old. There is every reason to believe that Isabella knew and liked him before the proposal was put forward.

Yet the accounts of his selection agree he was a reluctant candidate for the crown of Jerusalem. On the one hand, he wanted to return home. On the other hand, Isabella was pregnant by Montferrat, which meant that if she bore a son, this boy would take precedence over any of Champagne's children. The Lyon continuation of Tyre claims that Champagne was only persuaded to take up the burden of Jerusalem and marry Isabella because of promises made to him by Richard of England; the English king allegedly vowed to return with an even greater army in a couple of years and conquer all the former Kingdom of Jerusalem and more. The *Itinerarium*, on the other hand, claims that while the magnates of the kingdom were attempting to persuade a reluctant Henri to become their king, Isabella herself 'came to the count of her own accord and offered him the keys of the city'.[29] It goes on to say the marriage was hastily prepared and celebrated on 5 May 1192 (seven days after Conrad's death). The author, who was so ready to insult Isabella, her mother and her stepfather a few pages earlier, now writes approvingly: 'I don't think that those who persuaded the count to do this had much to do, for it is no effort to force the willing'![30]

The important point is that Isabella, with astonishing fortitude under the circumstances, was prepared to do the right thing for her kingdom: marry a man acceptable to her barons and do so without insisting on a year of mourning or other conditions. Henri proved his worth immediately; he persuaded his uncle Richard, and so, the entire crusading host, to remain in the Holy Land throughout the summer rather than return to the West at once. Although a second march on Jerusalem ended like the first and for the same reason, the English king's dramatic victory over Saladin at Jaffa, at last, forced the sultan to the negotiating table. On 2 September 1192, Richard the Lionheart's envoys, headed by Isabella's husband and stepfather, signed a three-year truce with Saladin. As one of the last crusaders to depart, Richard the Lionheart sailed from Acre on 9 October 1192. Less than six months later, Saladin was dead. Isabella's kingdom had been saved, if in a more compact form.

The following five years of Isabella's life may have been amongst her happiest. She gave birth to Montferrat's posthumous daughter, who she named after her mother, Maria. She also gave Champagne three daughters, Marguerite, Alice and Philippa; the latter two lived to adulthood. Because of the truce with Saladin, the kingdom was at peace, and the first steps towards economic recovery were possible. As the ceasefire neared its end, large contingents of crusaders started to arrive to the Holy Land in anticipation of a crusade led by the Holy Roman Emperor Henry VI. Although the emperor died before he reached the Holy Land, German nobles and knights succeeded in recapturing the important coastal city of Beirut and, with it, established Frankish control of the entire coastline from Arsur (Jaffa had since been lost again) to the County of Tripoli. Perhaps because they were still hoping to recapture Jerusalem, Isabella and Henri had not been ceremoniously crowned and anointed, yet they were otherwise treated as king and queen.

In a freak accident, Henri de Champagne tragically died falling from a balcony (or when the balcony or its railing collapsed), leaving Isabella a widow in October 1197. Henri was just 31 at his death, and his widow Isabella was 25.

Again, as an adult widow and reigning queen, Isabella could have insisted on her right to remain single. It is unlikely that the barons would have taken action against her had she asserted her rights. Yet Isabella was a queen first and a woman second. She knew that her kingdom was still exceedingly vulnerable. Only weeks before, Saladin's brother al-Adil had been threatening at the gates of Acre; his army had barely been beaten off by the German crusaders and Isabella's army. Now his forces had seized Jaffa. She did not have the luxury to mourn or vacillate if she wanted to have a kingdom. The kingdom needed a strong king capable of defending it.

Isabella's choice – and it was undoubtedly her choice – fell on a man whom she had known long and well, namely Aimery de Lusignan, the older brother of her sister's disgraced consort Guy. Aimery had come to the Holy Land earlier than Guy. He had been appointed constable in the reign of Baldwin IV. For roughly thirty years, he had been married to her step-father's niece, Eschiva d'Ibelin. But Eschiva had recently died, leaving Aimery a widower with several young children. Furthermore, Aimery had succeeded his brother as lord of Cyprus, a rich island with substantial resources that would be of use to Jerusalem. Last but not least, in a savvy move, Aimery had done homage for Cyprus to the Holy Roman Emperor, thereby elevating the island lordship into a kingdom. This made him equal in status to the queen of Jerusalem.

There is every reason to believe that Isabella personally liked and respected Aimery. Yet she unquestionably chose him as her consort because he was well-suited to please her barons and secure their enthusiastic support. Aimery de Lusignan had already demonstrated his extraordinary capabilities. He had decades of experience fighting in the Holy Land and had already commanded Jerusalem's armies as constable under Baldwin IV. More recently, he had turned a rebellious island into a secure and prosperous kingdom. Equally importantly, Aimery was an outstanding administrator. In addition to elevating his lordship to a kingdom, he had wisely adopted the Greek administrative apparatus left behind by the Byzantines. This worked like a well-oiled machine to generate revenues and reduce local tensions and resentment. With the Greek bureaucracy behind him, Aimery rapidly established peace with the natives while consciously encouraging more settlement from the disenfranchised Franks of Syria. Lastly, he was economically savvy and pursued a policy of economic diversification, which led almost immediately to burgeoning prosperity.

Isabella and Aimery married in December 1197 and were crowned jointly in Acre's cathedral in January 1198. Afterwards, Aimery turned his many talents to the benefit of what remained of the Kingdom of Jerusalem. He secured a six-year truce with al-Adil in the first year of his reign which he later renewed. He thereby created the peace needed to concentrate on the reconstruction of institutions, infrastructure and the economy. He also commissioned scholars to collect information and record as much as possible from as many sources as possible about the laws of the Kingdom of Jerusalem to re-establish a legal basis for society. Meanwhile, Isabella gave birth to Sibylla in October 1198, a second daughter Melisende in 1200 and, at long last, a son in 1201. The boy was named Aimery after his father.

Yet tragedy struck again in early 1205. On 2 February, little Aimery died in Acre of unknown causes. Less than two months later, on 1 April, King Aimery fell victim to food poisoning after eating fish that was apparently off. Isabella may have partaken of the same meal or developed another illness. At roughly 33 years of age, she died on 5 May 1205, leaving her eldest daughter, Maria de Montferrat, as her heir.

Isabella may not have put herself in the limelight as much as Queen Melisende, yet her judicious choices for consort in 1192 and again in 1197 assured that her kingdom survived as a political entity. She chose to remain in the background, but that is not synonymous with being powerless. She most certainly guided Champagne as he navigated in a unique and, to him, unfamiliar legal environment, and he was reportedly devoted and reluctant to be parted from her. While Aimery was more independent, there is no indication that he ever attempted to raise himself above his wife, as Fulk had done. They were crowned and reigned jointly only to die little more than a month apart.

The Bartered Brides

Maria de Montferrat

Isabella's heir was Maria, her daughter by Conrad de Montferrat. She was at most 13 and more likely 12 when her stepfather and mother died in early 1205. She was also still a maiden, and the High Court immediately appointed a regent to rule for her until a suitable candidate for her husband and consort could be identified. The High Court's choice fell on her closest adult relative, her mother's half-brother, John d'Ibelin.

John was the son of the Dowager Queen Maria Comnena by her second husband, Balian d'Ibelin. He had been appointed constable of the kingdom by King Aimery in 1197. However, he exchanged this post for the lordship of Beirut sometime before 1200, although the exact date is unknown. Beirut was one of the few cities in the kingdom to defy Saladin in 1187, and it paid a terrible price in assault, slaughter and plunder. German crusaders had recaptured the city from a Saracen garrison in 1197, but the city and surrounding countryside were in such a ruinous state that even the military orders did not want to assume the cost of restoring it. John d'Ibelin, however, succeeded in making it a functioning port that was soon producing immense revenues. It was probably this, as well as his blood ties to the young queen, that encouraged the High Court to appoint him regent, although he was, at most, 27 years old at the time.

The Lord of Beirut maintained the truces with the Ayyubids and acted as a conscientious caretaker of his niece's kingdom, while representatives from the High Court requested that the French king select a suitable nobleman to be their queen's consort. By 1208, a candidate had been identified, namely John de Brienne. Brienne's title derived from a subsidiary county inside the County of Champagne, and John was, technically, only the regent of Brienne for his deceased elder brother's minor heir. As such, he was at best of secondary rank, and the French king's choice of this relatively obscure nobleman bordered on an insult to the once proud Kingdom of Jerusalem.

Yet Jerusalem was proud no more. It was symbolically and emotionally significant. It still commanded material wealth. But it was vulnerable and short of manpower. Beggars, as the expression goes, cannot be choosers. Besides, John de Brienne was a young and vigorous man, roughly 31, with a glamorous reputation on the tourney circuit. Furthermore, his cousin Walter of Montbéliard was then regent of Cyprus for King Hugh I, who was a minor. (Montbéliard had married the eldest of Hugh's sisters.) Very likely, Montbéliard put in a good word for Brienne.

Yet, while Brienne's reputation at arms was high, he was not a powerful lord with a large entourage or an extensive feudal base. To make up for this deficit, King Philip of France and the pope granted him large sums of money to hire mercenaries. In 1210, after almost two years of recruiting, John de Brienne arrived in the Kingdom of Jerusalem with an entourage estimated at 300 knights and an unknown number of squires, sergeants and archers. Although significant, this was not a vast crusading army likely to tip the balance of power in the Near East in favour of the Christians. Therefore, from the start, John was something of a disappointment to his subjects in Outremer.

Whether he was also a disappointment to his bride, the now 18-year-old Maria de Montferrat, is unknown. There is no reason to assume so. Not only was he a successful tournament champion, but he also came from the heartland of chivalry and was a writer of poetry and song. The couple was crowned jointly in Tyre, with most of the High Court in attendance.

This latter fact tempted the Saracens into launching an attack on Acre. Although the attack was beaten off, it was an inauspicious start to John and Maria's reign. Maria's new husband retaliated with a chevauchée (cavalry raid) of his own. Yet, while this did some damage and the participants returned loaded with loot, they achieved no lasting benefit for the kingdom. John next attempted to strike at Egypt with a sea-borne expedition into the Nile Delta. Unfortunately, he did not have sufficient force to do more than moderate damage to secondary targets. The Ayyubids concluded that John de Brienne was no Richard the Lionheart and was unlikely to do them serious harm. They brazenly began the construction of fortifications on Mount Tabor. These commanding heights threatened Nazareth, which the Christians had only recovered in 1204.

Meanwhile, John's small host of crusaders had fulfilled their vows and returned home to France. John had little choice but to conclude a new six-year truce with the Saracens without territorial gains – the first time a treaty without territorial gain had been concluded since the Third Crusade. There can be little doubt that many men in John's new kingdom were less than impressed by his performance. However, all might have been forgiven had he at least done his dynastic duty and produced a male heir. Instead, in November of 1212, Queen Maria gave birth to a daughter and died shortly afterwards. She was too young and had ruled too short a time to leave any notable mark on the kingdom; we have no idea what kind of queen she might have been. She left behind an infant, a female heir, the worst possible scenario. It immediately produced a constitutional crisis.

Isabella II (Yolanda)

As king-consort, John's right to the throne of Jerusalem was derived through his wife. Already in 1190–1192, the precedent had been set that the consort of a ruling queen did not retain his position after her death. Unsurprisingly, Brienne followed Guy de Lusignan's precedent of refusing to accept his dismissal. Like Guy before him, Brienne insisted that he had been crowned and anointed for life, or at least until his infant daughter came of age and married.

Brienne's daughter, known in history as Yolanda or Isabella II, made Brienne's situation materially different from that of Guy de Lusignan. Guy's daughters by Sibylla of Jerusalem had died before she did, leaving him no claim to a regency. Brienne, on the other hand, could reasonably argue that he was still 'king' of Jerusalem as long as his daughter was a minor. The argument won over most of the barons, with the notable exception of the former regent, the lord of Beirut and other members of the Ibelin clan.

Ibelin opposition to John de Brienne may have been based on principle. John d'Ibelin was famous for his understanding of the law. His legal opinion was highly respected and sought after in court cases. According to Philip de Novare, the famous legal scholar of the thirteenth century, Ibelin's legal views were widely considered definitive. Furthermore, his parents had been Guy de Lusignan's chief opponents when he claimed the crown after Queen Sibylla's death. Yet, it was common practice for a minor's closest relative, male or female, to serve as regent. In this case, the closest relative to the infant heiress, Yolanda, was her father. Beirut's opposition was almost certainly more about self-interest than legal technicalities. When the rest of the High Court recognised Brienne as regent and continued to treat him as their king, the Ibelins withdrew to Cyprus. They expanded their power base and position of influence there without, of course, surrendering their mainland fiefs.

Meanwhile, Pope Innocent III was actively advocating a new crusade to regain Jerusalem by putting pressure on the sultan of Egypt. By now, the king of Sicily, king of the Germans and the Holy Roman Emperor, Frederick II Hohenstaufen, had come of age and dramatically taken the cross twice. There was a general expectation that he would lead this crusade and put the full financial and military might of the Holy Roman Empire behind it. However, Frederick II proved himself a reluctant crusader, easily distracted by other matters. He repeatedly postponed crusading for fifteen years. Instead, he sent others to fight for him, and the crusade, numbered by historians centuries later as the Fifth, was launched without him in 1217.

It was not until mid-1218 that enough men and troops arrived from the West for the crusade to begin in earnest. Chief among them, although not in command of any but his own contingent of vassals and their men, was the acting king of Jerusalem, John de Brienne. He was supported by virtually all the kingdom's noblemen, except the Ibelins, who participated in the crusade under the banner of the Cypriot king. Surprisingly, Brienne succeeded in convincing his fellow crusaders from across Europe that any territorial gains made in Egypt would be ceded to the Kingdom of Jerusalem rather than individual leaders fighting in the crusade. As a result, when the crusaders captured the Egyptian city of Damietta after a siege lasting roughly a year and a half, Brienne was declared king in Damietta.

More importantly, the crusader capture of Damietta induced Egypt's Sultan al-Kamil to offer to restore all the territory that had once been part of the

Kingdom of Jerusalem – including Jerusalem and Bethlehem – to Christian control in exchange for the crusaders' evacuation of Damietta. Brienne vigorously advocated for the acceptance of this offer. He was supported by the Templars, Hospitallers and Teutonic Knights, but overruled by the other crusading leaders, most notably the papal legate Pelagius and Frederick II's deputy and representative, the Duke of Bavaria. This decision revealed all too clearly that the 'king' of Jerusalem was not taken particularly seriously by either the pope or the Holy Roman Emperor.

Furthermore, the Ayyubids, trying to ease the pressure of the crusade on the Nile, struck at the Kingdom of Jerusalem. In a devastating raid, Saracen forces destroyed the coastal city of Caesarea and were soon threatening the Templar's new stronghold at Athlit. The Templars and many barons and knights from Outremer abandoned the crusade in Egypt to hasten back to the Kingdom of Jerusalem and repulse the threat.

To Brienne's credit, he did not despair. Instead, he undertook renewed efforts to bring the necessary financial and military resources to his beleaguered kingdom that would enable it to beat back its enemies and re-establish viable borders. To do so, he played his 'trump card', namely his daughter's undeniable status as heiress to the kingdom. Brienne sought to improve his deficits as a king-consort (i.e., a man without significant financial or military resources) by marrying his daughter to the most powerful Western nobleman imaginable: the Holy Roman Emperor himself. While the strategy appeared to make sense, it ultimately backfired with disastrous consequences for Brienne, his daughter Yolanda and the entire kingdom.

In the summer of 1225, envoys arrived in Acre with the news that Yolanda's father had negotiated her marriage to the most powerful monarch on earth, a man already calling himself 'the Wonder of the World'. A proxy marriage was staged in Acre followed by a coronation in Tyre. Immediately afterwards, Yolanda set sail with a large escort of prelates and noblemen for Apulia. She arrived at Brindisi and married Frederick II in person on November 9, 1225; it was just days before or after her thirteenth birthday. Her bridegroom was a 30-year-old widower who maintained a harem in the Sicilian tradition.

Furthermore, the marriage got off to a terrible start. Yolanda's father had negotiated for the marriage with implicit or explicit assurances from the emperor that John would remain king of Jerusalem until his death. Frederick Hohenstaufen had other ideas. He declared himself king of Jerusalem the day after the wedding and made the barons who had escorted Yolanda to Italy swear fealty to him at once.

Yolanda's father was outraged, and so was the Master of the Teutonic Knights, Herman von Salza, who had been instrumental in the marriage negotiations. The latter strongly suggests that Brienne had not simply been deluding himself about retaining the crown after his daughter's marriage. Frederick instantly made an enemy of his father-in-law, and the breach ensured that Yolanda never saw her father again before she died. Perhaps she did not miss him, given how little she had seen of him during her short life, but she certainly found no comfort or companionship in her husband. Although it is hard to distinguish facts from slander, the tales of Yolanda's marriage are unremittingly negative.

Meanwhile, Frederick was under increasing pressure to fulfil his repeated promises to go to the aid of the Holy Land. He had first taken crusading vows in 1215 and eleven years later had nothing but excuses to show for it. During the negotiations for his marriage to Yolanda, he had promised to set out on crusade no later than August 1227 or face excommunication. In the summer of 1227, a great army assembled in Apulia to sail to the defence of Christian Syria, but before the crusaders could embark, a contagious disease spread among them, killing thousands. Frederick boarded a vessel but was so ill his companions urged him to return. Frederick put about and landed not in the Holy Land but in the Kingdom of Sicily. The pope promptly excommunicated him.

Throughout this, Yolanda – technically, the reigning queen of Jerusalem – was imprisoned in Frederick's harem. Her husband and consort had not thought to take her with him when he set out for her kingdom. On 25 April 1228, Yolanda gave birth to a son, christened Conrad. Ten days later, on 5 May 1228, Yolanda of Jerusalem died. She was not yet 16 years old. Although she had been a queen almost from the day of her birth, not once had she exercised the authority to which she had been born.

To add insult to death, her husband Frederick II hardly took any notice of this fact. He continued to claim her kingdom as his right, despite denying his father-in-law the same dignity. Because of his disregard for the laws and customs of Yolanda's kingdom, Frederick soon found himself at loggerheads with Jerusalem's barons. In the end, Yolanda's subjects defeated her husband, but only decades after she had been sacrificed on the altar of her father and husband's ambitions.

Jerusalem Again Without a Queen: The Absentee Kings 1228–1268

Yolanda's infant son was exactly one-month old when his father finally embarked on his long-anticipated crusade. On 21 July 1228, Frederick II landed in Cyprus, where he made a crude attempt to disseize and extort money from the regent of Cyprus, John d'Ibelin – the same John d'Ibelin, Lord of

Beirut, who had been regent of Jerusalem for Maria de Montferrat. Frederick's bullying, which included surrounding unarmed knights and barons attending a banquet with mercenaries wielding naked swords, met with granite resistance. Beirut bluntly told the emperor that he could arrest or kill him, but he would not surrender his barony nor give an account of his regency unless there was a judgement by the respective High Court against him. He then turned and walked out of the emperor's banquet with most of the Cypriot knights and nobles in his wake. The battle lines had been drawn.

For the next twenty-two years, Frederick tried to assert authoritarian control over the Kingdom of Jerusalem without regard for the kingdom's constitution. The fundamental problem was that Frederick II viewed the Kingdom of Jerusalem as just one of his many possessions without recognising it as an independent kingdom with unique traditions, customs and laws. He believed he could dispose of it and rule it as he liked. Most egregiously, he acted as if the inhabitants held their lands and titles not by hereditary right or royal charter but simply at his personal whim. He thereby violated the fundamental principles of feudalism that recognised that even a serf could not be expelled from his land without due process and just cause. Equally offensively, he also rejected the feudal principle of ruling with the advice and consent of the barons of the realm.

The Kingdom of Jerusalem, however, was a feudal state *par excellance*, frequently held up by scholars as the 'ideal' feudal kingdom. (See, for example, John La Monte's work, *Feudal Monarchy in the Latin Kingdom of Jerusalem, 1100 to 1291*, or John Riley Smith's *The Feudal Nobility and the Kingdom of Jerusalem, 1174–1277*.) The nobility of Outremer in the age of Frederick II had already developed highly sophisticated constitutional views. Based on the history of Jerusalem, they viewed their kings as no more than the 'first among equals'. Furthermore, they upheld the concept of government as a contract between the king and his subjects, requiring the consent of the ruled in the form of the High Court.

Historians have rightly pointed out that, as the struggle between the Hohenstaufen and the barons dragged on, the baronial faction became ever more creative in inventing laws and customs designed to undermine Hohenstaufen rule. This overlooks the fact that the emperor had already squandered all credibility by repeatedly breaking his word and behaving like a despot. The baronial opposition became increasingly desperate and inventive in finding the means to prevent a proven tyrant from gaining control of the kingdom. They were creative in finding legal pretexts for achieving that aim. Yet that should not obscure the fact that at the core of the baronial opposition to Frederick stood the belief in rule-of-law as opposed to rule-by-imperial-whim.

Frederick proved his contempt for the laws and constitution of Jerusalem within the first four years of his reign by the following actions: (1) refusing to recognise that his title to Jerusalem was derived through his wife rather than a divine right; (2) demanding the surrender of Beirut and nearly a dozen other lordships without due process; and (3) ignoring the High Court of Jerusalem and its functions, which included approving treaties.

Of these actions, the second has received the most attention because Frederick's attempt to disseize the Lord of Beirut without due process was the spark that ignited the civil war. Because the Lord of Beirut was a highly respected, powerful and learned nobleman, the emperor's arrogant, arbitrary and unconstitutional attempt to disseize him met with widespread outrage and, finally, armed opposition. Beirut rallied a majority of the kingdom – and not just the nobility, but the Genoese, Templars and commons of Acre – to his cause. After each bitter defeat, Frederick tried to find a means of placating the opposition, yet he refused to budge on the principle of his right to arbitrarily disseize lords without due process. To the end, he insisted that Beirut abdicate his lordship without due process. To the end, Beirut insisted on due process before surrendering anything.

Unfortunately, because the clash between Beirut and the emperor is the focus of a lively, colourful and detailed contemporary account by the jurist and philosopher Philip de Novare, most historians (if they look at the conflict at all) reduce the baronial resistance to a struggle over land and titles. This dramatically oversimplifies the opposition's concerns and overlooks the other two constitutional principles that Frederick II blatantly violated.

The issue of where he derived his right to rule in Jerusalem surfaced first. As noted above, the very day after his wedding to Queen Yolanda of Jerusalem, Frederick demanded the lords of Jerusalem do homage to him as king in direct violation of the marriage agreement he had negotiated with his father-in-law, King John. Yet after Yolanda's death, Frederick abruptly – and without a trace of shame or embarrassment – adopted Brienne's position that his rule continued despite his wife's demise. He refused to recognise his son by Yolanda as king of Jerusalem and continued calling himself by that title until the day he died. On his deathbed in December 1250, Frederick II bequeathed Italy, Germany and Sicily to Yolanda's son Conrad. Still, he suggested that Conrad give the Kingdom of Jerusalem to his half-brother Henry, the son of his third wife, Isabella of England. This proves that Frederick utterly failed to acknowledge or accept that the crown of Jerusalem was not his to give away. It had derived from his wife and could *only* pass to *her* heirs and *only with the consent of the High Court*. Frederick's attempt to give Jerusalem away to someone with no right to it was a final insult to the bride he neglected and possibly abused. It also demonstrates that to his last breath, he remained ignorant of or indifferent to the constitution of the Kingdom of Jerusalem.

Last but not least, in the general enthusiasm for Frederick's 'bloodless crusade' of 1228–1229, historians and novelists generally overlook the fact that the constitution of Jerusalem gave the High Court the right to make treaties. Frederick II Hohenstaufen blissfully ignored this constitutional right when he secretly negotiated with the Sultan al Kamil and presented the High Court of Jerusalem with a fait accompli. This, as much as the seriously flawed terms of the treaty, outraged the local nobility.

Admirers of Frederick II appear to believe that constitutional concerns should not be allowed to inhibit a 'genius' who could 'retake' Jerusalem without any loss of life. Yet they conveniently forget that the kings and regents of Jerusalem had been making treaties with the Saracens for more than a hundred years before Frederick arrived. There was nothing exceptional, much less revolutionary, about making treaties with the Saracens. Frederick II did nothing inherently different from what every king of Jerusalem had done for the previous 128 years. The fact that his treaty included nominal control of Jerusalem for ten years did not make it exceptionally brilliant. It was a treaty doomed to failure; Richard of England had been too intelligent to fall into a similar trap by taking control of a city he would not be able to hold in the long run. Because Frederick II's truce (not a treaty, but a temporary truce) left Jerusalem naked of every kind of defence, it left the city so vulnerable that none of the military orders bothered to move their headquarters back to the Holy City. Indeed, Frederick II's terms were so terrible they led directly to the slaughter of some 40,000 Christians soon after the treaty expired.

The entire era of Hohenstaufen rule, including the reigns of Frederick's son and grandson, was characterised by absentee rule. In the quarter-century in which Frederick II called himself king of Jerusalem, he spent only eight months in the Holy Land. Neither his son nor grandson ever set foot in the kingdom for a single day. Thus, from November 1225 until 28 October 1268, Jerusalem was ruled by various, sometimes competing, baillies, i.e., deputy regents, sometimes appointed by the distant Hohenstaufens and sometimes elected by the local barons. Such men could never exert the authority of a king, not even a weak king like John de Brienne. More than anything, this doomed the Kingdom of Jerusalem to annihilation.

This was not immediately apparent, however. Through clever exploitation of the rivalries between the various Ayyubid princes, the Franks had by 1244 managed to restore the borders of the Kingdom of Jerusalem almost to what they had been in 1187 before the catastrophe at Hattin. Unfortunately, that year, the kingdom allied itself with the losing side in squabble between two

Ayyubid princes. As a result, a large part of the kingdom's army was wiped out at the Battle of La Forbie on 11 July 1244. Fortunately, the victors were not jihadists, and the kingdom was not immediately overrun. Nevertheless, it was once again vulnerable.

Soon other external factors began to undermine the kingdom's viability. Starting in 1250, the Ayyubids, with their practical interest in trade and economic development, were one after another murdered and replaced by fanatical Mamluks, who preferred to cut off their own sources of revenues rather than maintain mutually beneficial ties with their Christian neighbours. Meanwhile, the Mongols swept in from the Far East and were intent on subjugating the entire world with a level of brutality unprecedented in Europe.

By the time Hohenstaufen rule ended in 1268, the kingdom was beginning to unravel. The Genoese were openly at war with the Venetians in the streets of Acre. The Templar, Hospitaller and Teutonic Knights were at each other's throats. The Mamluks had captured Caesarea, Haifa and Arsuf, then Galilee, and in 1268, Jaffa. In the north, Antioch was overwhelmed in 1268 and subjected to slaughter and plunder on a scale comparable to the Mongol capture of Baghdad, Aleppo and Damascus eight years earlier.

Nor did the death of the last titular Hohenstaufen king pave the way for a better era. On the contrary, both Hugh III of Cyprus and Marie of Antioch laid claim to Jerusalem and vied for support. Yet neither was present in the kingdom. Marie eventually sold her claim to Charles of Anjou, the unscrupulous younger brother of King Louis IX of France. It was not until the death of Anjou in 1286 that the various factions in the kingdom could agree to crown Henry II of Cyprus as their king. By then, the kingdom existed in name only. Only a few cities along the coastline remained. Some of these, like the always quasi-independent Tripoli and the isolated Beirut, concluded independent treaties with the Mamluks to buy themselves time.

In April 1289, Tripoli fell, and two years later, on 6 April 1291, the Mamluk siege of Acre began. The greatest and wealthiest city of Outremer, once the rival of Alexandria and Constantinople, fell on 18 May. Sidon surrendered in June, Beirut in July, and the Templars voluntarily abandoned their last castles in the Levant, Tartus and Athlit, on 3 August and 14 August, respectively. The original crusader states were no more. Only the latecomer, Cyprus, remained.

It was merely a coincidence that this period of slow decay was also an era without queens or other notable female figures, with one exception noted in the next section. Although Frederick II remarried, his third wife had no claim to call herself queen of Jerusalem. In any case, she was confined to Frederick's harem just as Yolanda had been, a slave more than a queen. Conrad I married Elizabeth of Bavaria in 1246, and technically, she had the right to the title of queen of Jerusalem. Yet, Conrad never travelled to his inherited kingdom, so neither he nor his wife was crowned or anointed there before his death in 1254. The claim to the title then passed to his infant son Conrad the Younger or Conradin, who was executed at the age of 16 by Charles of Anjou after an unsuccessful armed attempt to reclaim his parental inheritance of Sicily from the Frenchman. Conradin never married. Although Henry II of Cyprus was acclaimed and crowned king of Jerusalem in 1286, he was, at the time, 16 and unmarried, so no queen was crowned with him. He was still unmarried when Acre fell five years later, although he subsequently married Constance of Sicily.

The Regent: Alice de Champagne in Cyprus and Jerusalem

Yet while Jerusalem rotted slowly away on the coast of the Levant, savaged by self-inflicted wounds and external forces, the last of the crusader states – the Kingdom of Cyprus – was prospering as never before. Here, the Lusignan dynasty was sinking deep roots.

Cyprus is roughly 3,500 square miles, 225 miles long and 95 miles wide. At the time of Richard the Lionheart's invasion in 1191, the population was approximately 100,000 strong and composed mostly of Greek peasants. There was only a small ruling elite of Greek aristocrats, bureaucrats and clergy, and even smaller communities of foreigners, mostly Armenians, Maronites, Syrian Christians and Jews. A province of only secondary or tertiary importance to the Eastern Roman Empire ruled from Constantinople, the economic base of Byzantine Cyprus was agriculture with small quantities of commodity exports.

Richard the Lionheart's conquest leading to the establishment of the Lusignan dynasty in Cyprus two years later, initially had little or no impact on the economy. The conquest neither dislocated large numbers of people nor altered the structure of land tenure or the means of production. For the vast majority of the Cypriot rural population, the change in regime only meant that the landlords changed. Where once the landlords had been (often absentee) Greek aristocrats, after the establishment of Lusignan rule, they were Latin noblemen predominantly from the crusader states, also often absentee. These landlords now held their estates as feudal fiefs with obligations to the crown, but for the peasants, little changed. Likewise, imperial lands became part of the royal domain, but the tenants' duties and dues remained the same.

What changed was the explosion in commercial activity in the wake of Frankish control of the island, which coincided with the loss of the interior of the Kingdom of Jerusalem to Saladin, followed by the recovery of the Levantine coast during the Third Crusade. Because the populous urban centres of the Levant remained in Christian hands while their rural hinterland fell to the

Saracens, the inhabitants of these cities turned to Cyprus for imports. The demands of the mainland triggered a diversification of the Cypriot economy. Thus, in addition to its traditional agricultural products of wheat, barley and pulses, Cyprus began to produce and export carob, fish, meat, flax, cotton, onions and rice in quantity, along with minor exports of saffron, nutmeg, pepper and other spices, including salt. In addition, a shift away from raw agricultural products to agricultural processing began. Under the Lusignans, Cyprus produced and exported various processed agricultural goods such as wine, olive oil, wax, honey, soap, cheese and, above all, sugar. Indeed, sugar production on an industrial scale became one of Cyprus' most important revenue sources.

Furthermore, under the Lusignans, Cyprus developed entire new industries. The manufacturing of pottery flourished at Paphos, Lemba, Lapithos and Engomi. Textile production is also documented from the mid-thirteenth century onwards, including samite, camlets and silk, and the textiles were often dyed locally, increasing the value-added captured on the island. Other examples of high-value export products were icons and manuscripts. Excavations also show that Cyprus employed the cutting-edge technologies of the age, notably highly sophisticated waterworks to power mills, followed by the reuse of this water to irrigate surrounding fields.[31]

The entire population benefitted from these changes, but none more so than the feudal elite and, above all, the crown. As much as one-third of Cyprus' arable land belonged to the royal domain, and Lusignan control did not end there. The Lusignans were more Byzantine than Western in their tight control over the Cypriot economy, building on a system of centralised administration they inherited from Constantinople, which included Orthodox and Greek-speaking personnel. In contrast to the Kingdom of Jerusalem, the kings of Cyprus maintained a monopoly on minting coins and established kingdom-wide standards for a variety of wares. They instituted selected price controls and maintained control of public highways. They granted far fewer privileges to the Italian city-states than the crusader states on the mainland. In addition, they fostered shipbuilding and financial services, two of the most lucrative economic sectors of the age.

Cyprus was set on this course by the competent Aimery de Lusignan. Aimery had assumed the lordship of Cyprus at the death of his brother Guy in 1194. At that time, he was already a mature man who had been married for roughly two decades to Eschiva d'Ibelin, the daughter of Baldwin of Ramla. The couple had six children – three sons and three daughters – three of whom died young. Eschiva died just before she and Aimery were to be crowned king and queen of Cyprus. Although she founded the dynasty that would rule Cyprus for almost 300 years, she never wore a crown.

Not long after her death, Aimery married Isabella of Jerusalem, becoming king of Jerusalem as well as king of Cyprus. At his death, this personal union of the kingdoms was dissolved. Isabella's eldest daughter, Maria de Montferrat, succeeded to the crown of Jerusalem, while Aimery's only surviving son by Eschiva, Hugh, ascended to the throne of Cyprus. The two monarchs were minors when they ascended their respective thrones. At his father's death, Hugh was only 9 years old, while Maria was 13. Both required regents. As noted earlier, Maria's uncle John d'Ibelin was selected as her regent, while in Cyprus, the High Court chose Walter de Montbéliard, the husband of Hugh's eldest sister, Burgundia. The latter was also his heir apparent. The heir apparent in Jerusalem, on the other hand, was Alice, the sister of the queen and daughter of Isabella I, by her third husband, Henri de Champagne. She has gone down in history as Alice de Champagne and was undoubtedly an ambitious and influential figure who left a colourful mark in the history of thirteenth-century Outremer.

In 1210, Alice was escorted to Cyprus by her uncles John and Philip d'Ibelin, where she formally married Hugh de Lusignan and was crowned queen of Cyprus. She would have been roughly 17 years old at the time, while her husband Hugh was just 14. Shortly afterwards, Hugh assumed his majority – with a vengeance. He immediately accused his brother-in-law of embezzlement and exiled him outright or forced him to flee. In either case, Walter de Montbéliard quit the kingdom and went to the court of his cousin John de Brienne in Acre.

In 1217, at age 22, Hugh joined what we know as the Fifth Crusade. He led a contingent of Cypriot crusaders to the mainland, where they made incursions into Saracen territory preliminary at the start of the main crusade against Egypt. During the winter lull in the fighting, Hugh travelled north to attend the wedding of his half-sister Melisende, his father's daughter by Isabella of Jerusalem, to Bohemond IV of Antioch. During the festivities, Hugh became ill and died on 10 January 1218.

He left behind two small daughters and an eight-month-old son, Henry. Alice de Champagne was a 25-year-old widow. By all accounts, she was immediately recognised by her vassals as the regent for her infant son. Yet, either at the advice of the High Court or in accordance with the dying king's wishes – or possibly of her own accord – Alice publicly appointed her uncle Philip d'Ibelin as her baillie. Significantly, after all the liegemen did homage to Queen Alice as regent, she had the barons swear to obey Philip d'Ibelin 'until her son Henry came of age'.[32]

According to the chronicles, the kingdom's revenues largely went to Alice, who thereby controlled patronage, while the day-to-day business of administration and the critical task of leading the armies of Cyprus devolved to her appointed baillie, Philip d'Ibelin. However, by no means was Alice's role passive or nominal. In 1220, Alice was actively involved in negotiating the settlement of a dispute between the Latin and Orthodox Churches in Cyprus. Meanwhile, Alice's baillie Philip d'Ibelin rebuffed efforts by the Duke of Austria to disinherit the Lusignan kings altogether. The Austrian duke spuriously alleged that Cyprus was a part of the ransom Richard the Lionheart owed his family. In addition, Ibelin repelled an Ayyubid raid on Cyprus' principal southern port of Limassol. Ships were burnt in the harbour, and allegedly 13,000 Cypriots were killed or captured. This was the first Arab attack on Cyprus in roughly 200 years and must have terrified the population and shaken the government under Ibelin, who very likely recalled vassals involved in the crusade in Egypt to defend Cyprus. Two years later, Cyprus was devastated by a severe earthquake, damaging three major cities, Nicosia, Limassol and Paphos. The latter was particularly ravaged, with the castle and much of the city levelled.

Perhaps the costs of rebuilding and repair caused by these calamities put Ibelin on a collision course with Queen Alice. Thirteenth-century historian Philip de Novare, an intimate and supporter of the House of Ibelin, claims that Alice spent money 'freely', implying irresponsibly.[33] Another chronicle is even more specific, saying: 'Queen Alice was very generous and spent the revenues of the kingdom liberally, and disposed of them entirely as seemed good to her'.[34] Ibelin evidently disagreed about how the revenues should be spent and tried to curb the queen. Alice resented his interference, leading to a rupture between them.

The High Court sided decisively with Ibelin. In 1223, Queen Alice abandoned her three children and went into voluntary exile in Tripoli, but not with any intention of giving up the fight. On the contrary, there she married the eldest son of the Prince of Antioch, Bohemond V, with the probable aim of returning to Cyprus with Bohemond as her consort in order to dismiss Ibelin. Queen Alice's plans foundered on a papal dissolution of her marriage to Bohemond based on consanguinity.

Alice next tried to outflank Ibelin by appointing a different baillie, a Cypriot lord by the name of Aimery Barlais. The High Court of Cyprus rejected Barlais' claims by citing their oath to obey Ibelin until King Henry came of age. Meanwhile – and ominously – Alice faced opposition from a different and more powerful quarter. Namely, the Holy Roman Emperor, Frederick II Hohenstaufen, rejected Alice's right to be regent; he proclaimed his exclusive right to this position. As with his claim to be king of Jerusalem after his wife's death and his attempt to force the Prince of Antioch to do homage to him, his presumption of the regency of Cyprus violated the constitution of the kingdom and the will of the High Court.

Indeed, despite Alice's friction with Ibelin and the High Court of Cyprus, the barons of Cyprus (including Ibelin) remained loyal to her. When Frederick II tried to make them do homage to him, they refused on the grounds that they had already done homage to Alice, and she was the legal regent. As always, the legality of his position was of no interest to the autocratic emperor. Frederick II ignored Alice and the High Court and imperiously appointed his own baillies for Cyprus, five men whose rapaciousness soon led to bloodshed and the only instance of violence against Orthodox clergy in the history of Frankish Cyprus.

Just as Frederick II's arrogance and disregard for the law had turned the Ibelins, the Prince of Antioch and the common citizens of Acre against him, his treatment of Alice pushed her into open rebellion as well. As soon as Frederick had sailed away (still drenched in the offal and innards the people of Acre had thrown at him as he walked down to his galley), Alice went before the High Court of Jerusalem and laid claim to the crown of Jerusalem. It was early May 1229.

Her reasoning was compelling and highly sophisticated. Queen Yolanda of Jerusalem had died on May 5, 1228. Her infant son, Conrad, was her heir apparent, and it was only as his regent that the barons of Jerusalem had submitted to Frederick II. However, Alice now pointed out, in accordance with the laws of the kingdom, the heir to a fief not resident in the domain was required to claim his inheritance within one year. A year had passed since Conrad had inherited his title, and he had not yet claimed it. In consequence, Alice argued, his claim had lapsed, and the next in line to the throne should be recognised as the rightful heir. After Conrad, Alice was the closest blood relative to the last queen, her niece Yolanda.

Alice's legal reasoning was based on the laws of inheritance for fiefs and, up to this point, had not been applied to the crown itself, but her arguments could not be dismissed out of hand. The High Court sent word to Frederick II, informing him of the kingdom's customs and demanding that he send Conrad east to enforce his claim. Frederick, of course, ignored the High Court as he always did. Yet while the emperor's attitude inflamed anti-imperial sentiment in Outremer, it did nothing to help Alice. Instead, a full-scale civil war exploded in which Alice's abandoned son, King Henry of Cyprus, played a prominent role on the side of the rebellious barons. He and his supporters (headed by the Ibelins) had no desire to complicate things by doing homage to a woman who had earlier tried to push an Ibelin from power – and possibly sought to depose her son as well. Alice had made the wrong enemies in 1223–24.

After her initiative had come to nothing, Alice turned her attention to an ultimately futile attempt to lay claim to her father's County of Champagne in France. Then in 1239, a young nobleman in the king of Navarre's entourage approached Alice and proposed (or accepted a proposal of) marriage. Alice was 47 years old, and her bridegroom, Ralph Count of Soissons, is thought to have been roughly half her age. Presumably, he was most attracted to her because she was the queen-mother of Cyprus and heir presumptive to Jerusalem since Conrad Hohenstaufen had no heirs of his body..

It is hard to imagine that what happened next was entirely coincidental. By 1243, the conflict between Frederick II and the leading rebels of Outremer had been frozen for roughly a decade. The emperor had lost all influence in Cyprus with the victory of King Henry over the Imperial Forces at the 1232 Battle of Agridi. On the mainland, Frederick's baillie Richard de Filangieri held sway only in Tyre, while the rest of the kingdom recognised the baillies appointed by the High Court. In early 1243, the rebel barons were told there was disaffection in Tyre and that elements within the city would welcome them if they could liberate it from imperial control.

Suddenly, the legal advisors to the leading barons of the anti-imperial faction remembered that a minor king had just one year to claim his inheritance after coming of age. If he failed to do so, his right to exercise power lapsed. Since Conrad had come of age in 1242 (or some say 1243), Frederick II could no longer call himself regent and no longer had the right to appoint baillies. On the other hand, Conrad had no right to appoint baillies either, or at least not until he had come to the kingdom and been properly crowned and anointed. Instead of the absentee monarch, power in the kingdom, so the argument went, should be exercised by the king's closest relative resident in Outremer, who would become monarch if the heir failed to appear within one year of coming of age. Conrad Hohenstaufen's closest relative resident in Outremer was none other than Alice de Champagne.

At once a written agreement was drawn up in which the leaders of the baronial faction, Balian d'Ibelin of Beirut (the son of John d'Ibelin, the former regent of the kingdom), and Philip de Montfort, Lord of Toron, agreed to swear homage to Alice as regent of Jerusalem. She promised to invest the named lords with all the fortresses in the kingdom, that is, to delegate the defence of the realm to them. On 5 June, an assembly was held, attended not only by the members of the High Court but also representatives of the Catholic Church, the military orders and the Italian communes. Alice was formally invested as regent, and those present swore homage to her, starting with Balian of Beirut, the foremost baron in the Kingdom of Jerusalem at this time, followed by his cousin, Philip of Toron (a cousin of the English Earl of Leicester).

A week later, Beirut led a military assault on Tyre, slipping through a postern with a few men and opening the chain to the harbour to admit a fleet loyal to the barons. The Imperial Forces were driven back to the citadel and soon agreed to surrender. They were granted free passage out of the city and returned to Sicily to face the wrath of the Hohenstaufen. Ralph de Soissons immediately demanded the victors turn Tyre over to him in his capacity as regent-consort.

Beirut and Toron did not share his interpretation of his role as husband to the regent Alice. They could legitimately argue that they had been entrusted with the defence of the realm, which naturally included such a vital and nearly impregnable city as Tyre. Furthermore, as an immature newcomer from France who had not been held hostage and tortured by Frederick II as Balian of Beirut had been, nor fought in the vicious, violent phase of civil war from 1228–1232, Soissons was not taken seriously. The depth of Soisson's feelings for Alice was made apparent when he immediately sailed for France, complaining loudly about his lack of power and the double-dealing and treachery of the barons of Outremer. This narrative reinforced the steady whining of Western chroniclers against the Franks resident in the Holy Land. Alice, however, did not join her husband. Nor does she appear to have shared his indignation. She remained where she was enjoying the revenues and, when Conrad as expected failed to put in an appearance, the title as well of reigning queen of Jerusalem. She was the last of the powerful royal women of Outremer.

Part II

Crusading Women

Chapter 5

Crusading Women

Policies and Attitudes

The very concept of an armed pilgrimage to liberate the Holy Land, the activity that we have come to call crusading, was radical and innovative when it was first broached by Pope Urban II in 1095. It is hardly surprising, therefore, that the exact role of women in these pioneering, religiously motivated military expeditions had not been envisaged or properly considered.

Indeed, Pope Urban appears to have been taken entirely by surprise by the degree to which his appeal for fighting men to liberate the Holy Land by force of arms would resonate with women, just as he had not expected clerics, the sick, disabled or elderly to answer his call either. Yet in the wake of Urban's speech at Clermont, women by the thousands rushed to 'take the cross'. Furthermore, these women included venerable widows, devout nuns and powerful noblewomen, all of impeccable reputations. They could not be dismissed as camp followers, and they exhibited palpable piety in their desire to free the Holy Land.

Disconcerted and confused, Pope Urban started back-pedalling immediately. He attempted to restrict those who took crusader vows to individuals physically and financially capable of making a military contribution to what promised to be a difficult armed expedition. He forbade monks from taking crusader vows, although he accepted the need for secular clergy to accompany the fighting men to provide them with spiritual support (hear confessions, bury the dead, etc.). Yet while Urban sought to discourage all types of non-combatants, clerical concern about the participation of women was twofold.

In addition to being unable to make a military contribution to the crusade, commanders and clerics worried that women would become a distraction and temptation for the male participants who were supposed to be undertaking the expedition in the service of God. As envisaged by the papacy, participants were expected to focus on spiritual duties and rewards rather than carnal matters such as material gain and pleasure. Crusaders were admonished to avoid all forms of sin, which meant avoiding adultery and fornication no less than jealousy, greed, pride, etc. The mere presence of women was presumed to be a temptation that would lead to sin and, with it, divine displeasure. In an age when divine intervention in events was considered normal, many commanders were wary of conditions that might attract the wrath of God.

Urban tried to solve the problem created by unsuitable persons taking crusader vows by urging these individuals to obtain absolution for their vows from a cleric of appropriate rank. In at least one recorded case, the bishop of Toulouse 'converted' the crusader vow of a prominent noblewoman into a vow to build a hospice for the poor instead. That is, he promised the same level of spiritual benefit as Urban had promised to participants in the crusade for her act of charity at home.

This and other acts like it set a precedent so frequently followed that, by the mid-thirteenth century, transmuting crusader vows to financial payments had become a cynical source of clerical income. In 1213, Innocent III had already institutionalised 'proportional indulgences' for services in support of crusading yet short of actual participation and officially offered 'redemptions' of crusader vows – at a price. His successor Gregory IX took things further in 1243 when he eliminated all restrictions on those allowed to take a crusader vow, thereby dropping all considerations of suitability or probability. Instead, Gregory actively encouraged everyone – the old and infirm, the sick and disabled, the destitute and women – to take crusader vows and pay cash into the papal coffers to redeem those vows. As historian Christopher Tyreman put it, these thirteenth-century innovations 'transformed crusade finance'.[35]

Meanwhile, clerics and military leaders alike had to deal with another relevant phenomenon: whether women took crusader vows or not, they had a profound influence on recruitment. For one thing, in the early years of crusading history, the prevailing clerical view was that married men required the permission of their wives to undertake a crusade. This derived from mediaeval marital theology, which argued that married partners owed 'conjugal services' to one another (often referred to as 'the conjugal debt'). The inability to fulfil one's conjugal duties due to long periods of absence made both partners more vulnerable to the temptations of adultery. Thus, the Church argued that both partners must consciously agree to the separation that crusading inherently entailed. Many clerical advocates of the crusade feared that wives might deny their consent to husbands keen to participate.

These fears were not entirely fabricated. Enough men blamed their wives for their failure to take crusading vows that the papacy concluded a remedy was needed. In 1201, Innocent III officially ended the need for a crusader to obtain his wife's consent. However, this only aided those men keen to undertake a crusade. As the Church knew all too well, many more men were reluctant to join a crusade because of strong emotional attachments and a sense of responsibility for wives and children. Men who loved their families were disinclined to be separated for years.

The immediate solution was to allow men and women to travel together on crusades. Since sex within marriage was not a sin, married couples could fulfil their mutual conjugal debt without sinning and would not incur the wrath of God. By travelling together, they were also presumed to avoid the temptation of adultery. The tradition of married couples crusading together was thus born during the First Crusade and became increasingly popular in the various expeditions that followed.

At the same time, contemporary sources also noted that if some women held their menfolk back, others actively encouraged crusading. The *Itinerarium Peregrinorum et Gesta Regis Ricardi*, for example, underlines the popularity of the Third Crusade by claiming that 'brides urged their husbands and mothers incited their sons to go'.[36] While such statements are easily dismissed as propaganda and are unquantifiable, they are unlikely to have been entirely without basis. Jonathan Riley-Smith, furthermore, documented the degree to which women served as catalysts for crusading by tracing family connections between prominent crusaders. His work demonstrates that noblemen who participated in the crusades tended to come from interrelated families. While sons followed in the footsteps of their fathers and grandfathers, the sisters and daughters of crusaders spread crusading enthusiasm to their husbands and in-laws, systematically expanding the circle of crusading nobility.

The more established the concept of crusading became, the more women shared enthusiasm for it. Women of this era, like their fathers, brothers and husbands, viewed the Holy Land as Christ's homeland and believed it should be under Christian control. Furthermore, pious women no less than devout men longed for the spiritual benefits associated with a pilgrimage to Jerusalem. Consequently, women supported and participated in crusading in one form or another from the first to the last crusade.

Supporting Roles

Before looking more closely at the women who participated in the crusades, it is worthwhile taking a brief look at the supporting roles played by the many women who remained in the West. The most obvious way these women supported crusading was by assuming the burdens and responsibilities of their crusading male family members. In some cases, wives or mothers took over the family business, oversaw workshops and staff, maintained commercial ties, conducted business correspondence and managed estates. At the pinnacle of society, for example, Queen Eleanor of England was instrumental in rebuffing her younger son John's attempts to usurp her elder son Richard's throne while the latter was in the East. She was certainly tireless in gathering her son's ransom after Richard was taken captive by the Duke of Austria on his return from the Third Crusade. Queen Blanche of France, another queen mother, was more powerful still. She assumed the full regency of France during Louis IX's crusade. In the opinion of some scholars, she ruthlessly enforced ecclesiastical tithes and otherwise marshalled resources to support her son's disastrous crusade and his subsequent activities in the Holy Land. Likewise, the dowager Countess of Champagne, Marie, governed Champagne for her son Henri while forwarding him the bulk of the revenues from his estates to finance his crusading activities and pay the debts he incurred in Acre. More commonly, knights' and nobles' wives assumed the role of lord during their husband's absence, a precedent set in the First Crusade by, for example, the daughter of William of Conqueror, who ruled Blois and Chartres whilst her husband Stephen took part in it. Such activity, however, was not exclusive to crusading. Under feudalism, women routinely assumed the role of lord for absent male relatives, regardless of the reason for that absenteeism.

More specific to crusading was the large number of women who provided financial assistance directly to crusaders. In some cases, this entailed agreeing to sell lands held jointly or even dower properties to finance the costs of a husband's or son's expedition. In other instances, it entailed direct donations to cover the costs of outfitting and provisioning foot soldiers or knights who wished to participate in a crusade but could not afford it. During the Third Crusade, Richard I's sister Joanna, the dowager queen of Sicily, agreed to sell her entire dower to help finance her brother's crusade in exchange for a promise to reimburse her from holdings inside his continental empire at a later date. At a smaller scale, yet completely without a guarantee of material compensation, the widow of Balian d'Ibelin of Beirut, Eschiva de Montbeliard, outfitted an entire ship at her own expense to transport crusaders of the Seventh Crusade to Egypt. There is also evidence that the women of Genoa raised more charitable donations in support of the crusades than their men. Lastly, after the establishment of the militant orders dedicated to maintaining Christian control of the Holy Land (the Templars, Hospitallers and Teutonic Knights), women contributed to crusading objectives by donating and endowing these institutions. While the total sum of these contributions has never been calculated, anecdotal evidence of grants to individual houses suggests that women played a significant role in bolstering the financial position of the militant – and indeed all – religious orders.

Participation

Regardless of what Pope Urban II had intended, wanted, said or done to prevent it, women took part in all the armed expeditions to the Holy Land that we call crusades. Chronicles, family histories and Muslim sources attest to the presence of women in the various crusading hosts, and it is a moot point whether these women were true crusaders or merely pilgrims. Undoubtedly, some women who travelled with each crusading host were traditional camp followers (whores, washerwomen, servants in attendance on more affluent female pilgrims, etc.). However, many more appear to have been religiously motivated pilgrims who had either officially taken the cross, were widows fulfilling vows made by their deceased husbands, or were the wives of crusaders who accompanied their husbands on their expeditions.

As noted above, the religious motivations driving the crusades – the desire for personal salvation, the feudal obligation to 'ransom' Christ's homeland from the Muslims, or the commitment to end the oppression of fellow Christians – appealed to women no less than to men. Precisely because women were more vulnerable to violence and less likely to be able to defend themselves, many female pilgrims preferred to join armed expeditions with large numbers of fighting men rather than travel independently, whether they took a crusading vow or not.

The most common pattern of female participation was in the form of wives accompanying their husbands, and there are many recorded instances of men and women taking vows simultaneously. Nevertheless, we also know of cases where sisters went with their brothers (e.g., Joanna Plantagenet and Richard I cited above) and daughters accompanied their parents. There is also evidence of unaccompanied women going on crusades, although the majority of these were presumably widows because wives needed the permission of their husbands to travel, and nuns were doubly discouraged both as cloistered clergy and as females. Whatever their status, women unaccompanied by a male relative usually travelled with other women for greater safety. Whether with male companions or alone, the women who set out on crusade came from all segments of society, from the richest to the poorest. Inherently, we possess more information about queens and noblewomen than their impoverished or less well-off sisters. Nevertheless, there is enough anecdotal reference to poorer women to suggest that upper-class women were not disproportionally present on crusades.

Two leaders of the First Crusade, Baldwin of Boulogne and Raymond of Toulouse, set out with their wives. A total of fifteen women of high birth are known by name to have taken part in the several armed pilgrimages carried out between 1096 and 1101. These include Ida of Austria, who led her own military contingent in the expedition of 1101. In the Second Crusade, Eleanor of Aquitaine famously took the cross publicly in front of the assembled nobility of France and, furthermore, did so in her own right as Duchess of Aquitaine rather than queen of France to encourage participation by her vassals. Eleanor was notoriously accompanied on the Second Crusade by an unspecified number of noble ladies, who were derogatively referred to as 'amazons'. Joanna Plantagenet and Berengaria of Navara, the sister and betrothed/wife of Richard of England, respectively, both joined him on the Third Crusade. The widow of King Bela III of Hungary, the sister of Philip II of France and former Queen of England and consort of Henry the Young King, likewise took crusader vows in 1196 and succeeded in making it to Jerusalem, where she died.

In the next century, Eleanor of Castile, Princess of Wales, took the cross in her own right in 1267, and in 1287 Alice Countess of Blois took crusading vows and led a large contingent of knights to the Holy Land. Incidentally, by this time, the papacy had not only institutionalised the practice of allowing women to take crusader vows to redeem them with a cash payment, but it also explicitly condoned or encouraged female crusading, provided the women were accompanying their husbands or were wealthy enough to 'lead (ducere) warriors to the East at their own expense'.[37]

It is fair to ask, however, what these women actually did while on these crusades. Starting with the high-profile cases, later sources blamed Eleanor of Aquitaine for the disaster we know as the Second Crusade or at least one severe setback during it. The popular legend that Eleanor and the women who accompanied her dressed and behaved scandalously, calling down the vengeance of God, is pure fiction. It is a hybrid construction based on allegations of an inappropriate relationship between Eleanor and her uncle Raymond of Poitiers, the Prince of Antioch, and a Byzantine account of German female crusaders who wore armour. (The Second Crusade was composed of two main contingents; the German component led by Conrad III of Germany passed through Constantinople before the French contingent.)

On the other hand, accusations by some sources that Eleanor was responsible for a disaster during the advance cannot be entirely dismissed. When passing through Anatolia in January 1248, Eleanor allegedly urged the vanguard under the command of one of her vassals to disregard orders from her husband, the king. Allegedly she convinced her vassal not to halt in a mountain pass but instead to continue down into the valley where it would be more pleasant to camp. As a result, a wide gap developed between the advance guard and the main body of troops. Exploiting this fact, the Turks attacked the main force while it was in the pass and inflicted heavy losses. King Louis' horse was killed under him, and he was nearly taken captive. Nightfall spared the crusaders from complete destruction, but as many as 7,000 men and hundreds of horses had died and the baggage train was looted. As in any military debacle, multiple mistakes were made, and it seems somewhat illogical to blame the French queen alone. Nevertheless, she may, indeed, bear some share of the guilt.

Yet, other sources note that the Byzantine empress corresponded with Eleanor during the French advance. Some have suggested that the women managed to mitigate growing tensions between the Greek emperor and the French king. If this is the case, both women served as mediators, thereby facilitating the progress of the crusade.

It is challenging to identify any specific role played by Queen Berengaria or Queen Joanna during the Third Crusade beyond the financial support given by Joanna to her brother noted earlier. On the other hand, Marguerite de Provence, the queen of Louis IX of France, played an extraordinary role in the Seventh Crusade. First, she commanded the forces that remained behind in Damietta while the main body of crusaders advanced up the Nile. After the debacle at Mansourah, Louis' army was cut off from supplies and devastated by various diseases, including scurvy and dysentery. Eventually, Louis was forced to surrender from his sickbed. Needless to say, news of this catastrophic development soon reached Damietta, carried by an Egyptian army bearing the captured arms of the French knights and nobles.

While the Muslims singularly failed to terrify Marguerite into surrender, they invested the city by land, and panic duly set in among the crusader garrison. The troops left behind consisted primarily of sailors and archers from Pisa and Genoa. Believing the crusade was over and the French army killed and captured, they wanted to sail away. Despite being unable to stand after giving birth to a son, Jean Tristan, Marguerite summoned the leaders to her chamber. Here she implored the men not to abandon her and those in captivity. Presciently she noted that the city of Damietta was the most important bargaining chip the crusaders had for negotiating a ransom for the captive men. The Italians countered by claiming they were starving. The queen promptly offered to buy all the provisions of the city with her own resources and undertook to keep every man at the crown's expense. The ploy worked, and the Italian sailors and archers remained in Damietta.

Yet, Marguerite's role was not over. Louis and the other surviving noblemen were in an extremely precarious position. Early in the ransom negotiations, the sultan threatened to torture Louis unless he surrendered certain castles in Outremer. The castles in question, however, had been built and maintained by the Templars, Hospitallers and barons of Outremer. Louis replied that he could not surrender castles that he did not control. When he was shown the instruments of torture his captors intended to employ, Louis answered that they could do what they liked, but he still could not surrender castles held by men not subject to the French crown. Eventually, the sultan offered to release him and the other prisoners in exchange for the surrender of Damietta and an enormous cash ransom payment of 400,000 livres. Louis agreed to 'advise' his queen to accept these terms but refused to swear an oath because, he told the sultan, he did not know if Marguerite would consent. To the sultan's astonishment, he explained that he could not compel her because she was his consort and the Queen of France. Marguerite agreed and complied without haggling, although the sum requested was astronomical.

Turning to the activities of nameless, non-noble women who joined crusading hosts, the chronicles tell us that they, too, played important roles. Women are described and praised, for example, for bringing water and refreshment to the men defending the shield wall at the Battle of Dorylaeum. At the siege of Jerusalem in 1099, women wove panels to protect the siege engines from missiles. At the siege of Acre, they helped fill in the ditches that protected the city and took their turn on guard duty protecting the siege camp. The women with crusading hosts reportedly provided first aid to the wounded, cleaned clothes, removed lice, ground corn, cooked and baked. At times, they donned improvised armour (such as putting pots on their heads) and used whatever came to hand (such as kitchen and butcher knives) to take an active part in the fighting – usually defensive fighting amidst a crisis.

None of these actions represented decisive undertakings that men could not have fulfilled. Indeed, most of the activities, with the possible exception of laundering, were routinely carried out by both men and women. Yet, while women with the crusading host may not have been indispensable, they were not merely dead weight either.

Part III

The Women of Outremer

Chapter 6

Mortar for a Multicultural Society

Putting Down Roots: Local Brides for Foreign Settlers

The moment the first crusade mutated from a military campaign intent on conquest into an attempt to maintain permanent and stable political control over the Holy Land, the role of women was transformed from incidental and supportive to essential and central. Permanent control depended not on soldiers but on settlers. Settlers, by definition, come to make their living in a new place, put down roots and find families. In short, settlers needed wives.

To be sure, many crusaders had been married men. Most of them had left their wives and families behind when they took the cross and set out on this exceptional expedition to the East. However, the majority of married crusaders returned home to their wives and families rather than remaining in the Holy Land. There were also a few crusaders who travelled in the company of their wives. If both survived the long hazardous journey – and only one in five did – they might have opted to remain together in the Holy Land. But the number of such couples would have been dismissively small. There can be little doubt that most of the crusaders who elected to remain in Outremer at the end of the First Crusade were bachelors or widowers, men without wives at home or in Outremer.

As these men turned to peaceful pursuits and thought of founding families, they turned – as men always have and always will – to the women closest at hand. Unlike the settlers of the sparsely populated 'New World' centuries later, the Latin settlers to the Near East in the early twelfth century found themselves in a well-populated region. Equally important in the twelfth-century context, the women around them were, for the most part, fellow Christians.

The importance of this fact cannot be overstated. Pope Urban II had called the First Crusade, in part, to rescue the native Christians from Muslim oppression. The papal legate on the crusade, Adhemar Bishop of Le Puy, had maintained close ties with the Greek Orthodox Patriarch throughout the campaign, and the Latin and Orthodox authorities had issued what we would nowadays call 'joint communiques' about the progress. The Greek Patriarch had sent the starving crusaders supplies from Cyprus during the siege of

Antioch. The Crusaders reinstated the Orthodox Patriarch of Antioch after their victory. Orthodox priests assumed the role of confessor to some of the crusade's leaders. In the first crusader state established in Edessa, the Latin count was first adopted and installed in accordance with Armenian customs and with the blessings of the Armenian church. Although the Latin and Orthodox hierarchies later engaged in squabbling over titles and tithes, the salient point with respect to inter-church relations was made by the Jacobite patriarch, Michael the Great. Writing in the second half of the twelfth century (that is, after a half-century of Frankish rule) Michael stated unequivocally: '[the Franks] never sought a single formula for all the Christian people and languages, but they considered as Christian anyone who worshipped the cross without investigation or examination'.[38]

This policy was decisive to the success and survival of the crusader states. It demonstrates additionally that the crusader states were never apartheid-like societies in which the new elites attempted to segregate themselves from the local population or viewed intermarriage with other ethnic, linguistic and cultural groups as undesirable. The reverse was true. From their inception, intermarriage with the native population was accepted and practised without approbation in all four crusader states. Indeed, far from being aloof and apart from the native residents, the Latin settlers were integrated and absorbed into the broader family networks of the local (Christian) inhabitants from the very start.

Writing in the first quarter-century after the establishment of the Kingdom of Jerusalem, Fulcher of Chartres, chaplain to Baldwin I, approvingly reported that the settlers 'have taken wives not only of our own people but Syrians or Armenians or even Saracens who have obtained the grace of baptism'.[39] He goes on to say: 'Some [settlers] already possess homes or households by inheritance. ... One has his father-in-law as well as his daughter-in-law living with him, or his own child if not his stepson or stepfather'.[40]

This Western cleric stresses – unconsciously because to him it was self-evident – the advantages these marriages with local women brought. Marriage in the mediaeval context was not only about 'taking a wife'; it was about acquiring a father-in-law who already had land or businesses. As Chartres notes, it was about brothers-in-law who could help tend the vineyard and till the fields. It meant obtaining mothers-in-law to help look after the children, stepsons who could herd the goats, and stepdaughters to help spin and weave. As Chartres enthusiastically points out in his description of settler society, settlers were already starting to inherit lands and benefit from the broader networks afforded by family ties. In mediaeval society, a man alone was always poorer than a man with a family.

In the context of Outremer, however, the value of these family ties was materially greater than in the West. The Western European settlers to Outremer found themselves in an alien environment with a seemingly hostile climate characterised by infrequent rains and completely different growing seasons than they had known at home. The Westerners confronted unusual crops, exotic insects and unfamiliar vermin, strange diseases and unexpected dangers. Alone, the settlers would have found it very difficult to survive; supported by a native family familiar with the crops, livestock, weather and hazards, they had far less to fear.

Soon, as Chartres records, the settlers started to 'go native' as well. Thus, they 'use the eloquence and idioms of diverse languages in conversing back and forth. Words of different languages have become common property known to each nationality'.[41] Significantly, Chartres claims:

> He who was a Roman or a Frank has in this land been made into a Galilean or Palestinian. He who was of Rheims or Chartres has now become a citizen of Tyre or Antioch ... Indeed it is written, 'the lion and the ox shall eat straw together'. He who was born a stranger is now as one born here; he who was born an alien has become a native.[42]

This description highlights that while the Franks did not attempt to set themselves apart, the native population did not reject them, either. The picture Chartres paints is one of mutual acceptance. The key is Chartres' phrase in his description noting that 'mutual faith unites'. As Michael the Syrian stressed from the other perspective, the common bond of Christianity – regardless of the exact form that religion took, whether Maronite, Melkite, Jacobite, Armenian or Latin – transcended and trumped all differences of ethnicity, race, language, culture and tradition.

The common bond of Christianity enabled intermarriage. Intermarriage, in turn, gave the new settlers the tools to adapt to their new environment and command of the local languages and fostered identification with their new home. Intermarriage, more than anything else, turned immigrants from France, Germany, Italy and England into Galileans and Palestinians. By the second generation, the children of these marriages also had a new identity. Regardless of where their fathers had come from, the second generation of Latin residents in the Holy Land was not only called Franks but also viewed themselves as such. In all this, it was the women – the native women – who played the crucial role in binding the settlers to their new homes.

Eastern Brides for Frankish Lords

While Chartres eloquently depicts the situation of the common settler, strikingly those at the highest level of society – the kings, counts and barons of the Holy Land – likewise initially sought their wives among the local nobility rather than sending to the West for consorts. This may, in part, have been because, as relative parvenus, they could not expect to obtain the hand of daughters of the higher European nobility. Yet it also reflected the need and desire to secure the aid of in-laws embedded in existing power structures and familiar with local conditions.

As Count of Edessa, Baldwin I immediately realised an Armenian wife was indispensable. When he became King of Jerusalem, he found the Armenian connection less useful and attempted to put his Armenian wife aside. He sought, instead, to forge an alliance with Sicily by marrying the Dowager Queen Adelaide. Although Adelaide's principal attraction was her wealth, troops and the Sicilian fleet, she had already proven herself an able and prudent ruler of a multicultural state with Greek and Muslim minorities when she served as regent of Sicily from 1101 to 1112. In short, she brought more to the marriage than money and troops; she brought invaluable experience.

Baldwin II also married into the Armenian aristocracy as Count of Edessa, but he made no attempt to rid himself of his Armenian wife Morphia when he became King of Jerusalem. Thus, Morphia was crowned queen and ruled as Baldwin II's consort until his death. Baldwin II's successor was his daughter Melisende, but the next time Jerusalem needed a queen consort for a ruling king, the kingdom was sufficiently established and powerful to seek – and receive – a marriage alliance with the most powerful Christian state in the Near East: the Byzantine Empire. Both of Melisende's sons married brides from the ruling Byzantine dynasty, the Comnenus.

Again, the principal political advantage of these marriage alliances with Constantinople was military. Kings Baldwin III and Amalric I sought and received Byzantine armies and fleets to assist them in confronting their Muslim foes and, in Amalric's case, pursuing geopolitical ambitions in Egypt as well. Yet the influence of the Greek brides extended beyond the military sphere. The Byzantine princesses went to Jerusalem accompanied by scribes, artists and craftsmen. They brought trousseaus whose transport required entire caravans. Their wardrobes and generous gifts were intended to inspire admiration for Byzantine culture and craftsmanship. Under Maria Comnena especially, Greek money poured into the kingdom to construct churches and monasteries, and an influx of Greek artisans followed the money. It was also while Maria Comnena was queen that Amalric visited Constantinople and did homage to the Byzantine Emperor. This significant political act was largely obscured by the Christian defeat at Hattin only sixteen years later. The disaster at Hattin rendered any implied subservience to Constantinople irrelevant, while Constantinople's subsequent alliance with Saladin justified the Latin conquest of the Byzantine capital a few decades later.

After the fall of Jerusalem to Saladin in 1187, there followed almost a century in which the crown of Jerusalem passed to daughters or was held by absentee kings with no interest in the kingdom's welfare. It is notable, however, that for most of the thirteenth century, the Kings of Cyprus sought their brides from among the local nobility of Outremer rather than the West. King Aimery married an Ibelin first and the queen of Jerusalem second. His successor Hugh I, also married a Princess of Jerusalem. Not until the third generation was a foreign bride sought; Henry I of Cyprus first married a Montferrat (a family tied to the crown of Jerusalem by marriage twice in the previous century) and took an Armenian princess as his second wife. His successor died before reaching the age for marriage, and the next king of Cyprus to take a queen, Hugh III, married yet another Ibelin.

Almost prophetically, the last ruling king of Jerusalem, Henry II of Cyprus, was the first ruler of a crusader kingdom to take a Western European bride. Henry married Constance of Aragon, but there was no issue from this union, and his successor reverted to the usual pattern of local brides, marrying two different daughters of the House of Ibelin in succession. It was not until the fourteenth century that the princes of Cyprus consistently sought western brides. Guy (who died before his father) married Maria de Bourbon. Peter I married a local heiress Eschiva de Montfort first but then took Eleanor of Aragon as his second wife. John first married Constance of Aragon but took an Ibelin for his second wife. Finally, James I married a German bride, Helvis of Braunschweig. All these alliances with Western royalty occurred in the second half of the fourteenth century when all serious hope of re-establishing Christian control of the Holy Land proper had evaporated. The earlier alliances with Armenian, Greek, and even Sicilian woman, had served to anchor the crusader states in the Eastern Mediterranean and had contributed significantly to giving the kingdoms in Outremer a hybrid or multicultural character.

Western Consorts for Frankish Heiresses

The situation with respect to female heiresses was the exact reverse – and arguably led to the kingdom's destruction. Although the right of heiresses to inherit the crown was established early in the kingdom's history, it was also recognised that a ruling queen needed a male consort capable of leading –

physically and in person – the feudal army of the kingdom. The importance of this military role undoubtedly led the High Court of Jerusalem to assert its right to select husbands for heiresses to the crown. Perhaps out of a desire not to elevate any of its own members to a higher status, the High Court consistently looked to Western Europe for fitting consorts.

This precedent was set very early when Baldwin II designated his eldest daughter Melisende as his heir. Almost at once, the High Court requested the King of France select a suitable nobleman to come to Jerusalem and marry their future queen. At roughly the same time, the High Court in Antioch rejected attempts by the dowager Princess Alice to marry her daughter to the Byzantine Emperor, preferring to invite Raymond of Poitiers to Antioch instead. Obviously and understandably, the barons of Antioch feared increased Byzantine interference in their affairs and possibly a complete loss of independence had the powerful Byzantine Emperor married the heiress of the principality. Yet, it is noteworthy that they preferred a French candidate over a nobleman from Armenia, Tripoli or Jerusalem.

The next female heiress in the Kingdom of Jerusalem was Sibylla, the sister of Baldwin IV. Again, the High Court sought to find an appropriate Western nobleman, although they rejected attempts by the Count of Flanders to impose unworthy candidates upon them. Nevertheless, the Archbishop of Tyre was dispatched to the West to identify a husband for Sibylla and returned with Stephen of Sancerre of the House of Blois. Stephen was clearly of sufficient rank; his sister was married to Louis VII of France, and his brothers were married to Eleanor of Aquitaine's daughters by Louis VII. But Stephen unexpectedly refused to marry Sibylla and returned to France.

Evidently disenchanted with the French king, the High Court turned next to the Holy Roman Empire and invited William Marquis de Montferrat to become their next king. William was first cousin to both Louis VII of France and the Holy Roman Emperor Friedrich I. Furthermore, his family had a long tradition of crusading. He arrived in the Holy Land in October 1176 and married the then 16-year-old Sibylla within six weeks. He was invested with the title of Count of Jaffa and Ascalon, the traditional title for the heir apparent to the throne. Unfortunately, he died just eight months later, in June 1177. Sibylla gave birth in August to a posthumous son named Baldwin, after her brother.

Meanwhile, the High Court again appealed to the King of France to select a consort for their future queen. Louis VII's choice fell this time on the Duke of Burgundy, who agreed and announced his intention to arrive in Jerusalem in the spring of 1180. However, before Burgundy set out on the journey to Jerusalem, King Louis died, leaving the 14-year-old Philip II as his heir. With the predatory Plantagenets licking their chops, Burgundy evidently believed it was his duty to remain in France. Sibylla had been jilted a second time, which may explain why, at this juncture, she took things into her own hands and married a man of her own choice. Despite his obvious unsuitability as the younger son of the Lord de la March, Sibylla married Guy de Lusignan with the disastrous consequences discussed earlier in this book.

The next time the High Court exerted its influence over the choice of king consort, it turned yet again to Western Europe, selecting Conrad de Montferrat (from the Holy Roman Empire) as Isabella I's second consort. Isabella's third and fourth husbands, in contrast, were her own choices and in both cases, she chose French men already in the Holy Land. Her fourth husband was a man who had been in the Latin East for decades and had risen to be King of Cyprus largely on his merits. The marriage of Isabella I to Aimery de Lusignan was undoubtedly a means to shore up both kingdoms. Yet it may also reflect the fact that Jerusalem was so fragile and vulnerable at this time that the prospects of finding a high-ranking Western nobleman willing to abandon his secure titles to assume the august but uncertain post of King of Jerusalem were undoubtedly slim.

This political reality is underscored by the High Court's difficulty finding a consort for Isabella's heir, Maria de Montferrat. Eventually, John de Brienne came to Jerusalem, but he was unquestionably a nobleman of tertiary rank without great fortune or following. Yet if he proved a disappointment to the barons of Jerusalem, the 'coup' of marrying Maria's successor Yolanda (Isabella II) to the greatest of all Western monarchs, the Holy Roman Emperor Frederick II Hohenstaufen, proved utterly disastrous.

The marriage of Yolanda to Frederick II demonstrated the drawbacks of the High Court's predilection for seeking Western consorts in the hope of obtaining greater military protection for the kingdom. Although Fulk d'Anjou, Raymond de Poitiers, Henri de Champagne and the Montferrat brothers William and Conrad were all Western magnates, they had been willing to renounce their lands in the West and resettle in the Holy Land to defend Jerusalem in person. That changed with Yolanda's marriage to Frederick II. He neither renounced his other titles (king of Sicily, king of the Germans, Holy Roman Emperor) nor took up residence in the Latin East. Altogether, he spent less than one year of his 25-year reign in the Kingdom of Jerusalem. More disruptive yet, he took the ruling hereditary queen away from her kingdom (she travelled to his Kingdom of Sicily to marry him) and denied her her hereditary rights as ruling queen from that day forward. Instead, he confined her to his harem and usurped her authority until she died aged 15. He then usurped the authority of her infant son.

The kingdom never recovered from the consequences of this disastrous marriage, and historians can only speculate on what course history might have taken had the spouses of queens consistently been men resident in and committed to Outremer. Isabella's choice of Aimery de Lusignan was brilliant, and it is tempting to picture the fate of the kingdom had Yolanda married, say, the heir of Beirut, an extremely competent fighting man, or his nephew, the brilliant jurist John of Jaffa.

Women at the Crossroads of History: Three Case Studies

The role of women in holding together the different cultures that collided in Outremer can perhaps best be illustrated by case studies. Below are three examples of women who forged critical alliances yet whose role has been largely overlooked in more general histories.

Eschiva d'Ibelin: Founder of a Dynasty

Eschiva d'Ibelin, the daughter of Baldwin d'Ibelin, Lord of Ramla, was married at an unknown but undoubtedly early age to a noble but penniless adventurer from France, Aimery de Lusignan. At the time of her marriage, she was not an heiress, and the union was indicative of her husband's desire to settle in the East and forge ties with the local feudal elite. Why the Lord of Ramla found the third son of the Lord de la March a suitable match for his daughter is unclear, but Aimery must have been a man of considerable charm; King Amalric of Jerusalem had been willing to pay his ransom when he was taken captive by the Saracens, a generosity that was far from common. Indeed, some sources allege Aimery de Lusignan was so charming he became the paramour of the Queen Mother, Agnes de Courtenay.

As time went on, however, Eschiva's husband and father came into irreconcilable conflict. Eschiva's brother-in-law Guy had married the heiress of the kingdom, Sibylla, the woman her father had hoped to marry himself. Furthermore, Guy, as Count of Jaffa, became the Lord of Ramla's overlord, causing him further resentment. When Sibylla usurped the throne and crowned the widely unpopular Guy her consort, Eschiva's father could take no more. He abdicated his lordships and departed the kingdom. Such a dramatic breach between her father and husband must have been extremely painful for Eschiva, but on the surface, she sided with her husband and remained at his side.

Less than a year later, Aimery and Guy were both prisoners of Saladin, and Eschiva had lost everything. She had several small children, no means to raise her husband's ransom and was a refugee. With the Lusignans in a Saracen prison, Eschiva almost certainly found support and refuge with her father's younger brother, her uncle Balian d'Ibelin. Balian was one of only three barons not in Saracen captivity, but arguably more importantly, he was married to a Byzantine princess. She had access to resources outside Saladin's grasp.

When Saladin released the Lusignan brothers, Eschiva was reunited with Aimery. There is no evidence Eschiva joined him at the siege of Acre, and relations between the Lusignan brothers appeared to have soured. Certainly, when Guy first went to Cyprus after being deposed as king of Jerusalem, Aimery conspicuously did not accompany him. Even more striking, when Guy died within the next year, he left Cyprus not to Aimery – who had endured so much with him at and after Hattin – but to their elder brother, Hugh. Aimery acquired Cyprus from the barons who had settled (and fought) with him in Cyprus rather than his ever-incompetent younger brother Guy.

Then a remarkable thing happened. Cyprus, which had been in open revolt, was pacified in a mere five years. An island that had defied the most powerful militant order in the world (the Templars) became a model of harmonious co-existence between Latin and Orthodox, Frank and Greek. It became an island kingdom famous for its luxury, prosperity and self-indulgent aristocracy. The laws and policies that set it on that course were promulgated by Aimery de Lusignan. No historian has adequately explained this, and the fairy tale repeated in most books that Guy de Lusignan asked and received advice from Saladin is exactly that: a fairy tale. The real key lies with Eschiva and her Ibelin connections.

Eschiva's pivotal role in reconciling her family the Ibelins with the Cypriot Lusignans cannot be overstated, and the importance of the Ibelins in Cyprus, something historians have puzzled over for centuries, can best be explained by her. It is generally assumed that because the Ibelins opposed Guy de Lusignan, they were also inveterate opponents of Aimery. Yet the Ibelins were perfectly capable of distinguishing between the two Lusignan brothers and, therefore, able to judge Aimery for his strengths rather than condemning him for his brother's weaknesses.

Eschiva's role as a mediator between her uncle and her husband explains another mystery that has long baffled historians: how the Ibelins became so powerful in Cyprus so fast. Historians such as Peter Edbury express perplexity at the fact that an Ibelin (Balian's second son Philip) was named regent of Cyprus by the Cypriot High Court only seven years after the first written reference to the presence of Ibelins on Cyprus. However, in the decade following the Third Crusade, the Kingdom of Jerusalem struggled to re-establish its institutions while the Kingdom of Cyprus was completely inchoate. In short, the first recorded presence of an Ibelin need not be the first actual presence of the Ibelins. It is more likely that Balian d'Ibelin and his wife, Maria Comnena, played an active role in the pacification of Cyprus. This would explain how the Ibelins came to possess vast estates in the island kingdom and the influence they held on the Cypriot High Court.

Indeed, the very fact that Balian d'Ibelin disappeared from the records of the Kingdom of Jerusalem in 1193, usually assumed to mean he died at this time, more probably reflects the fact that he was active in Cyprus rather than on the mainland. The same thing happened a quarter-century later when the Lord of Beirut disappeared from the witness lists after being regent of Jerusalem during King John's reign. Despite disappearing from the witness lists, Beirut was very much alive and well. Indeed, he would return to lead the baronial revolt against Frederick II. In short, the fact that Balian d'Ibelin disappears from the witness lists at the court of his stepdaughter Isabella I does not mean he was necessarily dead. It does no more than suggest he was absent from Isabella's kingdom. The most logical place for him to have been in this period was in Cyprus at the invitation of his niece, Eschiva. The reason Eschiva would seek her uncle's support for her husband at this juncture brings us to the second woman whose critical role in the history of the Latin East has been neglected: Maria Comnena.

Maria Comnena: The Key to Cyprus?
As noted above, Maria Comnena had already played a key role in forging an alliance between her first husband, King Amalric and the Comnena dynasty in Constantinople. She had arrived in Jerusalem with a large entourage of Byzantine artists and artisans, fostering the spread of Byzantine culture in her new homeland.

In 1190, Maria Comnena played a critical role in re-establishing a viable monarchy in the Kingdom of Jerusalem by convincing her daughter Isabella to put the welfare of her battered and bleeding kingdom ahead of her personal feelings. Maria's intervention at this time shows the wisdom of the daughter of the Byzantine imperial family. She understood political and military realities and correctly conveyed to her daughter the imperative of meeting the demands of her barons for a militarily competent king. In doing so, Maria Comnena saved the crown of Jerusalem for her dynasty. Had Isabella instead clung to Humphrey de Toron as her husband, the barons would almost certainly have abandoned Isabella altogether and elected Montferrat (or another candidate) as their king. The kingdom would have been fragmented even further by the competing claims to the crown put forward by Lusignan, Isabella/Toron and the barons' candidate. Maria ought to be praised and admired for her statesmanship rather than vilified for browbeating her 18-year-old daughter into making a rational rather than an emotional decision.

Once the succession was settled by the departure of Guy de Lusignan for Cyprus and Isabella's marriage to Henri de Champagne, Maria Comnena – like her second husband – seems almost to disappear from the history books. Yet, nothing would have been more logical than for her to go to Cyprus to assist in the pacification of this formerly Byzantine and still Greek Orthodox island. Maria Comnena was related to the island's last Greek 'emperor', Isaac Comnenus. She spoke Greek, understood the mentality of the population, and probably had good ties (or could forge them) to the secular and ecclesiastical Greek Orthodox elites on the island. She had the means to help Aimery pacify his unruly realm, while her husband Balian was a proven diplomat par excellence, who would also have been a great asset to Aimery.

We know that Maria was later credited with brokering a reconciliation between Aimery de Lusignan and her son-in-law, Henri de Champagne. Maria's tool in this case was a marriage alliance between Lusignan's eldest son (and heir) and Champagne's eldest daughter. Yet while Maria's influence with her son-in-law is logical, it is hard to see what influence she would have had with Aimery de Lusiginan unless she had earlier helped him establish himself in Cyprus by serving as a mediator to his Greek subjects during his early years in Cyprus.

Marguerite d'Ibelin: Bridge Between Rebels

Finally, there is Marguerite d'Ibelin, the eldest daughter of Balian d'Ibelin and Maria Comnena. Marguerite married the Lord of Sidon at an early age and her eldest son by that marriage became one of the most powerful barons in Jerusalem in the thirteenth century. He was appointed regent of the kingdom by Frederick II on two separate occasions and made serious attempts to mediate between his uncle and cousin of Beirut and the Holy Roman Emperor. Meanwhile, his mother had been widowed at a young age and married a second time.

Since she was a widow, Marguerite's second marriage could not have been imposed on her, and we can assume that she chose her second husband freely. Her choice fell on a certain Guy de Montfort, a crusader from the West. Guy and his elder brother Simon took the cross in or about 1203 but refused to attack fellow Christians at Zara or Constantinople. Instead, they had distanced themselves from the campaign financed by Venice that ended with the capture of Constantinople and travelled independently to the Holy Land. Simon soon returned to France and took command of a different crusade, the crusade against the Albigensians in Southern France. Guy remained in the Holy Land, married Marguerite, and had three children with her, two daughters and a son, Philip.

Marguerite died while these children were all still small, so Guy returned to France, taking his children with him. He turned the upbringing of his children over to his sister-in-law, Alice de Montmorency, wife of his brother Simon. Alice was the mother of Simon de Montfort, later Earl of Leicester. Philip and Simon appear to have been quite close, and nearly half a century later, they took the cross and set out to the Holy Land together. They participated in what became known as 'the Baron's Crusade' of 1239–1241. Like his father, Philip remained in the Holy Land and married there. Unlike his father, he married an heiress and became baron of Toron by right of his wife. He was also one of the staunchest and most steadfast supporters of his cousin Balian d'Ibelin, Lord of Beirut, in the latter's fight against the Holy Roman Emperor.

The connection between the rebels of Outremer and the rebel Simon de Montfort is a chapter of mediaeval history that has not yet been adequately explored and illuminated. It is, however, hard to believe that Simon de Montfort's stance against arbitrary and authoritarian monarchy was not, in part, inspired and encouraged by the successful stand of his Ibelin cousins against Frederick II. It is even more notable that the barons of Outremer under the Ibelins had experimented with harnessing the support of the commoners (e.g., the Commune of Acre, non-feudal observers to the High Court) before Montfort did. The fact that the Montforts and Ibelins were cousins made exchanging ideas and sentiments easier than between strangers. Family ties were forged by women like Marguerite d'Ibelin, who brought the ideas and customs of the East and West together in the same household. She was only one of scores of such women, most of whom escape the notice of chroniclers and historians.

Chapter 7

The Legal Status of Women
in the Crusader States

Feudal Lords

As noted earlier, the crusader states embodied developed feudalism before it began to degenerate into absolutism. Under feudalism, the monarch sat at the pinnacle of a pyramid of contractual relationships based on oaths of fealty; a person's status in society depended first and foremost upon one's place within that pyramid. The barons or 'tenants-in-chief' held their lands and titles directly from the king, forming the second tier of society. The barons' vassals formed the third tier, their vassals' vassals the fourth, and so on, to the bottom of the pyramid inhabited by those without land, e.g., farm labourers, itinerant workers, etc. Wealthy merchants and tradesmen represented a rising non-feudal economic sector that, on the one hand, integrated into feudal society via marriage and land purchases and, on the other hand, undermined and brought down the system over time.

In the crusader states, however, feudalism was at its apogee. The key indicator of legal status was the ability to give and receive homage, i.e., to take the feudal oath that elevated the oath taker into the feudal elite of the realm. Within decades of their establishment, the crusader states had recognised the right of women to hold the crown and so receive oaths of homage. It logically followed that women could also give oaths of homage, i.e., as barons and lords right down to the sergeant's fiefs at the bottom of the pyramid. There are numerous examples in the historical record illustrating this.

The right of women to give and receive homage derived from the laws of inheritance that recognised the right of female inheritance. In the crusader states, inheritance law explicitly gave the direct female descendants of the deceased lord precedence over male relatives from a collateral line. (For example, the lord's daughter took precedence over the lord's brothers or nephews.) Furthermore, if a man held more fiefs than male heirs, daughters inherited after their brothers. For example, if a man held three fiefs but had only two sons and one or more daughters, the eldest son would receive the largest and most prestigious fief, his second son the next fief and the eldest daughter the third.[43]

However, women could not fight in the feudal army. As the entire point of feudalism was to create a structure to defend the kingdom, one of the critical obligations incumbent upon a vassal was to fight in the entourage of his lord. Since women could not fulfil this fundamental feudal duty, the right of female inheritance was limited. First, male heirs were given precedence over female heirs, except in cases where the male was, for some reason, incapable of fulfilling his military obligations.[44] This could be because of physical or mental handicaps or due to religious vows. Second, female heirs over age 12 yet under 60 were required to be married to men capable of fulfilling the military obligations that went with the fief, e.g., serving as a sergeant (if it were a sergeant's fief), as a knight (in a knight's fief), or personally leading multiple knights as a banneret, if the fief owed more than one knight to the feudal host. (For example, the barony of Ibelin owed 10 knights, the barony of Transjordan owed 40, and the barony of Galilee owed 100.)

In the absence of a suitable male heir, the rights of the eldest daughter were initially accepted as equal to the rights of the eldest son. That is, for the first seventy years, the eldest female heiress received the entire fief just as the most senior male heir would have. However, in 1171, in the reign of King Amalric, the High Court ruled that, except for the kingdom itself and the tenants-in-chief, fiefs should be divided equally among the female heiresses. At the same time, the High Court stipulated that the younger sisters should do homage to their eldest sister for their shares of the fief, making them rear vassals of their elder sister. The point was to increase the number of men who could be called upon to render military service in the feudal host. An unintended consequence was to fragment the holding and possibly impoverish it.

Naturally, the husbands of heiresses not only fulfilled the feudal obligations that went with their wives' fiefs, but they also enjoyed the wealth and prestige that went with their wives' titles and properties. One need only think of Reynald de Châtillion becoming 'Prince of Antioch', Balian d'Ibelin styling himself 'Lord of Nablus', or Raymond of Tripoli's controversial role as Lord of Tiberias – all titles that derived from marriage rather than through inheritance or bestowal from the crown. Yet these husbands of heiresses, who held the titles and enjoyed the revenues, castles and prestige of fiefs 'by right of their wife', lost all when their wife died. At an heiress' death, her title and control of her fief passed to her heirs (male or female) rather than her husband. There are many prominent examples of this, the most famous of which was Reynald de Chatillon's 'loss' of Antioch after his wife's death and, of course, Guy de Lusignan's loss of the Kingdom of Jerusalem after Queen Sibylla died.

The status of a feudal lord, however, was not confined to heiresses alone. The consorts of kings, barons, lords and knights likewise served as the deputies of their husbands. This meant that if their husbands were either absent or incapacitated, their wives took on the role of lord and acted in their husbands' stead. They managed the household and finances, presided over the feudal court and commanded the garrison and any other fighting men left in the domain. Most important and astonishing, perhaps, in Outremer, women could and did attend the High Court of the Kingdom to represent their fief. They did this as heiresses if they were temporarily without a husband, as guardians for minor heirs or heiresses, or if their husband was incapacitated either by illness or being held in captivity and thus prevented from attending a session of the High Court.

This astonishing right of Frankish women has largely been overlooked in the literature probably because, as a rule, the number of women attending any one session of the High Court was too few to evoke comment. However, in 1261, in the Frankish Principality of Achaea, a situation arose that sheds light on this privilege. In 1259, the Byzantine Despot of Epirus, Michael Comnenus Doukas, allied with the Kingdom of Sicily and the Frankish Prince of Achaea to attack his Byzantine rival, Michael VIII Palaiologos. Doukas took the offensive and was forced to retreat with substantial losses, but when reinforced by his allies, he prepared to take a stand. In July 1259, it came to a battle known alternatively as the Battle of Pelagonia or Kastoria. Due to the discrepancies between the five existing accounts of the battle (three Byzantine and two Frankish), it is challenging to form a clear picture of what happened. The only thing beyond doubt is that mistrust between the Greeks and the Franks resulted in Doukas' army abandoning the field on the eve of battle. Palaiologos' forces then greatly outnumbered the Franks and achieved a resounding victory in which the Prince of Achaea, William of Villehardrouin, and thirty of his barons were taken captive. Many other Frankish knights were also killed or imprisoned, leaving the Latin Empire of Constantinople virtually defenceless. Within two years, Constantinople fell to the Greeks under Michael VIII Palaiologos, who re-established the Byzantine Empire and founded his dynasty.

Once he was secure in Constantinople, Michael VIII opened ransom negotiations with William de Villehardoin and the other Frankish nobles still in captivity since the Battle of Pelagonia. The deal struck was that the prisoners would be set free in exchange for oaths never to fight against Emperor Michael again and the surrender of three key fortresses in the Peloponnese (Maina, Monemvasia and Mystras). However, as with Louis IX of France when negotiating with the Mamluks, the Prince of Achaea and his nobles could only recommend the ransom terms. They did not have the power to enforce them. Instead, the terms were referred to the High Court of the Principality, which had the duty to reject or ratify the terms negotiated by men in captivity.

Guy Duke of Athens, the highest ranking of the Frankish lords still at liberty, convened the High Court of the principality 'as was his duty'.[45] Yet only two men attended. Women represented the remaining fiefs. These were either the widows of the dead lords and knights acting in their capacity as regents for minor heirs or the consorts of the men held captive in Constantinople. The latter, just like Queen Marguerite of France after King Louis IX's capture in Egypt, controlled the fiefs of their husbands for as long as they were prisoners.

The decision of the High Court was no rubber stamp. Guy of Athens himself firmly opposed acceptance of the negotiated settlement. He feared the surrender of the three fortresses would so weaken the Frankish hold on the Peloponnese that it would crumble altogether. Indeed, he offered to take Villehardouin's place in the dungeon rather than accept the loss of the castles.

The majority of the High Court chose instead to accept the negotiated terms in order to set free all of those who still lived (several Franks had already died in captivity). Furthermore, as guarantees of their good intent, two ladies were sent as hostages to the Greeks. The history of this so-called 'Ladies Parliament' demonstrates that women of the feudal elite in the crusader states were expected to fulfil the feudal duty of advising the king (i.e., attending parliament) if their husbands could not do so. It further demonstrates that their advice and vote were equal in weight to that of any male fief holder.

The legal privileges of Frankish women did not, however, extend to the entire population. On the contrary, Muslim women were still subject to Sharia Law, Jewish women to Talmudic Law, while the women from the various Italian mercantile states lived under the laws of their respective metropolitan cities, be it Venice, Pisa or Genoa. Nuns, naturally, were subject to canon law. Yet it is still noteworthy that women enjoyed extraordinary and prominent rights at the highest echelons of society, something which was bound to influence the attitudes and behaviour at lower levels as well.

The Marriage of Heiresses

As noted above, due to the need for the holder of a fief to fulfil military obligations, any woman who held a fief in her own right was required to have a husband capable of performing those military duties. In most cases, heiresses were betrothed at a young age (the legal minimum was seven for both boys and girls) by their parents or guardian and, as a rule, were already married when they succeeded to their inheritance. Among royal heiresses, we see this was the case with Queen Melisende, who wed Fulk de Anjou before her father's death, with Sibylla, who wed before the death of her brother, and with Isabella I. It was also true of baronial heiresses such as Eschiva of Tiberias and Stephanie de Milly, the heiress to Transjordan.

The marriages of royal heiresses were supposed to require the consent of the High Court, and those of baronial heiresses were supposed to be approved by the feudal overlord. However, in practice, most baronial marriages contracted before an heiress came into her inheritance were made without the consent of the feudal overlord, i.e., the families alone selected spouses for their children. Philip de Novare claims that under King Amalric in the 1160s, an attempt was made to give the feudal overlord a say in selecting husbands for heiresses. He admits, however, that this met with resistance from the barons, who wished to retain complete control over the marriage of their daughters, suggesting this practice may not have been universally implemented. Most likely, some barons avoided surrendering control over the marriages of their offspring or obtained the nominal consent of their overlords for their own choices. Nevertheless, Amalric asserted his right in at least one case, namely that of Stephanie, the widow of Humphrey of Toron the younger, who Tyre claims King Amalric gave to Miles de Plancy.[46] Likewise, his son Baldwin IV successfully asserted this right to select the husband of his half-sister, Isabella, taking her away from her mother and stepfather against their wishes and forcing her into a betrothal at the age of 8 that ended in an illegal marriage at 11 years. In both cases, however, the heiresses involved were half-orphans with no father capable of withstanding the king's will.

Curiously, in cases of orphans who came into their estate without already being betrothed or married, the laws of Jerusalem provided clear guidance on what was to happen next. Namely, as soon as the heiress reached the marriageable age of 12, her feudal lord would propose three suitable candidates, from which she was to select her husband. The legal scholars of the thirteenth century explained further that if she refused to marry any of the three, she would lose her fief (the revenues and privileges) for a year and a day, after which she would be re-summoned and again offered three candidates. Likewise, if a woman held a fief in her own right and was a widow without an adult male heir, she was required to remarry, albeit not until one year of mourning had passed. In both cases, 'suitable' candidates meant men of equal rank and status who were young, fit and strong enough to fight. Widows over the age of 60 were exempt from the mandate to remarry.

Edbury points out that such a practice was an invitation to corruption. Anyone keen to obtain the fief (or the bride) would be inclined to bribe the feudal overlord to become a 'candidate'. The heiress might also bribe her lord to ensure he included her preferred candidate among the three he would present. Or, the heiress' guardian, who enjoyed control of her estates until her marriage, might bribe the overlord to forget to summon the heiress altogether.[47]

Nevertheless, the practice was considerably more favourable to heiresses than prevailing law elsewhere, as a quick comparison to the contemporary customs in England and France demonstrates. In England and France, heiresses could not marry anyone without the permission of their feudal overlord. This meant women were, in effect, forced to bribe their overlord before they could contract a marriage with the candidate of their choice. In France, it was not until the middle of the thirteenth century that King Louis IX introduced into French law the custom of giving an heiress a choice between three candidates presented by the feudal overlord. Notably, this custom was introduced after King Louis' four-year sojourn in the crusader states. Before that, as in England, the feudal overlord selected an heiress' husband without giving her any choice whatsoever.

Practice, however, can vary substantially from theory. There can be little doubt that mediaeval noble children, whether male or female, rarely enjoyed anything more than nominal consent to their marriages. Betrothed as children and married in puberty, most lacked the power or courage to withhold consent from a marriage arranged by their parents or guardians. Furthermore, while the High Court of Jerusalem rejected the Count of Flanders' demeaning candidate for Sibylla's second husband on the grounds that her year of mourning was not yet over, Isabella I was married to her third husband only a week after the assassination of her second. Admittedly, this was during the Third Crusade, and it could be argued that the High Court had not been formally reconstituted since the disaster at Hattin. Five years later, after the institutions of the Kingdom of Jerusalem had been re-established, however, Isabella married her fourth husband within just four months of losing her third. In both cases, she did so freely as an adult ruling queen and widow to whom her barons had already done homage.

Isabella was not the first widowed heiress to take her marriage into her own hands, regardless of law and custom. Another kinswoman, Constance of Antioch, had already provided a more spectacular example. Constance was the daughter of Queen Melisende's sister Alice and Alice's husband, Bohemond II of Antioch. Bohemond was killed in 1130, making Constance the ruling princess at age 2, long before she could either exercise her office or marry. The principality was governed by regents and the High Court, which in 1136 selected Raymond de Poitiers, the younger brother of the Duke of Aquitaine, as Constance's husband. Poitiers came to Antioch armed with a papal dispensation to marry the 8-year-old Constance. The issue of consent was brushed aside for dynastic reasons. The marriage lasted until 1149, when

Raymond de Poitiers died fighting against Nur ad-Din in the Battle of Inab. Constance was left a widow at 21 with four children, including a 5-year-old son, Bohemond, now Prince Bohemond III.

After her year of mourning, the king of Jerusalem – Constance's cousin Baldwin III – urged her 'repeatedly' (according to William of Tyre) to take a new husband. Tyre notes that 'there were in the land at that time a number of noble and distinguished men ... [anyone of whom] seemed with justice quite capable of protecting the region'. Tyre goes on to list the three candidates with their qualities and bloodlines to show they were worthy consorts for the Princess of Antioch. However, as Tyre says: 'The princess ... dreaded the yoke of marriage and preferred a free and independent life. She paid little heed to the needs of her people and was far more interested in enjoying the pleasures of life'.[48]

While Tyre's opinion of Constance's motives may be biased, the fact remains that the king singularly failed to convince or force Constance to take one of his 'suitable' candidates. Indeed, he summoned what Tyre calls a 'General Council' at Tripoli and sent for Constance's aunts, Queen Melisende and Countess Hodierna of Tripoli, as well. Yet, as Tyre laments, 'neither the king nor the count, her kinsmen, neither the queen nor the countess of Tripoli, her two aunts, was able to induce her to yield and thus provide for herself and her land'.[49] Yet, three years later, Constance remarried a man of her choosing – the soon-to-be notorious adventurer, Reynald de Châtillon. Less than twenty years later, the widowed Sibylla of Jerusalem followed Constance's example by marrying the man of her choice without the consent of the High Court, albeit with her brother's approval: Guy de Lusignan.

Finally, the case of Isabella d'Ibelin of Beirut is an interesting case study regarding heiress and marriage obligations. Isabella inherited this important lordship from her father, John d'Ibelin of Beirut II, in 1264, when she was just 12. Shortly afterwards, she was betrothed to Hugh II of Cyprus, a youth her age, who unfortunately died two years later in 1267. Isabella returned to Beirut, yet her feudal overlord undertook no measures to make her remarry, despite her being an heiress of marriageable age. Apparently of her own will, she married and was widowed a second time. Then, suddenly, ten years after she had left Cyprus, the Cypriot king, Hugh III, sought to enforce his feudal rights as overlord to compel a marriage on Isabella. He had misjudged her. Isabella took her case to the High Court and won with an ingenious defence that will feature later in this book.

What this tells us is that no matter how much the High Court of Jerusalem wanted to ensure that heiresses were always wed to spouses capable of fulfilling the military obligations of their fief, the Church requirement for consent to marriage gave women the means to refuse the political pressure to marry – if they had the backbone. It is doubtful if a maiden of 12 or 13 would have had the courage to resist pressure like Constance did at 21 or Isabella at 25. Yet there can be no doubt that mature women, notably widows, could – and did – ignore the legal niceties recorded by the scholars of the thirteenth century in order to marry who and when they wanted.

Wives and Widows: Rights of Property, Dower and Guardianship

Turning to the status of non-heiresses as wives and widows, the laws of the crusader kingdoms were again surprisingly progressive. First, property was held jointly by a married couple, and neither partner could dispose of it without the other's consent. Indeed, it was common for all documents involving property transfers to be witnessed not only by husband and wife but also by all potential heirs (i.e., children over 7).

When a man died, his widow received a dower amounting to fifty per cent of his property at the time of his death. In other words, only half of the estate went to the adult heir or heiress, while the widow retained the other half for her maintenance until her death. The only exceptions to this were for the kingdom and the four principal baronies (Jaffa and Ascalon, Galilee, Tripoli and Transjordan). Due to the size of these estates, it was deemed appropriate that a smaller dower would suffice. As we have seen, the widowed Queen Theodora Comnena received Acre, and Maria Comnena was given Nablus, both extremely wealthy lordships. Widows of all lesser fiefs, were entitled to half of their husband's estate at the time of his death.

For comparison, in English law, a widow's dower initially consisted of only those lands and properties that had been explicitly designated at the time of the marriage. These might be generous or paltry, depending on the ability of the bride's family to negotiate a dower portion for her. By the twelfth century, English law recognised that in the absence of a formal agreement a widow was entitled to one-third of her late husband's property. In France, however, the right of a widow to a dower (properties for her maintenance after the death of her husband) did not evolve until the middle of the thirteenth century. In France as in England, it was set at one-third rather than one-half (as in Outremer) of the husband's property at the time of his death.

In the crusader states, widows had complete and sole control of their dower lands, including the right to alienate property. There are many examples of widows granting lands and revenues, entirely on their own, particularly to the Church. Equally important, however, was the right to buy fiefs if they were for sale. (Although that sounds like a contradiction since the crown granted fiefs, there were circumstances in the crusader states under which a fief-holder was allowed to alienate his fief through a sale.) However, a widow could only acquire such a fief if she were married and her husband could fulfil the military obligations associated with the fief.

This brings us to the marriage of widows. As noted above, widowed heiresses were, at least theoretically, required to marry after one year of mourning. In contrast, widows who were not heiresses were not required to remarry. In England, however, widows throughout the crusader era could be compelled to remarry. This fact offended contemporary sensibilities sufficiently for a prohibition of the practice to be included in Magna Carta. This seminal document explicitly states: 'a widow should not be compelled to marry so long as she prefers to remain without a husband'.[50] Yet the custom persisted; the grievance was raised again in the baronial revolt of the mid-thirteenth century.

While they could not be compelled to remarry, widows in possession of fiefs either as dowagers or as regents for minor heirs required the permission of their feudal overlord to remarry. Thus, we find Reynald de Châtillon outside the siege camp at Ascalon in 1153, seeking the consent of King Baldwin III to marry Constance of Antioch. Likewise, William of Tyre reports in his history that 'Balian d'Ibelin … with the king's consent espoused Queen Maria, widow of King Amaury'.[51]

In sharp contrast to the custom in England and France, when a man was outlived by his wife in the crusader states, his minor heirs, whether male or female, did not become the ward of the feudal overlord. Instead, a man's widow acted as guardian and regent for minor heirs and all other children of the marriage. This meant that if a man died leaving a minor heir, his widow retained control of the entire estate until that heir came of age (if male) or married (if female), and only after that event, lived from her dower. Again, the exception was in the case of the crown. If a king left a minor heir, it was the responsibility of the High Court to appoint a regent. However, even the major baronies could be held by a widow as regent for the minor heir. This happened twice in the case of the Principality of Galilee; first, when Ermengard, the widow of Elinard of Bures held it from his death in 1153 until her eldest son Walter came of age in 1159, and again when Eschiva of Tiberias ruled the principality following Walter's death until 1174. Likewise, Stephanie de Milly, heiress of Transjordan, held Toron as guardian of her son Humphrey.

Judicial Status Before the Courts

As opposed to Islamic law, the laws of the Kingdom of Jerusalem recognised women as legal persons equal in status to males, albeit with some restrictions. On the one hand, women defendants were on an equal footing with male defendants. Likewise, in property disputes, issues of inheritance and cases we would treat as civil rather than criminal, women were treated equally with men, and their word was weighted equally with that of male witnesses.

However, in criminal cases in which the punishment could include mutilation or execution, the laws of the crusader states still recognised the right of the defendant to request trial by combat. This impacted the status of women before the law because, despite possible exceptions, women were generally disadvantaged when fighting men. Hence, women were exempted from personally engaging in judicial combat. Instead, they had to bring forth a champion. That did not exempt the woman from capital punishment in the event her champion was defeated. On the contrary, if her champion lost, the female litigant was deemed guilty by the judgement of God and hung.

Notably, members of the clergy and men over 60 enjoyed the same exemption from combat and the requirement to bring forth a champion capable of fighting to initiate a court case that might be referred to judicial combat for judgement. Since witnesses in criminal cases were not allowed to use champions, women – along with priests and men over 60 – were likewise debarred from bearing witness in cases that might be referred to the judgement of God, i.e., trial by combat. It is important to stress that these legal impediments to women were not misogynous because they applied equally to anyone deemed innately disadvantaged in physical combat, e.g., male clergy and males over 60.

In effect, a woman could only initiate proceedings that could go to judicial combat (e.g., rape, assault, highway robbery) if she had two witnesses willing to fight to the death on her behalf. This was because all those initiating proceedings required two people to testify to the truth of their accusation. A male litigant only had to find one companion willing to support his accusations because he offered his own body in judicial combat (unless too old, disabled or in holy orders). A woman had to find two men willing to back her allegations with their lives.

In the case of rape or other acts of violence against women, unmarried women and widows could initiate court proceedings on their own. Married women, however, needed their husband's consent, presumably because he was expected to serve as her champion; failure to do so (without good reason) would prejudice the case against her. Usually, in the case of a married woman, her husband initiated the proceedings on her behalf and served as her champion.

However, the law did allow a wife to choose a different champion because husbands might be old, injured or otherwise disabled. In fact, however, very few cases went to judicial combat; most were settled out of court.

It is worth quoting Peter Edbury's conclusion to his essay on the legal status of women based on his study of John d'Ibelin's treatise, *Le Livre des Assises*, one of the most definitive primary sources on the laws of the Kingdom of Jerusalem. Edbury writes:

> 'John's treatise contains a wealth of information about the status and activities of women in the High Court of Jerusalem, but that what he says gives rise to further questions that cannot easily be resolved. While it is clear that women had certain disabilities at law ... it is also clear that they had well-defined rights and that the legal system was able to guarantee them'.[52]

Edbury also notes that, like William of Tyre, Ibelin's work is devoid of 'pejorative remarks' about women. As one of the leading noblemen and jurists of his society, that too tells us a great deal about how women were perceived in the crusader states.

Hostages and Captives

Finally, in a kingdom surrounded by enemies and frequently at war, the status of women caught up in warfare is particularly important. In the crusader kingdoms of the Levant (though not in Cyprus or Frankish Greece), women were frequently caught up in warfare as will be explored in more detail in the chapter 'In Defence of the Holy Land: The Women of Outremer in Time of War'. In this chapter, only two legal aspects of women's status in warfare will be highlighted: their ability to serve as hostages and their right to ransom.

The most famous case of a female being pledged as a hostage for the good behaviour of a male released from captivity is Baldwin II's surrender of his daughter Iveta to secure his release in 1124. At the time, Iveta was just 4 or 5 years old. One can well imagine Muslim dismay and reluctance to accept a female hostage, but Baldwin had no male heirs or close male relatives in the Near East. He only had four daughters. Notably, Iveta was accompanied by other hostages, mostly male and female children.

Interestingly, the ransom negotiations were conducted by Baldwin's wife, Iveta's mother, Queen Morphia, and primary sources agree that Baldwin moved as rapidly as possible to raise the enormous ransom required to liberate his daughter. Altogether, she is believed to have spent no more than eighteen months in Saracen hands. In short, she and the other children fulfilled the role assigned them (passively, of course) of ensuring that the king of Jerusalem complied with the terms of the ransom agreement.

In the incident cited earlier, in which two noblewomen served as hostages to ensure William de Villehardouin's compliance with the terms of his release from captivity in Constantinople, it is possible that, again, there were no suitable male hostages. William himself only had two daughters, both already married and living outside Greece. Obviously, the bulk of the Frankish lords had been killed or captured, which was why women dominated the High Court in the first place. Nevertheless, the fact remains that women were viewed as sufficient security for a man's compliance with the terms of an agreement.

Yet while hostages were (out of self-interest) generally well-treated, the fate of those taken captive was almost invariably hellish. In the Eastern Mediterranean, in the era of the crusades, there were all too many ways in which a man or woman could find themselves enslaved. The pilgrim routes were notorious for being plagued by robbers, and in an age characterised by widespread slavery, humans were viewed as 'plunder' no less than gold or silver. Pirates made sea travel dangerous. The porous nature of mediaeval borders meant that hostile raiders – whether Bedouins or Saracen troops – could conduct raids into the crusader states and take away captives. In the wake of major invasions, villages, towns and even walled cities might be captured and the inhabitants taken away as slaves.

In fact, so many people were taken captive in the Near East during the era of the crusades that several religious orders were dedicated primarily to raising money from charity to buy back those who had been carried off into slavery. For the high born, however, it was more common for captives to be ransomed by their families. Here, again, the crusader states demonstrated a concern and respect for women above and beyond that of other contemporary kingdoms. Thus, while the Law of Provence, for example, decreed that a son lost his fief if he failed to ransom his father, and a father lost his fief if he failed to ransom a son who stood hostage for him, in Outremer, a son had the obligation to ransom both his father and mother, and a man was obliged to ransom both his sons and his daughters, or otherwise lose his fief.

Chapter 8

The Political Power of Women in the Crusader States

Women in the crusader states exercised significant political power. They did so first and foremost due to their legal status as feudal lords. This power was direct in the case of heiresses who held land and titles in their own right or delegated in the case of consorts acting on behalf of absent or incapacitated husbands or mothers acting on behalf of minor heirs. In addition, women also enjoyed a high degree of indirect power in their capacity as consorts or dowagers of living and politically active feudal lords. Yet not all influence was derived from feudal law. Women in Outremer also acted as intermediaries with the enemy, sometimes positively as envoys and sometimes negatively as spies. Finally, in the crusader era, women still enjoyed a notable degree of independence, respect and influence as churchwomen. These different types of power are examined below by providing prominent examples from the historical record.

Direct Power: Feudal Lords

Queen Melisende

Arguably no woman had more influence on the image and status of women in the crusader states than the first reigning queen of Jerusalem, Melisende. While her father opened the door for her by designating her as his heir, a different woman might have squandered this opportunity to exercise power or failed to set a precedent of female competence in a traditionally male role. Melisende neither neglected nor misused her rare opportunity.

As we have seen from the narrative description of Melisende's reign, her authority was almost immediately challenged by her older and politically more experienced husband, Fulk d'Anjou. At her father's death, Fulk stopped including her in his charters, ignored her advice and opinions and generally disregarded her status as co-monarch; i.e., he attempted to rule on his own. It is unclear if Melisende and the High Court would have tolerated this situation indefinitely if Fulk had not, in the third year of their joint reign, also sought to discredit his wife by accusing her of an affair with her cousin, Hugh of Jaffa, one of the most powerful of the local barons. The king's motives are unknown, although historians speculate that Fulk favoured Angevin lords over the local barons and possibly sought to install a son from his first marriage as his heir, thereby disinheriting his son by Melisende, Baldwin III.

Whatever his intentions, the attack on Melisende's honour, or the threat to her son, provoked a vigorous response. Rather than becoming a victim of her husband's intrigue and disappearing from history, Melisende rallied baronial and clerical support. Even when her chief supporter, the Count of Jaffa, made the tactical blunder of forming an alliance with the Saracens, Melisende's position was not weakened. The High Court found Jaffa guilty of treason yet sentenced him only to three years of exile, possibly in recognition of the extenuating circumstances that had driven him into that alliance – i.e., the king's actions. Hugh's assassination before he could leave the kingdom provoked even greater outrage from local elites who assumed the king was behind the murder.

Fulk had hopelessly overplayed his hand. The contemporary chroniclers, most notably William of Tyre, report that henceforth, Fulk recognised he must scrupulously respect Melisende's rights as hereditary queen – or risk losing his crown. Yet we know nothing about how Melisende brought about this change of attitude or how she managed to rally nearly unanimous support among her powerful subjects in her confrontation with her spouse.

Equally intriguing, Melisende did not seek revenge or humiliation for her consort after her victory. Having re-established her position as co-monarch, Melisende showed herself as gracious. Not only were Fulk and Melisende reconciled enough to have a second son, but they became an extremely effective team who divided the responsibilities of ruling between them. Erin Jordan, writing in the *Royal Studies Journal*, notes that:

'Gender norms that divided the various duties associated with ruling, reserving military action for men, were not detrimental to female participation in government. The frequent and extended absences of the king from the royal court in Jerusalem which resulted from his preoccupation with military activity could easily have strained the administration of domestic affairs … [Instead] the constant presence of the queen at court curbed any such disruption in the routine governing'.[53]

Presumably, Melisende's competence in dealing with the kingdom's internal affairs won her the enduring respect of her subjects, or at least the more sober and responsible of them. Indeed, her reputation spread all the way to France, where none other than the renowned abbot, St Bernard of Clairvaux – by far the most influential cleric of the age – received favourable reports about Melisende's wisdom and judgement from the Knights Templar. It is worth pausing to reflect on that: The Knights Templar, a militant monastic order that forbade all contact between its members and females, reported favourably to the founder of the Cistercian Order about a woman's rule. This prompted St Bernard to address himself to Melisende directly, saying he had learned that:

> 'You are behaving peacefully and kindly; that you are ruling yourself and the kingdom wisely with the advice of wise men; that you love the Brothers of the Temple and are on friendly terms with them; and that, according to the wisdom given you by God, you are providently and wisely meeting the dangers which threaten the Holy Land with sound counsels and help'.[54]

St Bernard, although a reformer, is generally viewed as a conservative. Yet here he demonstratively indicated no discomfort with a woman exercising supreme executive secular power over the kingdom with responsibility for, as he stressed, the protection of the most sacred sites in all of Christendom.

Another influential cleric, William Archbishop of Tyre, was equally laudatory of Melisende's rule. Tyre was later chancellor of the kingdom and is the principal source for Melisende's clashes with her husband Fulk and her eldest son Baldwin III. In both instances, Tyre sides with Melisende against her male co-monarchs. This is particularly important in the case of Baldwin III, whom Tyre otherwise depicts as an exemplary king. Indeed, Tyre casts Baldwin's conflict with his mother almost as an immature youth briefly led astray by bad company. He writes:

> 'Melisende, the king's mother, was a woman of great wisdom who had much experience in all kinds of secular matters. … As long as her son was willing to be ruled by her wise counsel, the people enjoyed a highly desirable state of tranquillity, and the affairs of the realm prospered. But the more frivolous elements in the kingdom soon found the queen's wise influence hindered their attempts to draw the king into their own pursuits'.[55]

Such an interpretation of events, despite the grave risks to the kingdom brought about by Baldwin briefly tearing the kingdom in two and laying siege to his mother in the Tower of David, is possible because, again, there was no permanent breach between the co-monarchs. Instead, Melisende managed a rapprochement even after her humiliating defeat. Far from disappearing into a convent or obscurity, Melisende remained active in the Kingdom of Jerusalem long after her son had violently asserted his right to a more dominant role. As had been the case with Fulk, the more engaged Baldwin III became in military affairs, the more Melisende exerted her leading role in internal policy. This included important negotiations with the Pisans concerning their rights in Tyre, issuing charters, settling disputes, dispensing patronage, conducting marriage negotiations (notably with the Byzantine Emperor), and, most strikingly, dispatching royal troops to attack a Muslim-controlled fortress on the Jordon River. All this was done by Melisende after her short but forceful clash with Baldwin III. Furthermore, these are not nominal acts; they represent the very essence of royal power.

In short, after her victory over Fulk and her defeat at the hands of her son, Melisende understood how to re-establish amicable relations with her co-monarch to such a degree that she remained in possession of real political power. Furthermore, she exercised that authority so effectively that she retained the loyalty of her subjects and the respect of contemporary, clerical commentators. At her death, William of Tyre reflected on her reign as follows:

> 'Queen Melisende, a woman of unusual wisdom and discretion, fell ill of an incurable disease for which there was no help except death. ... For thirty years and more, during the lifetime of her husband as well as afterwards in the reign of her son, Melisende had governed the kingdom with strength surpassing that of most women. Her rule had been wise and judicious'.[56]

Queen Sibylla

No such praise can be found for the next ruling queen, Sibylla. Yet while Sibylla was anything but wise or judicious, she undoubtedly – if inconsistently – exercised the full powers of her office. After being widowed very young in 1177, she chose her next husband without the consent of the High Court and clung to him despite dramatic efforts by her brother, King Baldwin IV, and the High Court to pressure her into a divorce. More spectacularly still, she cajoled a minority of the bishops and barons into crowning her without the consent of the full High Court. In other words, she usurped the throne. Significantly, this minority faction was only prepared to back Sibylla's usurpation if she set aside her unpopular husband, Guy de Lusignan. Sibylla agreed to comply, setting one condition of her own: that she choose her next husband. No sooner was she crowned, however, than she declared that her next husband was the same as her last husband, namely Guy de Lusignan. When the patriarch of

Another woman artist.

Knight pays Homage to his Lady.

Jerusalem, until this point, one of her staunch supporters, balked at crowning Guy, Sibylla, in a dramatic demonstration of regal power, crowned Guy herself.

There was no precedent in Jerusalem for monarchs crowning monarchs. In fact, it was not recognised anywhere in the world at this time as a legitimate procedure. In short, Guy's coronation not only followed a usurpation, it was itself fraudulent. Yet, curiously, once it was done, it was widely accepted. To be sure, a majority of the High Court sought to counter Sibylla's coup by crowning Sibylla's younger sister Isabella as the legitimate monarch. However, as described earlier, the High Court lost heart and accepted Sibylla's fait accompli when Isabella's weak husband rushed to do homage to Sibylla and Guy. Only two barons (Tripoli and Ramla) refused homage because they did not recognise Sibylla's legitimacy. In other words, Sibylla got away with snatching a crown for herself in violation of the laws and customs of the kingdom and with imposing her candidate for king upon her subjects as well – despite near universal opposition to him as an individual. Those are not the actions of a chattel or pawn; they demonstrate just how powerful Queen Sibylla of Jerusalem was.

Isabella d'Ibelin, Lady of Beirut

The power of heiresses was not confined to the ruling queens. Baronial heiresses in the crusader kingdoms also demonstrated their independence and power, as the case of Isabella of Beirut demonstrates. Isabella d'Ibelin succeeded to the barony of Beirut in 1264 on the death of her father, John II d'Ibelin of Beirut. She was 12 years old.

Before focusing on her exercise of power, it is useful to remember the context in which she lived. When she came into her inheritance, the titular king of Jerusalem was the 12-year-old grandson of Frederick II, a youth who, like his father, had never set foot in the kingdom. The Mongols, on the other hand, had captured Baghdad, Aleppo and Damascus, before being defeated by the Mamluks at the battle of Ain Jalut in 1260. The following year, in 1261, the Latins lost control of Constantinople. Before Isabella had held her fief a full year, the Mamluks had taken Caesarea, Haifa and Arsuf, cutting the Kingdom of Jerusalem in half. Two years after she succeeded to her fief, the Mamluks had overrun Galilee and expelled the Templars from the fortress of Safed. In short, Isabella came of age in an environment in which the enemies of the crusader states were gathering at the gates.

Isabella was betrothed to King Hugh II of Cyprus shortly after coming into her estate. Although he was a prince roughly her own age, he was dead two years later. Rather than becoming queen consort of Cyprus, Isabella remained the 'lady' – that is, the feudal lord of Beirut.

On 9 May 1269, at 16 years, Isabella made the dramatic decision to conclude a separate truce with the Mamluk Sultan Baybars. She may have been reviving or continuing the policy of her father, John of Beirut II, who had also dabbled with separate truces in 1263. However, in Isabella's case, the truce was for an entire decade. Meanwhile, the last of the Hohenstaufen kings had been executed by Charles d'Anjou, and there were two rival claimants to the crown of Jerusalem. Neither seemed interested in Beirut, so Isabella continued to rule unimpeded and, surprisingly, unmarried.

It was not until 1272, when Isabella was already 20, that she married a second time. Her husband was not imposed on her by her feudal overlord, the king. Instead, she married an English Marcher Lord known only in the records of Outremer as Haymo Letrange (i.e., the stranger). Within a year, he was dead, leaving Isabella a widow again with neither an heir nor a husband to fulfil the military obligations of her fief.

Yet it was not until 1277, when Isabella was 25, that Hugh III of Cyprus appears to have remembered her. He tardily decided to enforce his rights as her feudal overlord by demanding her marriage in accordance with the customs of the kingdom. He forced her to accompany him to Cyprus, but Isabella was not cowed. She demanded a judgement of the High Court, and, significantly, this was granted her. She defended herself with the extraordinary argument that the terms of her truce with Sultan Baybars made him, rather than Hugh, her feudal overlord. In a dramatic decision about which we know far too little, the High Court sided with Isabella. The High Court of Cyprus officially recognised a Mamluk sultan rather than a Christian king as the overlord of Beirut, thereby denying Hugh the right to insist upon Isabella's marriage.

Thereafter, Isabella enjoyed an escort of Mamluks to protect her from further interference from Hugh III. She returned to Beirut and promptly married the titular lord of Caesarea. Unfortunately for her, he was a hothead engaged in a feud with the Ibelins. After assassinating one of the many John d'Ibelins living at this time, he was murdered in revenge by the brother of the man he had killed. The latter happened to be the Constable of Cyprus, which (rightly or not) put him at an advantage before the law. His vengeance-killing was neither condemned nor punished.

Meanwhile, Isabella was once again a widow. She married one last time to William Barlais and died childless of unknown causes in 1282. She was succeeded as Lady of Beirut by her sister Eschiva d'Ibelin.

Although the historical record focuses unsurprisingly on Isabella's dramatic and successful plea before the High Court that resulted in recognition of a Muslim sultan rather than a Christian king as her overlord, the untold story behind that dramatic event is that of a woman who ruled her barony independently for the greater part of the eighteen years she held the fief. In those years, she did more than fend off unwanted marriages and conclude a separate truce with the archenemy. She also conducted all the barony's routine domestic business, from granting charters and extending patronage to sitting in judgement in the baronial court, commanding the garrison and overseeing the baronial exchequer.

Delegated Power: Consorts and Regents

Alice of Antioch, Regent for Constance of Antioch

Turning to the second kind of female power, that derived from a woman's spouse or children, the most spectacular example in the history of the crusader states was arguably that of Alice of Antioch, the second daughter of Baldwin II and his Armenian wife, Morphia. Alice was born c.1110. In 1126, at age 16, she married the Prince of Antioch, Bohemond II. She was given the coastal lordships of Latakia and Jabala as her dowery and dower. Only four years later, when Alice was roughly 20 years old, Bohemond II was killed, leaving her a widow with a 2-year-old infant daughter, Constance. As Constance was the heiress to the principality, Alice was free from the duty to remarry. Since Constance was still so small, however, the ever-vulnerable principality needed a regent capable of leading the feudal armies until Constant came of age or married.

Despite Alice's youth, as a princess of Jerusalem and mother of the heiress, there was nothing inherently absurd about Alice assuming the regency of Antioch for Constance until her marriage. Instead, Alice was shunted aside, first by her father, Baldwin II, and then by her brother-in-law, Fulk d'Anjou. The conventional explanation is that Alice, unlike her elder sister Queen Melisende, had a bad and untrustworthy character.

Historian Thomas Asbridge has convincingly challenged this popular narrative.[57] Asbridge suggests that, at the time of Bohemond's death, the High Court of Antioch was not as united in its opposition to Alice as is usually assumed. He notes that several key figures, such as the patriarch and the constable of the kingdom, appear to have sided with Alice. The majority, however, were less interested in legal technicalities and more concerned with effective government and defence. The 20-year-old Alice might have been the logical and legal regent, but she could not lead armies.

For the majority of Antioch's feudal elite, rule by a young woman while trusting in a truce with a notoriously treacherous enemy appeared a risky option compared to rule by a strong military leader such as Baldwin II. The latter was familiar and tested, which made him trusted as well. The majority faction, favouring a strong military leader, sent to Baldwin II requesting that he resume the regency he had ably held during the minority and absence of the late Bohemond II.

Baldwin II responded promptly to the appeal of the Antiochene nobility, riding north personally to see to affairs in the principality. Although Alice initially ordered the city gates closed against him, she did not resort to force. When supporters of the king inside the city opened the gates to him, she was persuaded to submit to him peaceably. According to Tyre, Baldwin II was initially 'indignant' with his daughter, yet he does not appear to have found her conduct outrageous. He advised her to retire to her generous and prosperous dower lands, the coastal lordships of Latakia and Jabala, which does not suggest he viewed his second daughter as fundamentally evil, irresponsible or dangerous.

Two years later, however, Baldwin II died and was succeeded by Fulk d'Anjou. Asbridge suggests this opened a welcome opportunity for the Counts of Tripoli and Edessa to assert greater autonomy from Jerusalem. The two counts, however, needed support from Antioch, which geographically separated them and formed the largest of the three crusader states outside the Kingdom of Jerusalem. United the three northern crusader states stood a fair chance of ending their de facto – albeit not de jure – subservience to the kings of Jerusalem.

Alice joined forces with Tripoli and Edessa, and Tyre acknowledged that she had the support of many Antiochene nobles in doing so. Other historians suggest that growing dissatisfaction with Fulk's rule enabled Alice to become a focal point for subjects opposed to the increasingly unpopular Angevin. Thus, Alice's court at Latakia attracted, in addition to Tripoli and Edessa, the rebels Hugh of Jaffa and Ralph of Fantanelle from Jerusalem. There is no evidence, however, that she was the ringleader of the rebels or that she induced them to rebel against their better judgement. On the contrary, the disaffected lords and autonomous counts may have exploited her youth and inexperience for their purposes. Certainly, her actions at this point were in no way indicative of plans to disinherit her daughter. The most that can be said with certainty was that she was a 22-year-old princess eager to control her destiny.

Unfortunately for Alice, Tripoli was defeated in the field by Fulk, weakening her coalition significantly. At the same time, Fulk, with the help of the feudal army of Antioch, defeated a Muslim threat lead by the sultan of Aleppo. This later event swayed public opinion in Antioch back in Fulk's favour. Yet, Alice continued to build her power base on the coast. There, she established a princely administration complete with chanceries, constables and other household officials – and steadfastly styled herself as the Princess of Antioch.

In the autumn of 1135, five years after the death of her husband, she rode back into Antioch and assumed the role of regent without protest on the part of the High Court, the Church or the population. Significantly, this occurred after Fulk's attempt to sideline Melisende had failed. It is hard to imagine that Alice's move in 1135 was not coordinated and approved by her sister Queen Melisende in advance. It appears that Melisende, now firmly back in the saddle, told her husband not to interfere in her sister's affairs, and Fulk obeyed.

Yet envoys had already been sent to Poitiers to seek a consort for Constance. In 1136, Raymond of Poitiers arrived in Antioch. As before, nobles and commons preferred a prince who could actively fight for them over a woman who could not. The fact that Antioch had suffered several military setbacks at their neighbours' hands in the six years since Bohemond II's death would have weighed heavily against Alice. Losses included Tausus, Adana and Mamistra to the Armenian king between February 1132 and January 1133 and four other cities to Zengi in 1135. Thus, although Constance was only 8 years old and below the age of consent, she was married to Raymond of Poitiers, and he assumed the title of Prince of Antioch (by right of his wife).

Stripped of Tyre's pejorative assessment, Alice's actions hardly seem particularly ill-advised or selfish, much less evil. That she failed to assert her position had less to do with her sex per se than the fact that, for whatever reasons, she scorned a second marriage. Had she married a man capable of leading Antioch's feudal host, she could almost certainly have replicated her sister's successful model of corporate rule. Alice's husband could have fulfilled the military duties of the regency while Alice herself held power internally until her daughter Constance came of age and married. Alice's regency was always bound to be temporary, but she might have enjoyed more power longer had she been willing to share it with a fighting man who satisfied the demands of the Antiochene feudal elite for a militarily capable leader.

Beatrice of Edessa, Regent for Joscelyn III

In 1144, Sultan Zengi captured the city of Edessa when the count and his family were absent. Zengi carried out a notoriously brutal slaughter of the population, including torturing prisoners, in violation of Sharia Law. He also sent a letter to Count Joscelyn bragging about his brutality, particularly the desecration of churches, the humiliation of women of all ages and classes and the mercilessness of his troops. This provoked a response that led to Joscelyn II being taken captive and Zengi conquering the lion's share of the county.

Left behind was Joscelyn's countess and soon-to-be widow, Beatrice, and three small children, two daughters and a son. The latter, the heir to Edessa, was just 7 years old at the time of his father's capture. Beatrice immediately

– and without opposition – assumed the regency of what remained of the County of Edessa.

The situation was catastrophic, given that many of Edessa's fighting men had been killed in the original occupation and sack of Edessa or in her husband's futile attempt to regain possession of the city. Beatrice could not salvage the situation merely by remarrying; she needed an entirely new army. Yet she neither despaired nor was she dismissed by a frightened population.

Tyre writes that: 'With the assistance of the principal men still left in the kingdom, [Beatrice] tried to govern the people to the best of her ability; and, far beyond the strength of a woman, she busied herself in strengthening the fortresses of the land and supplying them with arms, men, and food'.[58] Yet her situation remained precarious, and King Baldwin III rushed north with a part of his feudal host to try to shore it up. Notably, unlike when Baldwin II and Fulk hurried to Antioch, there was no suggestion that Baldwin came to Edessa to assume the regency.

Shortly after Baldwin's arrival, an envoy from the Byzantine Emperor Manuel I arrived with an offer to supply the Countess of Edessa with a suitable annuity in exchange for her surrender of the remaining cities and castles in the County of Edessa to Constantinople. The High Court of Edessa was summoned to discuss the proposal. Both Baldwin III and Beatrice attended the session. Although unstated, given the recent slaughter of the feudal fighting forces, many of those present were probably female, just as during the Ladies' Parliament in Frankish Greece a hundred years later.

In any case, the Byzantine offer was hotly debated, with many Edessan nobles reluctant to surrender their independence and accept Byzantine suzerainty. On the other hand, Baldwin III realised he could not provide the military assistance the county needed in the long run. He could not absent himself from Jerusalem perpetually, and his kingdom needed its feudal host for its own defence. He, therefore, advocated acceptance of the Byzantine offer. The decision, however, was made by Beatrice. After hearing the advice of her barons and the king of Jerusalem, she made the decision in her capacity as acting regent of Edessa; she agreed to the Byzantine proposal.

Once Beatrice had accepted the principle of handing over the remaining territories to the Byzantine Emperor, Baldwin III handled the details of the meeting with the Greek officials, negotiating the transfer of cities and castles. Finally,

'[King Baldwin] took under his protection the countess and her children and all others of both sexes, whether Latin or Armenians, who wished to leave … together with their pack animals and a great amount of baggage, for each man proposed to take with him his entire household and domestic staff as well as all his furniture. So, with this great crowd of unwarlike people and an enormous amount of baggage, the king hastened to depart, that he might lead them to a place of safety.'[59]

Thus ended Beatrice's brief 'reign.' Yet despite the refugee convoy being attacked repeatedly by Zengi's forces, Baldwin's troops beat off the assaults enabling the refugees from Edessa to make it safely to Jerusalem. Here they soon formed a large Armenian enclave. Beatrice's decision to abdicate to the Byzantine Emperor had undoubtedly saved most of their lives.

Indirect Power: Dowagers

Two dowagers stand out in the history of Jerusalem for having exerted a historically relevant influence upon reigning monarchs. Strikingly, one's impact was predominantly detrimental to the kingdom, while the other saved it.

Agnes de Courtenay

As noted above, when Baldwin III died in February 1163 without heirs of his body, Baldwin's younger brother Amalric became the heir apparent. Yet, the High Court of Jerusalem refused to recognise him as king unless he first set aside his wife, Agnes de Courtenay. Amalric wasted no time complying and was crowned within a week, while Agnes was sent back to her former betrothed, Hugh d'Ibelin. At Amalric's death, however, his son by Agnes ascended the throne as Baldwin IV. As the mother of the young, unmarried king, Agnes became the first lady of the land.

Agnes' influence on Baldwin IV was unquestionably significant. To her credit, she appears to have obtained that position of trust by giving her afflicted son motherly affection and care. Yet her motives for meddling in the affairs of her son's kingdom appear to have been largely venal or malign, while the impact of her advice was ultimately disastrous.

Her first act was to convince Baldwin IV to use royal revenues to ransom her brother Jocelyn III of Edessa from Saracen captivity. Once Edessa returned to the kingdom, Agnes successfully pressed her son into appointing him to the lucrative and influential post of seneschal. As his subsequent underwhelming and venal behaviour proved, the appointment was sheer nepotism untinged by any trace of wisdom.

Next, in 1179, Agnes persuaded Baldwin IV to appoint Aimery de Lusignan, a Frenchmen with limited experience in the Near East, to the most senior military post in the kingdom, that of constable. The position had become vacant after the venerable Humphrey of Toron II died defending Baldwin IV after he had been unhorsed in a skirmish with Saladin's forces. While nothing in Aimery's background suggested he was fit for this position and contemporaries explained the appointment with innuendos suggesting that Agnes was sleeping with Aimery, he proved himself an excellent constable. As described earlier, Aimery later established Latin rule in Cyprus and become one of Jerusalem's most competent kings. Yet given Agnes' other personnel choices, his success appears to have been a fluke.

In 1180, Agnes successfully imposed her candidate, Heraclius, Archbishop of Caesarea, on the patriarchal throne of Jerusalem. William, Archbishop of Tyre, who had expected this appointment himself, naturally disparaged his rival in his influential history, *A History of Deeds Done Beyond the Seas*. This work is one of the most important primary sources from this period and is widely considered fundamentally trustworthy. Yet, in this instance, because of the obvious and understandable personal enmity of the author towards Heraclius, it must be discounted. That said, there are objective reasons to view Heraclius as the lesser choice. First, he was a Frenchman, while Tyre was a native of the kingdom. Although they enjoyed the same formal education, Tyre was a scholar who wrote the aforementioned history of the crusader states and a history of Islam. The latter work, based on Arab sources, testifies to Tyre's profound understanding of the Arab language and the Muslim world in which the crusader states operated. Heraclius had no comparable accomplishments, and there is no evidence he spoke, much less read, Arabic or understood anything about Islam. Finally, Tyre was widely regarded as pious and not marked by scandal. Heraclius, in contrast, offended contemporaries by flaunting a mistress and fathering a child with her. Heraclius' appointment was, therefore, not logical, and contemporaries attributed it to the fact that he, too, slept with the queen mother. He remains a controversial figure.

Without doubt, Agnes' most disastrous interventions in the affairs of state were the husbands she chose for Baldwin IV's two sisters. Agnes persuaded her son to betroth his half-sister Isabella to Humphrey de Toron IV. Marrying a princess of the realm to a local nobleman was against the tradition of the kingdom and undoubtedly demeaning. Doing so when Isabella was still 8 years old was unusual, albeit not exceptional in this period. Removing Isabella entirely from her mother's home went a step further and appears to have been a vindictive act intended to hurt the woman who – quite involuntarily and as a puppet of her great-uncle – had taken Agnes' place as Amalric's consort.

To add injury to insult, Agnes negotiated marriage terms with Toron's guardian, Reynald de Châtillon, the former Prince of Antioch, which entailed Humphrey renouncing his hereditary lordships of Toron and Chastel-Neuf.

This impoverished both Humphrey (a minor at the time of the negotiations) and Isabella, further demeaning the princess. No sooner had these rich lordships reverted to the crown than the king bestowed them on his mother, making her the immediate beneficiary of the humiliating marriage she had arranged for the daughter of her hated successor.

Malevolent as this was, the consequences were more wide-ranging than the humiliation of the Dowager Queen Maria and Princess Isabella. The marriage had disastrous outcomes for the security and survival of the realm because Humphrey de Toron was fatally weak. Contemporary chronicles describe him as 'cowardly and effeminate'[60] or 'more like a woman than a man: he had a gentle manner and a stammer'.[61] Even as a youth, it was obvious he was patently unfit to lead the feudal army of Jerusalem, the most fundamental duty of the king in this besieged kingdom. It is hard to escape the conclusion that in addition to enriching herself and having the spiteful satisfaction of humiliating her rival and rival's daughter, Agnes knew that the marriage to Toron would effectively prevent Isabella from being considered a viable candidate for the crown. It appears that the entire point of this marriage was to ensure that Agnes' daughter Sibylla rather than Maria's daughter Isabella would succeed Baldwin IV at his anticipated early death.

However, Agnes' most significant legacy to the Kingdom of Jerusalem was its destruction. Agnes is credited with convincing her son to allow his sister Sibylla to take as her second husband Guy de Lusignan, the younger brother of the constable. Sibylla, as heir apparent, had been married at the behest of the High Court to William de Montferrat in 1176. However, Montferrat had died in 1177, probably of malaria, leaving Sibylla widowed with an infant son. At the time of her second marriage in 1180, Guy was the landless fourth son of a French noble family, who had, thus far, distinguished himself by trying to take the queen of England hostage and assisting in the murder of the Earl of Salisbury. The marriage between Guy and Sibylla was so obviously unsuitable that it took place in great haste and complete secrecy.

There are two possible reasons to explain this. Either Guy had already seduced Sibylla, as some accounts suggest, and there was a need to hastily 'put things right'. Or, far more likely, Agnes wanted to prevent the High Court from exercising its constitutional right to determine the husband of the heiress to the kingdom. By presenting the High Court with a *fait accompli*, she ensured not only that her choice for Sibylla's husband prevailed but also that Lusignan was indebted to her. Yet in no way was Guy de Lusignan a suitable husband for the heir apparent of the kingdom. As described earlier, he proved to be one of the most disastrous kings in the history of the realm.

Maria Comnena

Maria's role in persuading her daughter Isabella I to choose her kingdom over her husband has been described in detail earlier and need not be retold. Noteworthy is only that Maria used her influence with her daughter to support the High Court's endeavour to secure a militarily competent king consort amidst the kingdom's existential crisis in 1190. Her influence was not only benign; it was critical to the survival of the kingdom and the dynasty. It is an example of a mature woman using her influence on a teenage ruler for the benefit of the realm rather than for personal gain – in sharp contrast to Agnes' actions.

Non-Feudal Forms of Power: Abbesses, Envoys, and Spies

Abbesses

A significant number of mediaeval women chose to renounce the secular world, following a vocation in the Church. Here, as the brides of Christ, they escaped the dominance of mortal husbands and enjoyed both independence and empowerment in a uniquely feminine environment. The royal family of Jerusalem provides a prominent example of just such a woman who exercised authority not in the secular sphere but through the office of abbess.

Baldwin II had no sons, but four daughters. The eldest became his heir and the reigning queen of Jerusalem, Melisende. The second daughter, Alice, married the prince of Antioch, and the third, Hodierna, became Countess of Tripoli. When it came time to find a husband for his youngest daughter Iveta,* however, he had run out of candidates of suitable rank from among the nobility in the Latin East. It would have been logical and comparatively easy to marry her to a prominent European lord, bringing new resources to the kingdom. Alternatively, she could have been used to cement a relationship with the Armenian or Greek royal houses.

Instead, Iveta entered the Benedictine Convent of St Anne in 1134 at 14 years of age. Four years later, she transferred to the convent of St Lazarus of Bethany, which had been founded and generously endowed by her sister Queen Melisende. The Abbey of St Lazarus was located just east of Jerusalem at Bethany, where, according to Christian tradition, the home of Mary, Martha and Lazarus had been located. It was a major pilgrimage site as it was viewed as the venue for Christ's miracle of raising Lazarus from the dead. As early as the fourth century AD, a church had been built beside the alleged site of Lazarus' tomb, but it was replaced in the sixth century by a larger Byzantine church. It

---

* Iveta's name is also given as Ivetta, Joveta, Jovita, Jowita, Yvette and even Juditta.

was this sacred monument that Queen Melisende renovated at considerable expense. In parallel, however, she ordered the construction of a larger church to the south of the tomb of St Lazarus. While the Byzantine church was to be used by pilgrims, the modern church was consecrated to Saints Mary and Martha and served as the convent church of a nunnery founded on the site. In addition, other buildings necessary for monastic life and a defensible keep as a place of refuge if danger threatened were built at the queen's expense. Iveta transferred to this newly constructed abbey in 1138 and was elected abbess in 1144.

Subsequent chronicles invented the story that Iveta had been 'violated' by Muslims during her roughly eighteen months as a hostage for her father in 1124–1125 making her effectively unmarriable and insinuating that she was hidden away in the abbey of St. Lazarus in disgrace. This is nonsense. First, no contemporary source supports the allegations of abuse that would have been shocking (and commented upon) on three counts: her position as a hostage, her social status (princess) and her age (4–5). Second, the abbess of a wealthy monastic institution located between a popular pilgrimage site and the sacred city of Jerusalem is neither hidden away nor powerless.

On the contrary, abbesses enjoyed a degree of independence unknown by women in secular life except for wealthy widows. With her election to abbess, Iveta became a major landholder with the same power over the estates held by the abbey as a secular lord held over his fief, but notably without the obligation to render military service. The convent at Bethany was exceptionally wealthy and prominent. It was located on a pilgrimage site venerated by Christians, Jews and Muslims, a fact that ensured a steady stream of devotional gifts. Just a mile and a half from the Holy Sepulchre, it was also the departure point for the Palm Sunday processionals. Furthermore, it had been richly endowed by Melisende with the tax revenues from the city of Jericho and its dependencies, as well as an additional house and church inside Jerusalem. Indeed, Melisende lavished gifts such as chalices and crosses of gold and silver, rich ecclesiastical vestments, books and jewelled ornaments upon the institution. Tyre explicitly states, that '[Melisende] endowed the church with rich estates, so that in temporal possessions it should not be inferior to any monastery, either of men or women; or rather, as it is said, that it may be richer than any church'.[62] It was further enriched by gifts of properties scattered across the kingdom from various other lords in exchange for prayers.

At the age of 24, Iveta became the master of this establishment. She appears in various charters regarding property arrangements using her own seal, a rare phenomenon for a woman in the twelfth century; neither of her sisters Alice of Antioch nor Hodierna of Tripoli had seals, for example. Tyre also suggests that Iveta, in coordination with her elder sisters, was influential in assuring the elevation of the prior of the Church of the Holy Sepulchre to the patriarchy. Iveta is known to have sent sacred relics to other religious establishments, most notably the famous abbey of Fontevrault in France, the burial place of Kings Henry II and Richard I of England. The significance of this is hard to fathom nowadays, but relics were sincerely revered in this era, and access to them was a source of spiritual power. Finally, in 1163, Iveta was entrusted with rearing King Amalric's daughter Sibylla, who remained under her care until her first marriage to William de Montferrat in 1176.

Iveta died sometime between 1176 and 1178. The cause of her death and her burial place are unknown, but she would have been in her late 50s. For a woman who had not been subject to the hazards of childbirth, that seems surprisingly young, but she probably would not have wanted to live to see the siege and conquest of Jerusalem that destroyed the convent that had been her home for forty years.

Because of her royal birth, Iveta has left a record in the chronicles, but she was by no means alone. She was preceded and succeeded by other less exalted women, who would have enjoyed the same wealth and power, if not influence, that Iveta did. Furthermore, the Kingdom of Jerusalem was dotted with monasteries for men and women because all the religious orders wanted a presence near the places where Jesus had lived and died. The Benedictines, Premonstratensians, Cistercians, Augustines, Dominicans and Franciscans all built and maintained houses in the crusader states. Indeed, the Holy Land gave birth to several new religious orders, of which the most important were the Templars, Hospitallers, Teutonic Knights and Knights of St Lazarus.

With the notable exception of the Templars, all these monastic orders had women associated with them and maintained houses for women. The number of Cistercian convents was particularly high. Every convent had a woman in charge in the role of abbess or prioress. Convents also had other household officials, all women, who enjoyed status and power no less than their male counterparts in their respective houses. While none of these women attained the fame or influence of Heloise of Paraclete, Mathilda of Fontevrault, Hildegard of Bingen or other famous religious women in the West, they should not be dismissed as insignificant, much less powerless.

Envoys

The role of women as mediators between parties in both war and peace is well documented throughout the history of the crusader states. Queen Morphia oversaw the ransom negotiations for her husband, Baldwin II. Eschiva of Tiberias negotiated with Saladin to surrender the Citadel of Tiberias. Stephanie de Milly negotiated with Saladin regarding the fortresses of Transjordan. Maria Comnena negotiated rapprochement and marriage alliances between the antagonistic Henri de Champagne and Aimery de Lusignan. Marie of Brienne, the wife of the Latin Emperor of Constantinople, approached Louis IX during his sojourn in Cyprus on behalf of her husband. Isabella of Beirut concluded separate truces with the Muslim sultan.

Yet these famous examples are only the tip of the iceberg. Gordon Reynalds argues:

> Throughout the twelfth- and thirteenth-century crusades to the East, numerous women from a variety of social standings had leadership thrust upon them or used the opportunity that power-vacuums provided to lead negotiations, act as mediators between forces or as emissaries on diplomatic missions. ... Their continuous presence in inter-crusader mediation ... highlights the willingness of the Frankish people, both new arrivals in the East and established settlers, to rely on women for this role.[63]

Spies

Arab sources reference two cases of highly placed women acting as spies for the Muslims. Ibn al-Athir claims that a certain 'Lady of Bourzey' exchanged gifts with Saladin and informed him of many significant developments. It is unclear, however, if this woman is separate from or simply another name for Sybil of Antioch, the bigamous second wife of Bohemond III of Antioch. We know substantially more about this second case.

Bohemond's legal wife was Theodora Comnena, the sister of Maria Comnena, King Amalric's queen consort. Bohemond left Theodora as soon as her powerful great uncle, Emperor Manuel I, died in 1180. In her place, he took a woman, Sibyl, of unknown ancestry (possibly the above-named Lady of Bourzey) to 'wife'. This marriage was immediately condemned as bigamous and vehemently opposed by the Church. When Bohemond refused to separate from Sibyl, he was duly excommunicated. The conflict continued to escalate, with Bohemond openly attacking churchmen and their property and, at one point, laying siege to the patriarch and other leading clerics, when they sought refuge in a fortress. This incident and Bohemond's intransigence caused some of Antioch's feudal lords to withdraw their homage from Bohemond. Meanwhile, the patriarch of Antioch placed those loyal to Bohemond under interdict. At this juncture, fearing that the Saracens would take advantage of the situation, the patriarch of Jerusalem tried to mediate, but without success.

Bohemond refused to dismiss his concubine, and his support among his vassals crumbled further.

While Tyre attributed Sibyl's power over Bohemond to witchcraft, the truly remarkable and deplorable fact was that, according to Arab sources, Sibyl was on Saladin's payroll. In short, this single, well-placed and successful female spy single-handedly reduced the fighting capacity of Antioch in the critical years immediately before the battle of Hattin. If nothing else, through her correspondence, she kept Saladin informed of the disarray in the principality and its vulnerability. Few women in any era can be said to have enjoyed so much power.

Chapter 9

The Economic Position of Women in the Crusader States

In contrast to the political power of women in the Latin East, their economic role has left few traces in the historical record. The problem is not unique to the Latin East. Unlike political and military events, economic developments were rarely described by chroniclers and contemporary historians. The incremental and collective character of economic evolution made it difficult to detect, much less assess, by those experiencing it. As a result, modern economic historians rely heavily upon archaeological evidence, household accounts, land deeds, tax records, wills and sometimes oblique inferences in letters and chronicles to piece together a picture of the economy in any place or period. Such records are rarely systematic or comprehensive, leaving many blanks and questions. Even when economic factors and developments can be inferred, they are usually handled in broad terms without highlighting the role of individuals. Alternatively, data mining of tax records or household accounts, while specific, is generally too narrow to enable generalizations.

Given the dearth of sources pertaining to the economic role of women in the crusader states, this chapter is inevitably circumscribed. It first offers an overview of the economic role of women in contemporary Western Europe. It then highlights some of the factors and features of life in the Levant that might have impacted the economic position of women in the context of the crusader states. Finally, the chapter will highlight the importance of female patronage in the Latin East.

The Role of Women in the Western Mediaeval Economy

As noted above, feudalism inherently granted an economic role to women by making them major landholders. As heiresses, widows or deputies of their husbands, women acted as the overall manager or CEO of the economic activities on their lands. As we have seen, a substantial portion of all fiefs was held by women (as heiresses, dowagers or guardians of underage heirs) at any one time. In addition, the other obligations of noblemen (attending the king, administering justice or taking part in warfare) ensured that the daily management of noble estates fell to wives while their husbands were otherwise preoccupied.

Wealthier noblemen, of course, hired professional estate and household officials (almoners, chancellors, treasurers, comptrollers, stewards, marshals, constables, bailiffs and clerks, etc.), who were almost invariably men. The poorest (male) landowners were more personally involved in the daily oversight of agricultural production. Yet, the time-consuming and demanding nature of agriculture and agricultural processing (particularly preserving and storing) in the twelfth and thirteenth centuries made it nearly impossible for one individual to oversee all aspects of the process effectively. A lord's first and primary partner in direct management or in managing the managers was his lady. That role is largely invisible to us now simply because it was viewed as natural or self-evident, which meant it did not warrant mention. We find it reflected, however, in the plethora of household accounts and inventories in which wives and widows are the recipients or auditors and in tax records. In an age where agriculture was still the dominant sector of the economy, aristocratic women were directly involved in managing the largest share of the national economy.

In addition to overseeing the running of the feudal estates, women also almost invariably ran the lord's personal household. The only significant exception to this was the case of the greatest magnates, who maintained several households – one for themselves, one for their ladies and maybe one or more for their children. For most feudal lords, however, there was one household, and the lady of the fief ran it.

Mediaeval households were large and complex. They encompassed not only the family but servants, retainers and dependents as well. They served as the headquarters of all the lord's activities. A nobleman was seriously disadvantaged in politics and war if his household was not in order. He depended on men, horses and supplies being where he wanted them when he wanted them. He expected revenues to be delivered when demanded and payments to be made to his retainers and dependents when due. A nobleman also depended on his household for the care and education of his children and the spiritual wellbeing of the living and dead members of his affinity. In short, the lifestyle of nobles in the High Middle Ages revolved around the aristocratic household, and noblemen depended first and foremost on their wives to keep the household running smoothly. The activities of a noblewoman running a complex household resembled the management of a small business rather than the lifestyle of a modern housewife served by utilities and devices rather than people.

Middle-class women played a similar role in their husband's businesses. The role of wealthy merchant wives resembled that of noblewomen, with various subordinate officials, large staffs and managerial responsibilities. The farther down the economic scale one went, the more hands-on the wife's role became. The poorest men had neither servants nor apprentices, only their wives and children as helpers. Significantly, at a man's death, his widow could inherit his business in its entirety, and she was entitled to take up her husband's seat in his guild.

Manuscript illustrations are wonderfully revealing. There are images, for example, of a banker handing out loans while his wife collects them. An 'alewife' is pictured filling barrels with liquid under the direction of her husband. Another illustration shows a wife holding a helmet steady on a forge while her husband, the smith, smites it. Women are also shown aiding their husbands in butcher and cobbler shops, selling vegetables and so on.

Of course, many images are ambiguous. When workshops are depicted with multiple adults working together, the women may just as easily be apprentices or employees as wives. As noted earlier, women could and did learn a variety of trades in the era of the crusades and worked as apprentices, journeymen or masters of their trade throughout their lives. Some women established and ran independent businesses. Once qualified in a trade, women took part in the administration of the respective profession, both as guild members and on industrial tribunals that investigated allegations of fraud, malpractice and the like.

Women in the era of the crusades were free to engage in a wide variety of trades. Indeed, some trades such as brewing in England, baking in France and silk-making almost everywhere, were dominated by women. Women in the Middle Ages engaged in many service jobs we still associate with women today, such as hairdressing, laundering, waiting on tables (barmaids), cleaning, cooking, child-rearing and prostitution. Like today, women were frequently shopkeepers, selling everything from fruit and vegetables (not very lucrative) to spices and books (high-margin businesses). Yet they are also listed as providing services we don't generally associate with women, such as barbers, carters and farriers.

Furthermore, women were not confined to the service sector. Women also engaged in industry. Tax rolls reveal women confectioners, candle makers, cobblers, and buckle makers. Women are listed in town records as ironmongers and net makers, bookbinders and haberdashers, glove makers and butchers. They could also be musicians, copiers, illuminators and painters. More surprising to modern readers, women appear in mediaeval documents as coppersmiths, goldsmiths, locksmiths and armourers.

In the early Middle Ages, women could also be medical practitioners. All midwives were women, of course, and women provided most of the care for women patients at hospitals, hospices and infirmaries. Women could also be barbers (who performed medical procedures such as bloodletting), apothecaries, surgeons and physicians. A female doctor, for example, accompanied King Louis IX on crusade in the mid-thirteenth century. Women learned these trades in the traditional way by apprenticing with someone already practicing the profession. It wasn't until the fourteenth century that universities imposed the exclusive right to certify physicians while excluding women from universities.

Unique Economic Characteristics of the Latin East

Two factors in the Latin East may have significantly modified the above-generalised image of women in the economy. First, the fact that men were frequently called up to join military expeditions would have given women greater responsibility and opportunities for 'minding the store' while their men were absent. While the time spent campaigning should not be exaggerated, the fact that a man was liable for military service may have encouraged women to take a more active interest in their husband's business simply to ensure they could manage when he was called to the feudal host or engaged in garrison duties.

Second and more intriguing is the fact that the economy of Outremer was strong in fields in which women were particularly active, if not dominant. The most obvious example is silk making. The spinning and weaving of silk are described in many mediaeval sources as the preserve of women, and silk making was a major industry in Outremer. Records suggest that as many as 4,000 silk weavers worked in the County of Tripoli alone. Other centres of silk production in the Latin East were Tyre, Gaza and Ascalon. Tyre was famed for its white silk, while Beirut is known to have exported silk in significant quantities, silk that was presumably produced in the city or nearby.

One of the most luxurious textiles of the Middle Ages was a cloth known as siqlatin, or as we would say today, 'Latin Silk'. The name was probably derived from the fact that this textile was produced in the Latin East by or for Franks. It consists of silk interwoven with threads of pure gold. In addition, Cyprus became famous for patterned silk cloth and silk brocade. These products were so valuable they commanded the highest prices in the West and were treasured and preserved. As a result, we can still see examples of this work in the Vatican and other museums with artifacts from the royal courts of mediaeval Europe. All of this suggests that women were in control of one of the Levant's most lucrative economic sectors during the crusader era.

Although only silk making is consistently described as the preserve of women, women were undoubtedly active in other kinds of textile production. While both sexes appeared to have engaged in weaving, spinning was the typical work of ladies, even in a domestic context. In Outremer, textile production was a major and diverse industry. In addition to siqlatin, the crusader states produced pure silk, cotton, linen, felt and wool cloth. Fragments of material made from goat and camel hair have been found. Intriguingly, the Latin East appears to have experimented with hybrid fabrics in which the warp was formed by one kind of yarn and the weft another, including combinations of silk woven with wool, linen and cotton.

Another lucrative export of the crusader states was icons. We know that large workshops for the mass production of icons were established, particularly in Acre. These produced images of popular saints such as St George and the Virgin for sale to the religious tourists, who came to the Holy Land by the tens of thousands every year. Some icons were left half-finished, to allow purchasers to commission personal touches. Others were undertaken only on commission and were unique. While the latter may be deemed works of art, the former were mass-produced souvenirs.

Women were probably engaged in producing these valuable export products. There are many manuscript illustrations of women painting what appear to be icons, and the sedentary and detailed nature of the work made it well adapted to the employment of women. It was work that women could do in their homes, and they could be paid by the piece.

Similarly, the crusader states engaged in the mass production of books. Again, these could be commissioned works with elaborate illuminations in precious metals or simple devotional works devoid of all illustrations for the low end of the market. Books without illustrations were affordable objects among the middle class and literate portions of the working class. Collections of psalms, hagiographies, the gospels and even complete bibles were popular among pilgrims. Such books served devotional needs and provided a souvenir of the trip to the Holy Land. The number of women engaged in producing these books is unknown, but it would be foolish to presume they were insignificant. Nuns had copied books from the earliest days of the monastic movement. They established the precedent of women being good at copying and provided a role model for secular female copyists. If women were particularly well represented in this industrial sector, they were engaged in one of the most lucrative economic activities in the Latin East.

All in all, women were active participants in the rural and urban economies. While sparsely represented in some trades, they would have dominated others. They thereby contributed materially to the overall creation of wealth at the individual, family, community and national levels in a region infamous for its wealth. Even assuming that women earned less than their male colleagues, they could make and accumulate independent wealth by acquiring skills and qualifications. With that capability, independence and empowerment came automatically

Women as Patrons of the Arts and Church

Finally, women had an economic role as patrons of the arts and the Church. While the most famous female patrons were the great feudal lords such as the queens, princesses, countesses and baronesses, wealthy women of the merchant class also made donations according to their means.

Queen Melisende set the gold standard for such activities. As noted, she endowed the entire convent of St Lazarus and oversaw its construction. She commissioned a psalter with a jewel-studded ivory cover and exquisite illuminations, which is viewed to this day as one of the greatest masterpieces of mediaeval artistry. Melisende is also credited by Jaroslav Folda, the leading historian of crusader art, with contributing to the renovation of the Church of the Holy Sepulchre. As the daughter of a Frankish lord and an Armenian lady, she was uniquely suited to fostering a unique hybrid art and architectural style incorporating elements from early Christian, Byzantine, Syrian, Armenian, Italian and other traditions. Maria Comnena followed in her footsteps by overseeing the restoration of the Church of the Nativity in Bethlehem. Appropriately for a church built under the eye of a Byzantine princess, this magnificent architectural monument reveals many Byzantine stylistic elements and workmanship. The patronage of queens had an impact not only on artistic style but also on the economy. Major building projects, for example, employed hundreds of masons, carpenters, sculptors, mosaic workers, smiths, glaziers and more.

Far more common, however, were women of more modest means who commissioned works of art for their homes or churches. Women commissioned many tomb effigies, especially for husbands or children who pre-deceased them. Folda notes that one of the surprising characteristics of crusader art is the depiction of women as supplicants on icons, 'an important indication that women were involved as patrons'.[64] He also notes that amazons are depicted more frequently in manuscripts produced in the Latin East than elsewhere. This, he suggests, is either an indication of female patronage or of the more prominent role women played in the defence of the Latin East. That role is the subject of the next chapter.

Chapter 10

In Defence of the Holy Land:
The Women of Outremer in Times of War

lthough the crusader states were at peace for many more years than they were at war, they were created by the sword and would end by the sword. Eight major armed expeditions that we call crusades punctuated the history of the crusader states, and various smaller armed pilgrimages brought armies from the West, usually in response to Muslim incursions and attacks.

Yet these expeditions from the West represent only one aspect of the armed conflict that characterised the Middle East in this era. War came in many other forms as well. The founders of the crusader states fought back five major attempts to expel them in the first ten years following the capture of Jerusalem. In the same period, they took the offensive, capturing Haifa, Arsuf, Caesarea, Tortosa, Jubail, Acre, Tripoli, Beirut and Sidon. Shortly afterwards, a bloody struggle for control of Edessa began that ended in the complete expulsion of the Franks. Yet in the same period, the Franks took control of Tyre and Ascalon and laid siege to Aleppo and Damascus. All these military campaigns took place without any aid from the West.

Likewise, in the 1160s, the Franks undertook no less than five invasions of Egypt, usually in alliance with one or another Muslim faction and sometimes supported by the Byzantines, but all without Western crusaders. While these campaigns constituted offensive action on the part of the Franks against the Saracens, in the following decade, the roles were reversed. Saladin led six invasions of Frankish territory between 1177 and 1188; all were met exclusively by local military forces.

It took the Third Crusade to re-establish a viable crusader state on the coast of the Levant after Saladin's victory at the Battle of Hattin, but in the period following that crusade, most Frankish territorial gains were made by treaty rather than warfare. Nevertheless, Saracen raids into Frankish territory continued sporadically, such as the sack of Caesarea and Limassol in 1220 and 1221, respectively. Then, starting in 1261, the Mamluks kept up near-continuous military pressure on the crusader states, taking one city after another until they captured the last Frankish stronghold, the city of Acre, in 1291, thereby ending the Frankish presence in the Levant.

Contemporary accounts of crusades and warfare in the crusader states frequently refer to women. This was not because women warriors were commonplace but rather because circumstances in the Holy Land repeatedly resulted in situations requiring the response of every Christian, male and female. In short, women took part in the defence of the Holy Land largely in response to emergencies.

Furthermore, women are conspicuously absent from Christian accounts of mounted raids and invasions, i.e., mobile operations. Mobile operations were conducted in the crusader states by mounted troops of two kinds: knights (heavy cavalry) and turcopoles (light cavalry). Knights were expected to fight on horseback with lance and sword, while turcopoles were mounted archers who had to use a bow and arrow while controlling their horses with their legs only. No man or woman could obtain proficiency in these skills without years of intensive training. Such training was both time-consuming and expensive and could not be carried out without the approval and complicity of various actors. In contrast to mobile warfare, however, women were prominent in all forms and nearly all aspects of static warfare – that is, siege warfare – both in offensive and defensive situations.

This chapter explores the role of women in the Holy Land during armed conflict with the Saracens. It looks at the various activities women undertook during military engagements, including combat, support and command functions. Because a woman's social status was decisive in determining how they participated in warfare, the chapter looks first at the bulk of women fighters (the commoners) and then at the role of aristocratic women. First, however, it is useful to consider contemporary attitudes and how they influenced the sources.

Contemporary Perceptions of Women Warriors

The leading female historian of the crusades, Helen Nicholson, notes that contemporary European and Muslim cultures viewed warfare as a male preserve and rejected female warriors in principle as unnatural. It is precisely because female fighters were anathema to the Muslims that Muslim chroniclers delighted in depicting Christian women who violated 'natural laws'. Several Muslim accounts, for example, describe finding the corpses of women dressed fully in armour among the Christian dead. Yet, such voyeuristic accounts, Nicholson stresses, were intended to demonstrate the dishonourable and barbaric character of Christians. She writes: 'Muslims ... gladly depict

Christians as allowing their women to fight, as this would show that they were a barbarous, degenerate people'.[65] She further claims that Baha al-Din, a notoriously unreliable and melodramatic Muslim source, 'mentioned women fighting and the presence of women in the Christian forces to underline the perverted fanaticism of the Christians'.[66]

Christian sources, on the other hand, while sharing the view that the natural place of women was in non-combat roles, accepted and admired those extraordinary women who, in exceptional circumstances, took up arms and fought 'manfully'. Indeed, Christian chroniclers on the whole saw the martial qualities of Frankish women as remarkable – and admirable – because physically, women were viewed as the weaker sex. Nicholson points out that in contemporary literature (texts *not* intended to depict historical reality but purely fictional and even fantastical), women don armour and take up arms almost invariably to 'show the failings of the male characters'.[67] In the context of Outremer, however, the salient point was that women who fought were seen as defending Christendom and the Holy Land and their 'unwomanly' actions were considered minor miracles in which the holiness of their cause endowed the weak with unusual strength. While fighting for Christ made their 'manly' actions admirable, it did not make them 'natural' or 'normal'. Women taking an active part in warfare remained the exception rather than the norm.

In her study of women on crusade, Sabine Geldsetzer makes another important point. Muslim accounts of finding women dressed in armour and helmets like men, even if taken at face value, do not prove that the women were engaged in combat. Women are known to have donned armour merely to protect themselves while traveling in insecure territory or when bringing water, ammunition or food to men defending the walls of a city under siege or while on watch. While wearing armour was mostly for protection, it also served to deceive the enemy. Women standing watch on a wall would have signalled a vulnerability to the enemy. By wearing men's clothing, especially armour, women made the defending forces seem stronger than they were and therefore helped discourage attacks.

Women at War: Commoners

Based on the Christian accounts, it is fair to say women played an active role in warfare only in emergencies and that the military role of women in the crusading era was primarily supportive and auxiliary. Indeed, most references to women are incidental to the overall narrative depicting military events. Nevertheless, the historical record provides explicit references to women engaging in the following support activities that contributed to the fighting capacity of the Christian armies:

• Keeping watch and serving as lookouts;
• Conducting reconnaissance and reporting enemy activity and movements to the Christian leaders;
• Providing first aid to the wounded;
• Providing long-term medical care to the sick and wounded;
• Providing meals to the fighting men;
• Providing water to the fighting men;
• Bringing ammunition (rocks and arrows) to the fighting men;
• Putting out fires;
• Cleaning and repairing the clothes of combatants;
• Helping in the construction and deployment of siege engines;
• Digging ditches and constructing barriers to prevent enemy access; and
• Building up earthworks to facilitate attacks or protect against attacks.

The most famous offensive sieges in which women are depicted taking an active part were the initial siege of Jerusalem in 1099 and the siege of Acre in 1190–1191. Albert of Aachen recorded that during the initial siege of Jerusalem, women (along with children and older people) were tasked with sewing together hides from camels, cattle and horses to create protective coverings for the siege engines. The leather coverings reduced the risk of the siege engines being set alight by burning arrows. While sewing hides together could be done outside the range of enemy sharpshooters, Aachen notes that women also helped push the finished siege engines into position, a task that brought them within range of enemy missiles. Likewise, when the Saracens later managed to set one of the Frankish siege engines on fire, women were explicitly mentioned as being among the crowd that rushed forward with water in a futile attempt to put the fire out.

In 1190–1191, Guy de Lusignan undertook a siege of Acre, which soon turned into a war of attrition that consumed, as the chronicles tell us, 6 archbishops, 12 bishops, 40 counts and 500 barons along with 'countless' thousands, possibly tens of thousands, of ordinary men – and women. Most of the women lost during the siege fell to disease, the natural consequence of the highly unsanitary conditions in the siege camp. Thus, Queen Sibylla and both her daughters died in the siege camp at Acre. Other noblewomen were also present, notably Sibylla's younger sister and successor, Queen Isabella of Jerusalem, Richard of England's Queen Berengaria and his sister, the dowager queen of Sicily.

Yet it was the women of lesser rank who contributed to the siege. One such incident made it into the *Itinerarium Peregrinorum et Gesta Regis Ricardi*, a chronicle widely viewed as a biased eulogy of King Richard the Lionheart. It is hard to know if the anonymous chronicler included the below account because it was representative or exceptional, yet the tone is unquestionably one of admiration. The text reads:

> Among those carrying earth to fill the ditch around the city so that it could be captured more easily was a certain woman. With great care and persistence, she laboured on to get the job done. She worked without stopping, untiringly coming and going, encouraging the others as she went ... While this woman was busy depositing the load of earth she had brought, a Turkish sniper shot her with a dart, and she fell writhing to the ground ... [H]er husband and many others came running to her side, and in a weak voice she tearfully begged her husband for a favour. 'Dearest lord, ... I treat and implore you, my darling, not to let my corpse be removed from here when I am dead. No, because I may no longer live to labour towards the completion of this work, let my body have a place in the work so that I can feel I have achieved something.'... O admirable faith of the weaker sex! O zeal of woman worthy of imitation[68]

In another passage, the same source records the fate of 'Turks' who broke into the crusader camp. Not only were many killed by women, but the women were also specifically described as dispatching them with particular (desperate?) brutality. Reportedly, they grabbed the Turks by their hair and cut their throats with kitchen knives.

While some women took part in offensive sieges fulfilling largely subordinate and auxiliary roles, the part played by women in defensive sieges was, on the whole, both greater and more important. The most important defensive sieges at which women were present were Banyas in 1132, Edessa in 1144, Saladin's sieges of Kerak in 1183 and 1184, Saladin's sieges of Beirut, Jaffa and Jerusalem in 1187, Saladin's siege of Jaffa in 1192, al-Adil's siege of Jaffa in 1197, the siege of Ascalon in 1247, the Mamluk sieges of Caesarea, Haifa and Arsuf in 1265, the Mamluk sieges of Jaffa and Antioch in 1268, the siege of Tripoli 1289 and, of course, the siege of Acre in 1291.

In most of these sieges, women were trapped in cities alongside their menfolk and the regular garrison. In some cases, the besieged cities had been intentionally reinforced in advance of the siege and contained large numbers of additional, trained, fighting men. This was the case, for example, with most Mamluk sieges, particularly the siege of Acre in 1291. In these circumstances, i.e., when men were present in substantial numbers, the role of women remained subordinate to and supportive of the trained male fighters.

Yet in the sieges that Saladin undertook following his victory at the Battle of Hattin, the situation was radically different. King Guy had summoned the entire feudal host to fight off Saladin's invasion in late June 1187. He mustered one of the largest Christian army ever recorded in this era, including roughly 1,200 knights, an equal number of turcopoles and some 18,000 sergeants/infantry. In order to field such a large army, the garrisons of castles and towns had been stripped of fighting men. King Guy's defeat at Hattin resulted in the annihilation of the Christian field army as a fighting force. Along with King Guy, all but three barons were taken captive. Of the estimated 20,000 other troops, knights, turcopoles and infantry, only 3,000 are believed to have escaped. These survivors did not disperse to their home cities and villages but retreated as a body towards the nearly invincible stronghold of Tyre. This meant the other cities, towns and villages of the entire kingdom were without fighting men.

The news of the catastrophe at Hattin naturally spread panic among the civilian population, particularly those living in the kingdom's unwalled and indefensible rural communities. Non-combatants, mostly clerics and women with their children and ageing parents, fled from these villages to seek refuge behind city or castle walls. Consequently, the walled cities and castles of Outremer were overrun with refugees following the defeat at Hattin. As with refugees everywhere in any era, they arrived with little more than the clothes on their backs and without stores of food or water. They immediately became a burden to the residents of the towns they fled to and a liability in case of siege since they represented additional mouths to feed.

Furthermore, while walls provide a sense of security, walls alone offer insufficient protection against an attacking army. Antioch famously had 400 towers. The sheer size of such a perimeter consumed manpower merely to maintain a watch along it. The greater the perimeter, the larger the number of troops necessary to defend it. Even the mightiest of the crusader castles, such as the legendary Crak des Chevaliers, eventually fell not because the walls were weak or the design was ineffective, but because such elaborate structures required large garrisons to take advantage of their overlapping fields of fire and other defensive features. In short, the inhabitants were unsafe even after taking refuge in walled cities.

The laws of war in this period dictated that the inhabitants of a city that surrendered should be spared, while those that defended themselves but lost could be put to the sword or enslaved. It is, therefore, hardly surprising that in the aftermath of the catastrophe at Hattin, most cities in the Kingdom of Jerusalem, including Acre, opted for surrender. Beirut, Jaffa and Jerusalem were the exceptions.

While Jaffa and Beirut rapidly fell and their surviving inhabitants paid the price in death or slavery, Jerusalem put up such a spirited defence that it forced Saladin to come to terms. It is worth looking more closely at this defence because it tells us a great deal about the women of Outremer in a military crisis.

According to the primary sources, the defence of Jerusalem against Saladin was led by Balian d'Ibelin, a highly experienced native baron, who commanded one of the largest contingents of troops in the feudal army.* It was probably because of this that he was entrusted with the command of the rear guard at the Battle of Hattin. He had fought his way off the field separately from Tripoli and initially made his way to Tyre. From there, however, he approached Saladin and obtained a safe-conduct to go to Jerusalem to remove his wife and four small children from the city before hostilities against the city commenced. Saladin, however, stipulated that Ibelin must go to Jerusalem unarmed, accompanied by only one squire, and remain only one night. This was to ensure his arrival did not serve to reinforce the meagre garrison in the Holy City.

Notably, the inhabitants of Jerusalem had already rejected very generous terms from Saladin. According to the Lyon continuation of the History of William of Tyre, Saladin promised to give the citizens both 30,000 bezants to build up their fortifications and the land within a five-mile radius around the city to cultivate without interference. He even offered to send provisions and guaranteed a truce until Pentecost of the coming year. If Jerusalem had not received outside aid by that time, however, Jerusalem's citizens were to surrender the city peaceably to Saladin, and he would allow them to withdraw with all their moveable goods. The representatives of Jerusalem rejected Saladin's terms because, according to contemporary accounts, 'they would never surrender that city where God had shed His blood for them'.[69]

Significantly, the delegation that went to Saladin was composed exclusively of burghers, that is, non-nobles. Neither Queen Sibylla nor the Dowager Queen Maria, both of whom were in Jerusalem, were parties to the negotiations, although we do not know why. Given that the population of

---

* Ibelin commanded 85 knights from his wife's fief of Nablus, 40 from his brother's fief of Ramla and Mirabel, and 10 from Ibelin for a total of 135 knights. Only the Count of Tripoli commanded more. At least one squire accompanied every knight, and, as a rule of thumb, a banneret had at least as many light horsemen under his command as heavy cavalry. Barons also often had "household" knights, i.e. knights on a retainer rather than land-holding vassals. On top of these came the foot soldiers. Ibelin may have contributed as many as 1,500 men to the feudal host.

Jerusalem notoriously had a disproportionate number of clerics, churchmen may have dominated the delegation to Saladin. Possibly, it was this clerical component that preferred martyrdom to life. It is hard to imagine that a woman who faced a future of unremitting sexual abuse in slavery would be quite so sanctimonious about not surrendering the city. Whoever the Christian spokesmen were, Saladin's response was predictable and understandable. He vowed never to negotiate for the city again but to take it by force, with all that implied for the inhabitants.

Both the rejection of Saladin's offer and Saladin's vow to put Jerusalem to the sword occurred before Ibelin's arrival. The chronicles tell us the citizens of the Holy City pleaded with the baron to remain and assist them in repelling Saladin's army. When Ibelin demurred because of his oath to Saladin, they sought out the patriarch of Jerusalem and asked him to dissuade Ibelin from departing. The patriarch duly argued that an oath given to an infidel was secondary to a Christian nobleman's duty to protect the Christian inhabitants of Jerusalem. Ibelin relented and sent word to Saladin of his decision to stay. The sultan generously sent his own men to escort Ibelin's family (and, incidentally, Queen Sibylla) to safety outside Jerusalem.

For Ibelin himself, the decision to remain and take command of the defence must have seemed suicidal. Not only was Jerusalem flooded with as many as 60,000 refugees, bringing the total population to 80,000 or more, but in all that humanity, there were allegedly only fourteen 'fighting men'. Another account says there were just two knights. Ibelin is recorded knighting sixty to eighty youth of 'good birth', presumably the younger brothers and sons of men lost at Hattin or youth of the wealthy middle class. Yet when all was said and done, the ratio of women and children to men was noted as 50:1[70]

Even if the ratio of 50:1 was, in part, rhetorical hyperbole, there can be no question that women outnumbered men by an overwhelming number. Unlike the defence of Antioch in the First Crusade or Acre a hundred years later, Ibelin's defence of Jerusalem in 1187 was conducted *primarily* by women. While clerics in the crusader kingdoms were explicitly exempt from the usual prohibition against shedding blood and would also have fought in this fierce and religiously impassioned battle, women undoubtedly formed the greatest number of defenders.

Furthermore, Ibelin not only defended Jerusalem successfully for nine days, but he also mounted sorties out of the city. One of these resulted in the death of a prominent emir; another drove Saladin's troops back to their camp, and, in a third instance, some of Saladin's siege engines were set on fire. However, after the Saracens had undermined it and brought down a forty-metre-long segment of the wall, the city became indefensible.

At this point, when some of the men were calling for a fight to the death, the patriarch interceded on behalf of the women and children, arguing: 'If we [the men] are dead, the Saracens will take the women and children. They will not kill them but will make them renounce the faith of Jesus Christ, and they will be lost to God'.[71] For the sake of the women and children, therefore, the highest Church dignitary in the Holy Land abjured martyrdom and advocated instead for a negotiated settlement. Ibelin agreed to seek terms and after much bargaining, eventually succeeded in obtaining a deal with Saladin that saved the lives and freedom of something like 50,000 Christians.

Yet the chronicles are curiously coy about describing the activities of the female defenders of Jerusalem during the nine days in which they held off Saladin's vastly superior army. Only the biography of Margaret of Beverley, a Cistercian nun, includes a reference to her wearing men's armour while standing watch on the walls of Jerusalem in 1187. Whether she bore arms or not is unclear. In the absence of historical records, we can only speculate and imagine the courage of these women.

Women at War: Noblewomen

Yet, important as women must have been (anonymously) in defending Jerusalem in 1187, arguably, women's most significant contribution to the defence of the crusader states was the part played by aristocratic women in their capacity as feudal lords. As Nicolson summarises: 'A noblewoman was responsible for the defence of her own estates if they were threatened ... [She] was also deemed responsible for defending her husband's lands if he were unable to do so, and as a mother of an underage son, she was responsible for the defence of his inheritance'.[72] Unsurprisingly, given the vulnerability of fiefs in the crusader kingdoms and the right of female inheritance, we have numerous examples of noblewomen doing precisely this.

In 1119, a Frankish army from Antioch led by the regent Roger of Salerno was obliterated at the 'Field of Blood'. His widow, Cecilia le Bourcq, sister of Baldwin II, immediately took measures to shore up the defence of Antioch. She is specifically described as knighting squires to increase the number of fighting men available, an exceptional and possibly unprecedented act.

In 1144, after the fall of Edessa, the widow of Count Joscelyn II was praised explicitly by William of Tyre because: 'she busied herself in strengthening the fortresses of the land, supplying them with arms, men and food'.[73]

In 1184, Saladin laid siege for a second time to the mighty castle of Kerak, and once again, the feudal army of Jerusalem went to its relief. Although Saladin again avoided a direct confrontation with the army of Jerusalem, during the withdrawal he sent his troops out to do as much damage as possible to the undefended countryside along the route back to Damascus. Sebaste was sacked by marauding soldiers, and several nunneries and monasteries were laid waste. The unwalled city of Nablus was likewise attacked and sacked. However, contemporary reports claim that not a single Christian soul was lost because the inhabitants found refuge in the citadel. Commanding that citadel was its feudal lord, Queen Maria Comnena, the widow of King Amalric. Although Nablus owed 85 knights to the feudal army, most of those knights would have joined the feudal army under the banner of her second husband, Balian d'Ibelin. In short, Maria defended Nablus with a garrison composed primarily of native troops.

During Saladin's invasion of 1187, his first move was to lay siege to Tiberias, the main city in the Principality of Galilee, a fief held by Eschiva de Bures, in her right as heiress. When Saladin invested Tiberias, Eschiva's husband, Count Raymond of Tripoli, as well as her four sons and the knights of the barony, had mustered with the army of Jerusalem. Like Maria Comnena at Nablus three years earlier, Eschiva was left with a garrison composed primarily of native archers and infantry. These forces were insufficient to defend the entire town. So, just like at Nablus, the citizens of Tiberias withdrew into the citadel. Although the citadel withstood the first attacks, Eschiva believed her position was sufficiently precarious to justify requesting aid from the feudal army of Jerusalem. Although her husband argued against such action for the reasons noted above, King Guy decided to attempt her relief. This decision cost him his army and his kingdom, both of which he lost on the barren plains near Hattin en route to Tiberias. After the obliteration of the Christian army at the Battle of Hattin, Eschiva had no choice but to surrender the citadel of Tiberias. Saladin generously allowed her and the citizens to withdraw unmolested to the nearest Christian-held territory, Tripoli.

In the aftermath of Hattin, only the most powerful castles stood any chance of holding out until relief could come from Western Europe in the form of a new crusade. Most of the fortresses that succeeded in defying Saladin were held by the militant orders, that is, they were castles garrisoned by trained fighting men and unburdened by civilian refugees in significant numbers. Notably, the Hospitallers' modern and self-sufficient castles, such as Crak des Chevaliers, Belvoir, Castel Blanc and Margat (Marqab), were considered so impregnable that Saladin did not attempt to assault them, counting on time and isolation to force them to surrender eventually.

Initially, the powerful border fortresses in Transjordan, Montreal and Kerak also refused to surrender. Saladin was extremely keen to seize these castles threatening the lines of communication between Egypt and Syria. His eagerness to lay claim to them was no doubt further heightened by the fact that his nemesis, Reynaud de Châtillon, had successfully defended these castles against him, most notably Kerak in 1183 and again in 1184. Although Saladin took Châtillon captive at the Battle of Hattin and ordered him beheaded immediately, the castles did not automatically fall into his hands. Instead, they were held by Châtillon's wife, the hereditary heiress of Transjordan, Stephanie de Milly. Saladin, however, believed he had the means to force Stephanie to surrender these two fortresses because he had taken her son from her first marriage, Humphrey de Toron IV, captive at the Battle of Hattin.

Saladin offered to free Humphrey in exchange for Stephanie's castles. According to one popular legend, Stephanie agreed to the exchange, but the men of her garrison refused, so she dutifully sent her son back to Saladin and captivity. Ibn al-Athir reports more credibly that Stephanie went to Saladin and begged him to release her son, but Saladin made the surrender of Kerak the condition. Stephanie returned to Kerak (without her son), and it continued to hold out for almost two more years, with or without her consent.

The most credible account claims that only when supplies began to run out did Saladin bring the captive Humphrey out of his dungeon to plead in person with the garrison for surrender. Allegedly, 'Humphrey said:

> "Sirs, if you can maintain yourselves and the castle in the interests of Christendom, then stay as you are, but if you don't think you can hold out, I call on you to surrender it and free me". The men in the castle who by now were in great discomfort agreed among themselves that if Saladin would give them a safe-conduct to go securely with their wives, children and possessions to the Christian-held lands and would free their lord, they would surrender the castle'.[74]

Curiously, the passage ends with the statement that Saladin 'had Humphrey taken to his mother and escorted the people of the castle as far as the land of Antioch'.[75] It is unclear if this means Stephanie was inside the castle or not.

On the other hand, Philip de Novare's account of the civil war between the Holy Roman Emperor and the barons of Outremer in the mid-twelfth century contains an intriguing if oblique reference to another noblewoman seizing the initiative to secure a castle, thereby preventing its fall to the enemy. This is worth quoting in detail:

> Most of the ladies and damsels and children of Cyprus were taken so unawares that they were not able to go to [the castle of] Dieudamor and so they took refuge in the churches and houses of religion, and many

there were who took refuge and hid in the mountains and in caves. Lady Eschiva de Montbéliard, who was at that time the wife of Sir Balian d'Ibelin son of my lord of Beirut ... mounted a rock [castle] called Buffavento. Therein was she received by an old knight named Guinart de Conches who was there on behalf of the king, and she supplied herself so that she provisioned it [Buffavento] with food, of which it had none.[76]

What is particularly interesting about this incident is that Eschiva was not the feudal lord of Buffavento. The castle of Buffavento was a royal one. Also, she did not take command of the defence; that was in the hands of Sir Guinart. However, her wealth was such that it enabled her to provision the entire garrison. In this instance, the provisioning alone was decisive to victory because, as Novare states, the garrison had no food and implicitly would have been forced to surrender if Eschiva had not arrived and brought with her adequate supplies. Buffavento held out until the emperor's forces were defeated at the battle of Agridi and withdrew from Cyprus altogether.

This episode highlights how noblewomen repeatedly contributed to the defence of the Holy Land through donations or patronage. Two more examples will serve to emphasise this point. In his first-hand account of the Seventh Crusade, Jean de Joinville notes that the widow of Balian of Beirut, Eschiva de Montbéliard (yes, the same Eschiva who had taken supplies to Buffavento), financed a small ship for the Seventh Crusade and put this ship at his disposal. He used it to carry eight horses during the attack on Damietta.[77] Another example of female military patronage comes from Alice, Countess of Blois. In 1288, she travelled to Acre with a large military entourage, and funded the construction of a tower to help defend Acre from a Muslim attack.[78]

These few examples that have found their way into the chronicles are most likely only the tip of the iceberg. Unfortunately, we have too little data to quantify the magnitude, much less the overall impact, of such female financial support to the defence of the Holy Land. Furthermore, it must be remembered that women were also prominent patrons of the militant orders, providing land grants and other resources that contributed materially to the wealth and strength of these institutions dedicated to defending the Holy Land.

Chapter 11

Defeat and Captivity for the Women of Outremer

Defeats, as well as victories, punctuate the history of the crusader states. This meant that the possibility of death or capture could never have been far from the minds of the inhabitants of Outremer. After all, less than one in five of those who set out on what we call the First Crusade survived to reach Jerusalem, underscoring that even the costs of victory were great. Furthermore, warfare continued sporadically throughout the crusader period. Even when peace descended upon the region, the borders remained porous and the seas insecure. As a result, travel remained treacherous throughout the crusading era. Overland travel was dangerous due to the risk of enemy and criminal raids, while Muslim and Christian pirates plagued the seas of the Eastern Mediterranean throughout the Middle Ages. This prevailing insecurity had particular and unique consequences for women.

In the era of the crusades, the rules of warfare in the Near East were unambiguous concerning the fate of a conquered people: a defeated enemy was entirely and without restrictions at the mercy of the victors. Although rare exceptions were made for enemy leaders who might be more valuable as hostages or men who were wealthy enough to pay alluring ransoms, the fundamental rule was that all adult males would be killed. The fate of their women and children was equally unequivocal: they would be enslaved. Islamic authors are most explicit about recommending this course of action, and countless examples demonstrate the policy was ruthlessly implemented.

In warfare, women usually fell into the hands of the enemy after their men had been slaughtered. As noted above, Balian d'Ibelin was initially urged to sally forth to a martyr's death, but was persuaded to seek terms with Saladin to spare the women. Ibelin turned the threat on its head and promised Saladin that:

If we see that death is inevitable, then by God we shall kill our children and our wives, burn our possessions, so as not to leave you with a dinar or a drachma *or a single man or woman to enslave*. When this is done, we shall pull down the Sanctuary of the Rock and the Masjid al-Aqsa and the other places, slaughtering the Muslim prisoners we hold – 5,000 of them – and killing every horse and animal we possess. Then we shall come out to fight you like men fighting for their lives, when each man, before he falls dead, kills his equals; we shall die with honour, or win noble victory![79] [emphasis added]

Yet not all leaders were as courageous or as compassionate as Ibelin. Following the Battle of Paphlagenia in 1101, Albert of Aachen reports that the men simply fled to safety, leaving their tents, equipment, wagons – and wives – behind. According to William of Tyre, in 1126, the men in an unspecified besieged town likewise fled rather than risk sharing 'the wretched bonds of captivity along with their wives and children'.[80]

Furthermore, women in this era fell into captivity not only because of warfare but also due to low-scale raiding and criminal activity. Attacks on travellers by Bedouins, highwaymen and marauding troops from the neighbouring territories were commonplace. Some raids were explicitly undertaken to seize slaves. Yvonne Friedman, who has undertaken extensive research on the topic, claims that 'raids into hostile territory to take hostages and slaves were standard procedure, both in Muslim and Christian warfare; here, the women were valuable trophies and loomed large in the number of captives'.[81]

It was also common to attack merchant caravans for costly goods. In such attacks, any women seized were viewed as additional loot. At sea, the target was usually the ship and cargo, but again any women on board were treated as extra booty. Two women of royal rank were victims of piracy. Arda, the first wife of Baldwin I of Jerusalem, was taken by pirates when traveling from Edessa to Jerusalem to join him. Eschiva d'Ibelin, the wife of Aimery de Lusignan, was the victim of an even more audacious pirate attack. A Greek/Armenian pirate sailed into the cove beside the estate where she was recovering from an illness, stormed ashore and carried her and her children off to captivity in what was clearly a targeted attack on a prominent woman.

In exceptional circumstances, women of very high birth might be held for ransom rather than enslaved. Albert of Aachen records one case in which a lady was taken captive on the road after her husband, Folbert of Buillon, and his knights were all killed in a fierce clash. The lady was then taken to the fortress of Azaz, where the lord 'ordered her to be treated honourably while he found out if she might be worth some great sum of money in ransom'.[82] Although we know nothing about the intentions of the pirate Canaqui who seized Aimery de Lusignan's wife and children, Eschiva d'Ibelin was released to her husband quite promptly after the intercession of Leo of Armenia.

On the other hand, sex alone did not inherently protect a captive from slaughter. Contemporary accounts tell us that Kilij Arslan's men spared 'only young girls and nuns, whose faces and figures seemed pleasing to their eyes and beardless and attractive young men'.[83] In a similar fashion, Kerbogha offered to spare only 'beardless youths' and virgins.[84] Yet, if being held for ransom or slaughtered immediately represent the two extremes of treatment for female captives, the overwhelming mass of women in the mediaeval Near East faced a single fate: slavery.

Female Slaves

As the references to sparing only attractive and young women from slaughter suggest, the immediate fate of the overwhelming majority of female captives was rape and sexual abuse. Indeed, it was expected, taken for granted, and assumed to take place by all parties. Precisely because sexual abuse was the presumed fate of female slaves, many women, both Christian and Muslim, preferred death to slavery. After the capture of her husband, King Louis IX, Queen Marguerite of France kept an elderly knight in her bedchamber whose express purpose was to kill her rather than let her fall into Muslim hands. She was not going to risk rape, even if her rank would probably have spared her. On the other hand, some women chose the opposite course. In at least one recorded case when a crusader camp was overrun by Saracens, 'stunned and terrified by the cruelty of this most hideous killing, girls ... were offering themselves to the Turks so that at least, roused and appeased by love of their beautiful appearance, the Turks might learn to pity their prisoners'.[85]

The bottom line was that the Muslims of this period viewed the sexual abuse of female captives as the conqueror's right, 'regardless of the captive's former standing'.[86] This is illustrated best by the following passage describing the situation in Jerusalem in 1187 after the forty-days of grace ended. It was written by Saladin's secretary Imad ad-Din, an eye-witness:

There were more than 100,000 persons in the city, men, women and children. The gates were closed upon them all, and representatives appointed to make a census and demand the sum due. ... About 15,000 were unable to pay the tax, and slavery was their lot; there were about 7,000 men who had to accustom themselves to an unaccustomed humiliation, and whom slavery split up and dispersed as their buyers scattered through the hills and valleys. Women and children together came to 8,000 and were quickly divided up among us, bringing a smile to Muslim faces at their lamentations. How many well-guarded women were profaned, how many queens were ruled, and nubile girls married, and noble women given away, and miserly women forced to yield themselves, and women who had been kept hidden stripped of their modesty, and serious women made ridiculous, and women kept in private now set in public, and free women occupied, and precious ones used for hard work and pretty things put to the test, and virgins dishonoured and proud women deflowered, and lovely women's red lips kissed and dark women prostrated, and untamed ones tamed, and happy ones made to weep! How many noblemen took them as concubines, how many ardent men blazed for one of them, and celibates were satisfied by them, and thirsty men sated by them, and turbulent men able to give vent to their passion. How many lovely women were the exclusive property of one man, how many great ladies were sold at low prices, and close ones set at a distance, and lofty ones abased, and savage ones captured, and those accustomed to thrones dragged down![87]

It may surprise readers that there is no Christian equivalent to Imad ad-Din's glorification of rape. While it would be naïve to imagine that rape did not occur, it was not the official policy of the Christian leadership, and it was not institutionalised. Furthermore, it was condemned by the Church because it degraded the sanctity of the cause (fighting for the *Holy* Land) and constituted a mortal sin. Christian theology, it will be recalled, regarded sex outside of marriage as a sin for men as well as women. The difference in attitude towards the rape of captives is well illustrated by the first-hand account of Fulcher of Chartres, who proudly reports: 'In regard to the women found in the tents of the foe, the Franks did them no evil but drove lances into their bellies'.[88] For those who question if this was merely whitewashing or disingenuous propaganda, the Frankish custom of not raping female captives is corroborated by contemporary Jewish sources that reported, with evident surprise, that the Franks did not violate or rape women 'as others do'.[89]

The length to which Imad ad-Din goes to describe the sexual humiliations of the Christian women and the stress he puts on their misery, along with Muslim joy, eloquently illuminates Muslim attitudes to enslaved Christian women. Yet sexual abuse was only one aspect of the treatment to which women slaves were subjected. Albert of Aachen notes that the female captives were 'chained by the Turks, who sent them as slaves into countries where they could not speak the language, to be treated like dumb animals'.[90] Thomas of Froidmont's biography of his sister Margaret of Beverley stresses the physical work and the privations to which his sister was subjected while glossing over any sexual abuse she endured. Although it is possible she was so unattractive at the time of her capture that she escaped sexual abuse, it is far more likely that her brother, writing in Western Europe about a sister he wished to honour for her piety, chose intentionally to omit reference to something that might have discredited her in the eyes of readers.

As Froidman's account makes clear, enslaved women could be required to carry out tasks more commonly done by men, such as chopping wood or carrying stones for construction. Nevertheless, contemporary accounts show that most female slaves performed household tasks. They cleaned floors, baths and toilets. They spun, wove and did other needlework. They laundered clothes and worked as bath attendants. They harvested crops, preserved foods and cooked. They tended fowl and herds of livestock. They served as personal attendants, combing, coifing and bathing the wives and concubines of their masters. Slave girls were particularly useful for shopping, as they could venture out into the male-dominated exterior world, whereas Muslim women of any status could not. Lastly, slave women often looked after the children of their owners.

While such tasks did not, perhaps, differ substantially from what many of the captive women would have done at home, their condition as slaves was fundamentally different. First, they had no rights, not even the right to life itself. Second, they did not share in the profits of whatever business or estate their work supported. Third, they were subject to sexual and other forms of physical abuse. Fourth, most women did not speak the language of their captors and were, therefore, isolated. All this came on top of the circumstances which had delivered them into slavery in the first place, i.e., a traumatic event such as capture by pirates or robbers or a siege and assault that had destroyed their home and family.

The psychological condition of enslaved women in this era is eloquently illustrated by the following account left to us by Ibn al-Athir.

When I was in Aleppo I had a slave girl, one of the people of Jaffa. She had a child about a year old, and wept greatly when she dropped him, though he was not really hurt. I calmed her and told her there was no need to weep for so small an accident. She replied, 'it is not for my boy that I am weeping, but for what happened to us at Jaffa. I had six brothers all of whom perished. I had a husband and two sisters; what has happened to them? I have no idea'.[91]

Al-Athir explicitly states she is only one of many slave women in such a state. Indeed, he also tells another anecdote about two slave women meeting in Aleppo.

'Then he [the owner of the house] brought out another Frankish woman. When the first one caught sight of this other, they both cried out and embraced one another, screaming and weeping. They fell to the ground and sat talking. It transpired that they were two sisters. They had a number of family members but knew nothing about any one of them.[92]

Arguably, trauma experienced during a siege or sack and subsequent abuse, along with psychic stress associated with uncertainty about the fate of loved ones and the future, was far greater torture than sexual abuse or hard work.

Escaping Slavery

Opportunities to escape from slavery were extremely limited. Most captives were first taken in large slave caravans to distant slave markets in the major urban centres of the Near East. These slave caravans consisted of slaves chained together and forced to walk behind the beasts of burden of their captors. Along the way, they were often prodded, whipped, raped and taunted by those escorting them. On arrival in a major urban centre, which might be hundreds of miles from the point of capture, the slaves were led through the city triumphantly and subjected to further verbal and physical abuse. At the slave market, the 'goods' were sold without regard for keeping families together. Because slave markets drew customers from a wide radius, slaves were often transported substantial distances after purchase. Thus, slaves generally ended up isolated from everyone they had known before their capture. Typically, they found themselves living in towns and villages far from familiar geography among people speaking a language they did not understand. It would not have been uncommon for slaves to have no idea where they were until after some time in captivity when they gradually learned the language and more about their new environs.

With slim prospects of returning home, many slaves sought to adapt to their new circumstances. The easiest route out of slavery was conversion. Contemporary Christian and Muslim religious thought condemned the enslavement of co-religionists. Consequently, in the case of Christian women in Muslim captivity, conversion to Islam offered an escape from the status of slave. As noted above, Muslim women in the Near East had extremely limited rights and status in this era, but at least they weren't technically chattels, as were slaves. Furthermore, conversion opened the door to the status of wife rather than concubine. While precarious (the man only had to say, 'I divorce you' three times to get rid of an unwanted wife), this was better than complete subjugation and destitution. There are numerous references throughout contemporary accounts of Christian captives married to Muslim men.

Another route to freedom was through payment of compensation to the Muslim enslaver to release the slave. Effectively, this happened when a ransom was paid. Yet even for common prisoners subjected to the complete indignity of slavery, the prospect of being freed from slavery through a cash payment was a real possibility.

This came in three forms, private, religious and public. First, family members or entire communities sometimes raised money to purchase individuals taken into captivity. Indeed, Jewish law demanded the ransom of prisoners and gave precedence to women prisoners because they were presumed to suffer most (i.e., sexual abuse) in captivity. As we have seen, Frankish feudal law likewise stipulated that a man must ransom a mother or daughter or risk the loss of his fief. Farther down the social scale, some mediaeval marriage contracts explicitly included the obligation to ransom one's wife. For example, marriage contracts have survived that include the following clause: 'And if you are taken captive, I will ransom you with my possessions ... and I will take you back. And I will not wrong you concerning this'.[93]

Payment for a specific individual, however, assumed the person could be tracked down and identified. After a small-scale raid or pirate attack on a single ship, this might be reasonable; in the aftermath of a major military disaster, on the other hand, few family members remained in a position to make a payment. Furthermore, discovering the location and contacting the owner of any individual caught up in a major catastrophe was almost impossible.

Perhaps in recognition of this fact, or at least in acknowledgement of the limited resources available to the families of captives, the religious orders increasingly took responsibility for securing their release. The military orders took the lead in transforming the purchase of enslaved Christians into a pious duty. It was, after all, only a small step from protecting pilgrims (the *raison d'etre* of the Templars at their foundation) to rescuing pilgrims from captivity through their repurchase. Likewise, the Hospitallers were, from their inception, dedicated to serving the 'holy poor', and slaves were the incarnation of complete destitution because they owned not even their own bodies. Charitable activities to release Christians from Saracen slavery were a natural extension of the Hospitaller ethos.

The end of the twelfth century also saw the founding of an order specifically dedicated to the ransoming of Christian captives in the Muslim East. This was the Trinitarian order, founded in France in 1198 with strong papal backing. Significantly, a woman, Margaret I, Countess of Burgundy, was the leading patron, providing the initial land grant for the establishment of the order. Fully one-third of the order's income was set aside for the ransom of captives or, interestingly, the purchase of Muslim slaves who could be used in slave exchanges. Significantly, the order also set itself the task of establishing hospitals to assist the redeemed slaves both physically and mentally after their return to Christian society. Within twenty years, the Trinitarians had forty houses, including seventeen hospitals. Furthermore, the Trinitarians inspired imitators.

Within a short space of time, a fundamental change in public attitudes towards captives had taken place. By the thirteenth century, the release of prisoners from Muslim captivity was no longer viewed as the responsibility of their families but rather the responsibility of Christian society as a whole. Furthermore, the suffering of those Christian captives who did not convert to Islam was equated with the sufferings of Christ. No distinction was made between men and women in the activities of these charitable institutions.

Finally, public action by the state could lead to the wholesale release of captives. This could come in the form of military or diplomatic action. Whenever the Franks took Muslim-held territory, Christian slaves in these lands were automatically freed. More commonly, however, 'prisoner' exchanges were negotiated when military hostilities temporarily ceased and a truce was signed. Again and again, these truces included clauses that provided for the release of captives. Sometimes, the exchanges were one-for-one, a knight for a mounted Muslim fighting man, an infantryman for an infantryman, or a woman for a woman. In such circumstances, the fact that the Muslims placed a much higher value on men than women reduced the opportunities for the return of Christian women.

Nevertheless, there were circumstances in which the Christian negotiators could and did demand a wholesale return of slaves. In 1159, for example, a truce with Nur ad-Din secured the release of thousands of captives, including men held since the Second Crusade ten years earlier. Another truce imposed on Damascus in roughly the same period explicitly included women captives. Ibn al-Athir states:

The Franks sent to review those male *and female* slaves of their people who had been taken from all the Christian lands, and bade them choose whether they would stay with their lords or return to their homelands. Anyone who preferred to stay was left, and anyone who wanted to go home went there.[94] [emphasis added]

Women Post-Captivity

Christian theology might equate the suffering of Christian slaves in Muslim captivity with 'a living martyrdom' for Christ, but Christian husbands rarely viewed their wives' 'failure to respect the sanctity of the marriage bed' in the same light. The Trinitarian Order established their hospitals in recognition of the fact that captives – male and female – faced significant difficulties after their release. Similarly, the Hospitallers stipulated that freed male and female captives should be given a sum of money to help them start a new life. This custom highlights that many captives could not pick up their lives where they had left off. In many cases, the cities where they had lived had been destroyed or taken over by the enemy. In other cases, their entire family had been killed, captured or dispersed, leaving them without a family network in which to reintegrate. In other cases, individuals may simply have opted to attempt a new start in life in a new place where their past was unknown. Significantly, because Christian women, unlike their Muslim sisters, did not need a male guardian, women no less than men could take advantage of this option. Returned women slaves were free to purchase property, set themselves up in an independent business or accept employment.

Nevertheless, for women, the inherent difficulty of reintegration into society was aggravated by the universal assumption that a woman returning from Muslim slavery had been subjected to repeated sexual abuse. In some prominent cases, the wives of Frankish elites were sequestered in convents following their return from captivity. While this sounds like incarceration to our ears, it may have been exactly what these women wanted to avoid the looks, innuendos and voyeuristic questions of others. A key consideration here is that a wife's sequestration in a convent did *not* free the husband to remarry. Christian theology did not recognise captivity and any attendant sexual abuse as grounds for divorce. Thus, while Muslim women who won release from captivity were promptly set aside, Christian women retained their status of wife and lady – whether their husbands liked it or not. This also meant that a husband gained little by putting a wife away in a convent against her will.

Yet status alone does not create acceptance, much less respect or sympathy. Despite being the victims of abuse against their will, the Church still viewed sex outside marriage as a sin. As a result, former women captives had to confess, repent and seek absolution for the abuse they had suffered. Many would have found this an indignity; it certainly would have required mentally reliving the trauma. Not all priests would have shown understanding. The penance imposed might be burdensome or humiliating. Nor was it just husbands who might be reluctant to welcome returned captives. Parents might also be embarrassed by an unmarried but no longer virgin daughter. Not all siblings would have been as sympathetic to the sufferings of a sister as Margaret of Beverley's brother.

Depending on the individual's circumstances and expectations of treatment from family and society, women sometimes opted to remain in captivity. This explains why the terms of the truce cited above state explicitly that only those slaves who wished to return would be released to the Franks. Yet, there are also examples of women who gave up comparative luxury and status to return to a humble home. Usamah ibn-Munqidt tells the story of a beautiful Christian captive who was sent as a gift to the ruler of Ja'bar, Shihab al-Din Mulik ibn Salim. She joined his harem and, in due time, her son by Shihab al-Din became the ruler of Ja'bar. Yet, despite her exalted position as the ruler's mother, the 'ungrateful' Christian woman took advantage of her new status to escape back to her Christian husband. Usamah was outraged that this woman 'preferred life with a Frankish shoemaker, while her son was the lord of the castle of Ja'bar'.[95] Two things are striking about this account. First, the woman's Christian husband evidently welcomed her back. Second, the luxury of a golden cage was not inherently more attractive than freedom.

Summary and Conclusions

Fundamental to understanding the significant contribution of women to the history of the crusader states is recognising that human development is not linear. Because women in later ages suffered significant curtailments to their independence, enfranchisement and status, it is all too often assumed that women in the Middle Ages were even more restricted. The contrary is true. As French feminist historian Regine Pernoud noted, 'From the tenth to the thirteenth century … women incontestably exercised an influence that the lovely rebels of the seventeenth century or the severe anarchists of the nineteenth century were not able to achieve'.[96]

The deterioration in the status of women in more recent centuries can be traced to what we know as the Renaissance – the European rediscovery of all things Roman. Whatever benefits the Renaissance may have brought, the reintroduction of aspects of Roman Law resulted in women being denied the status of a legal entity, thereby making them subject to a male guardian. Women were effectively disenfranchised, losing the power, status and freedoms they had enjoyed in the feudal period.

The Latin kingdoms in the Levant were feudal states *par excellence*. Established at a time when feudalism was already an established and well-developed form of government, the crusader states of Outremer recognised the right of female inheritance from their inception. Women derived their status as overlords and vassals from that fundamental right. The right of women to own and run feudal fiefs, businesses and enterprises, from trading empires to workshops and market stands, followed logically. Women learned and exercised trades and professions, participating actively in a wide range of economic activities, many of which are nowadays more commonly associated with men.

Furthermore, women could vote. They voted in secular bodies such as professional guilds and the High Court. They also voted in the chapters of religious houses, where they could be elected to executive and leadership positions.

As a result, contemporary accounts describing the fate of Outremer is full of colourful examples of women, both prominent and humble, who contributed materially to the successes and failures of the crusader states. From Queen Melisende effectively thwarting her husband's attempt to sideline her to Queen Sibylla's crowning of her unpopular husband Guy, Jerusalem's reigning queens shaped the fortunes of the Holy Land. Yet, the nameless native women who married crusaders and integrated them into local families and communities, enabling them to survive and prosper in an alien environment, were just as crucial to forging the crusader states. The latter unnamed women made it possible for the transient crusaders to become settlers, enabled the settlements to become prosperous, and in so doing, secured the viability of the Frankish states for two centuries. It was the native wives of crusaders and pilgrims that created a multilingual second generation of Franks adept at navigating the shifting rivalries and alliances among the Muslim princes. Ultimately, the mixing of Frankish settlers with locals created the hybrid society that gave the Frankish states their unique character.

Daily life in the crusader states was fashioned as much by women as men. Women made up at least half the population and could be found in every walk of life. Unlike their sisters in the Muslim states around them, the women of Outremer did not live locked behind the walls of their guardians' homes but instead enlivened the streets by their presence as shopkeepers and customers, tradespeople and homemakers, pilgrims, nuns and patrons of the arts. Their public presence both scandalised and intrigued Muslim visitors such as the poet Ibn al-Qaysarani, who was enraptured by Frankish women and wrote effusive poems praising their beauty, or Ibn Jabayr, who, after feasting his eyes on the sight of unveiled women, felt the need to 'take refuge with God from the temptation of the sight!'[97]

The extent to which their presence was more pronounced than in contemporary Western societies is not the subject of this book and a conclusion in that regard must be deferred to scholars with a greater comparative perspective. It has been suggested that 'women were integrated into all aspects of the crusades, from preserving the home to participation in business and agriculture, from care of the sick and wounded to logistical support in wars, and from their role in religious life to active political leadership.'[98] If so, this may imply that the era of the crusades generally – or specifically – was conducive to female empowerment, irrespective of geography. This thesis rests on the notion that the extraordinary logistical, financial and military mobilisation necessary to carry out these massive campaigns over thousands of miles of territory was similar to a modern world war. As such, the societies involved in the pervasive struggle elevated the status of women out of the need to harness all available human resources. Yet, such a theory fails to explain why women's status as heiresses, reigning queens and guild masters, etc., was not confined to periods of conflict.

Rather than attempting to prove or disprove any particular theory, the objective of this work was to reveal the surprising number of famous and anonymous women who left a mark on the history of Outremer. The focus of the book has been on what women did as opposed to what others have said about them. The women are present in primary sources, but too often, they have been obscured by the subjective commentary of chroniclers or ignored by subsequent generations focused on the action and the heroes associated with military campaigns.

Therefore, it is vital to separate the subjective commentary of historians from the facts. A classic example is the 'abduction of Isabella' in Western European chronicles of the thirteenth century. Because Alice de Champagne, Queen Isabella's daughter by Henri de Champagne, laid claim to the County of Champagne, French chroniclers sought to discredit this 'foreign' woman who threatened the status and wealth of one of their most generous local patrons. They did so by alleging that Alice was the product of a bigamous marriage and, therefore, a bastard. To that end, they needed to prove that her mother, Queen Isabella I, had not been legally separated from Humphrey de Toron. The chroniclers outdid themselves in voicing outrage and employing melodramatic language. A committee of leading prelates deliberating on the validity of Isabella's marriage while keeping her sequestered in their protection becomes in their accounts an act 'more disgraceful than the rape of Helen'. Maria Comnena, a princess of the imperial Byzantine family, is described as 'steeped in Greek filth', 'godless' and 'fraudulent'. The man who offered himself as a hostage to Saladin to secure the release of 8,000 paupers is called 'cruel' and 'faithless'. The subjective opinions of the chroniclers originated decades after the events and were fabricated in France by people who had never met the subjects. Yet the core of the story reveals two strong-willed women, Isabella and her mother Maria, who together saved the crown of Jerusalem from Lusignan.

Similarly, the historian Philip de Novare was inclined to attribute base or contemptible motives to female characters. His Eschiva de Montbéliard, therefore, is in 'so great fear' that she leaves the security offered by the Knights Hospitaller and disguises herself as a man to go alone across twenty miles of territory controlled by notoriously brutal imperial mercenaries to provision a royal castle at risk of falling to the king's enemies. Moreover, to be sure his readers understood how reprehensible Eschiva's actions were, he invents children she did not have whom she allegedly left behind and talks of her 'abandoning her fiefs' at a time when the emperor's men had already confiscated them.

As these illustrations demonstrate, writers of history are subjective, and their opinions colour the historical record. It is necessary, therefore, to look more closely at what the women of Outremer did rather than what others say about them to find the real women beneath the sometimes disfiguring commentary. Although I have tried to do just that, I have also let the most eloquent contemporary historians speak because their voices also tell us much about the age and society that is the subject of this book. If nothing else, the praise for women we find in the pages of contemporary documents, while no less subjective than the insults, shows us this era was not consistently misogynous. William, Archbishop of Tyre, is a wonderful example of a cleric who reveals no consistent bias against women. He is equally quick to praise women such as Melisende or Beatrice of Edessa as he is to criticise other women such as Alice of Antioch.

Ultimately, all we have are fragments of a mosaic badly damaged by time. We have no comprehensive or systematic description of the society in which these women lived, much less their full contribution to it. Hopefully, this book has blown away some of the sand that hides the complete picture underneath, but there is still much to discover and reveal. The women who lived, worked and reigned in the crusader states deserve to be brought into the light and remembered.

Biographies

Agnes de Courtenay, Queen Mother (b. 1136–d. 1184)

Agnes de Courtenay, the mother of Baldwin IV, was a controversial and divisive figure in her lifetime. Despite revisionist attempts to paint her as a victim of a hostile press, Agnes was, by and large, the architect of her fate – and reputation. She bears a substantial portion of the blame for the near collapse of the Kingdom of Jerusalem in 1187.

Agnes de Courtenay was the daughter of the powerful Courtenay family. In France, the Courtenays ranked high enough for a daughter of the house to marry the younger brother of King Louis VII of France. In the crusader kingdoms, the family derived its prominence from the fact that Joscelyn de Courtenay was a first cousin of Baldwin de Bourcq, one of the leaders of the First Crusade, who ruled Jerusalem as Baldwin II. When Baldwin de Bourcq was elected to the crown, he invested his cousin, Joscelyn de Courtenay, with his former County of Edessa. Joscelyn thereby became Joscelyn I of Edessa, a position he fulfilled vigorously and successfully.

Under his son Joscelyn II, however, Edessa was overrun and lost to the Saracens due largely to the neglect and poor leadership of the new count. The city of Edessa was lost to Zengi in November 1144, and by 1150, those remnants of the once rich and powerful county that had not been overrun by the Saracens, had been ceded to the Byzantine Emperor. Joscelyn II was captured in that same year by Nur al-Din and tortured. He eventually died in captivity in 1159.

Joscelyn III inherited his father's title without the lands or income that went with it. As titular Count of Edessa, he was to prove a singularly ineffective (not to say incompetent) leader. He distinguished himself by getting captured at a disastrous battle in 1164, and playing a key part in the usurpation of the even more inept Guy de Lusignan. Finally, he surrendered Acre to Saladin in haste against the wishes of the population – who rioted in protest because Acre was defensible and could have received aid from the West by sea.

Agnes was the daughter of the ill-fated Joscelyn II and his admirable wife Beatrice, who dealt so competently with the disaster left by the loss of Edessa.

We do not know the year of Agnes' birth, but it was probably between 1135 and 1140. She had been married, possibly at the age of 8 or only slightly older, to Reynald of Marash. She was left a widow when he was killed in battle in 1149. The following year, Agnes' father was captured, never to be seen again. In just six years, her family had fallen from one of the richest and most powerful in the crusader states to the 'poor cousins' of royalty, living on a few estates in Antioch that belonged to Agnes' mother Beatrice from her first marriage. Agnes was a widow with no dower and a daughter with no dowry. She was possibly no more than 10 years old, although she was probably a little older.

Under these circumstances, it appears that Agnes languished for some time in her mother's much-reduced household and was eventually betrothed to a man of comparatively obscure origins and only recent prominence: Hugh d'Ibelin. Hugh was the son of an adventurer of unknown origin, Barisan, who had distinguished himself as a knight and administrator in the reign of Baldwin II and was first rewarded with the constableship of Jaffa, and, subsequently, the newly created barony of Ibelin. Ibelin was small. It owed only ten knights to the feudal levee and was a 'rear-tenancy'. That is, the Baron of Ibelin did not hold his fief directly from the crown but rather from the Count of Jaffa. Agnes may have felt, as the daughter of a count, that this marriage was demeaning. In any case, shortly after the betrothal, Hugh d'Ibelin was taken captive at Jacob's Ford. It was 1157.

Hugh's capture left Agnes in a difficult position. She was between 17 and 22 years of age, penniless, her father was still in a Saracen prison, her brother was probably even younger than she was, and now her betrothed was in captivity. She may have assumed he would suffer the same fate as her father and never return. Perhaps she felt vulnerable and desperate, or she may simply have been flattered to find the king's younger brother took an interest in her. Whether she was the seducer or the seduced or was outright abducted (as some historians have suggested, see H.E. Mayer, *The Origins of King Amalric*), sometime in 1157, she married Prince Amalric of Jerusalem, then Count of Jaffa and Ascalon.

There are no recorded objections to the marriage, which is significant. Furthermore, Agnes rapidly fulfilled her feudal obligations by giving the Count of Jaffa two children: a daughter, Sibylla, born in 1159, and a son, Baldwin, born in 1161. Then in February 1163, her brother-in-law, Baldwin III of Jerusalem, died childless. Amalric as the king's only brother, a young and vigorous man with experience in war and peace, seemed the obvious candidate to succeed him. Yet rather than being immediately acclaimed king, Amalric faced serious opposition – because of his wife.

As noted earlier, the High Court of Jerusalem had such strong objections to Agnes that they refused to recognise Amalric as king of Jerusalem unless he set Agnes aside. Officially, the Church had suddenly discovered (after six years of marriage) that Amalric and Agnes were related within the prohibited degrees. Yet even the highly educated church scholar and royal insider William of Tyre found this explanation so baffling that he had to conduct extra research to track down the relationship. Under the circumstances, the official grounds for nullifying the marriage appear dubious. A more credible canonical justification for the nullification of the marriage was the pre-contract Agnes had with Hugh d'Ibelin. Mediaeval law saw betrothals as akin to marriage, and if the betrothal had not been legally abrogated, the marriage to Amalric was technically bigamous. The fact that Agnes married Hugh d'Ibelin as soon as her marriage to Amalric was dissolved supports the thesis that her betrothal was deemed legally binding.

Yet, if this were the case, it is surprising that Amalric's children by Agnes were explicitly recognised as legitimate. Therefore, it is possible that the High Court did not so much question the validity of Amalric's marriage as the character of his wife. Possibly, she was viewed as too assertive a woman or was already known to be a notoriously grasping one. Alternatively, as M.R. Morgan's *Chronicle of Ernoul and the Continuations of William of Tyre* suggest, she was seen as insufficiently virtuous for the position of queen in the sacred territory associated with Christ. Ultimately, such speculation is pointless; Agnes was found unsuitable for a crown by the majority of the High Court. Even without knowing the reason, that was a judgement by the peers of the realm and not simply a matter of 'bad press'.

Agnes then married (or returned to) her betrothed, Hugh d'Ibelin. When he died in or about 1170, she married a fourth time. For a dowerless woman, that's quite a record and suggests she may have had charms not measured in land and titles and inadequately conveyed by the historical record. She had no children by any of her husbands (or alleged lovers) except King Amalric, and until his death, she had no contact with her children by him. Even after Amalric's death, during her son Baldwin's minority, she appears to have been excluded from the court.

Then in 1176, Baldwin IV took the reins of government for himself and invited his mother to his court. She rapidly established herself there as a key influence on her son; she had an affectionate relationship with the young king, who, by this point, was afflicted with leprosy. She travelled with him, even on campaigns, and appears to have taken a motherly interest in his health and welfare. Since Baldwin IV was unmarried, Agnes' influence was all the stronger. Thus, although she never wore a crown, she was undoubtedly the most powerful woman in his court and, by the end of Baldwin's reign, participated in sessions of the High Court.

At this stage in her life, Agnes was allegedly promiscuous. She would have been in her late 30s when her son invited her back to court, and she had been widowed three times. Although she had been married to Reginald of Sidon shortly after Hugh's death, there are some indications that this last marriage was also dissolved or ruled invalid. She did not live in Sidon but resided at court. Here she reputedly took the Archbishop of Caesarea, a native by the name of Heraclius, as her lover. Afterwards or simultaneously, she was said to have had an affair with Aimery de Lusignan.

While her morals were arguably her affair and modern sensibilities are not greatly offended by a mature woman finding sexual pleasure wherever she pleases, Agnes' influence on her son was unquestionably reprehensible. Within a few short years, Agnes de Courtenay had succeeded in imposing her candidates for seneschal, patriarch and constable upon her young, dying son. These were, respectively: (1) her underwhelming brother, Joscelyn III of Edessa, (2) the controversial figure Heraclius, who – whether or not he was as bad as his rival William of Tyre claims and regardless of whether he had been Agnes' lover as the *Chronicle of Ernoul* claims – was nevertheless an undistinguished churchman and patriarch, and (3) an obscure Frenchmen, also alleged to have been Agnes' lover, Aimery de Lusignan. Even if Aimery de Lusignan eventually proved capable, her candidates were not impressive.

However, the worst was yet to come. Agnes also engineered the marriage of Baldwin's two sisters, her daughter, Sibylla, and the daughter of Maria Comnena, King Amalric's second wife, Isabella. As noted above, no other actions in Agnes de Courtenay's life were as detrimental to the welfare of the Kingdom of Jerusalem as the marriages of the princesses of Jerusalem with Guy de Lusignan and Humphrey de Toron respectively.

Humphrey was a man of 'learning' who's most notable accomplishment was to betray his wife and the majority of the High Court by vowing allegiance to the usurpers Sibylla and Guy. Although Humphrey lived a comparatively long life and should have held an important barony, he never distinguished himself in any field and died in obscurity. He was not exactly a brilliant match or a wise choice of consort for a future queen of Jerusalem.

Agnes' other choice, the man she chose for her daughter, was even more disastrous. At best, Guy de Lusignan, freshly come from France, was young, inexperienced and utterly ignorant about the crusader kingdoms. At worst, he was not only ignorant but also arrogant and a murderer. He rapidly alienated his brother-in-law, King Baldwin IV, and he never enjoyed the confidence of the barons of Jerusalem. The dying king preferred to drag his decaying body around in a litter – and his barons preferred to follow a leper – rather than trust Guy de Lusignan with the command of the feudal army.

Nor was this mistrust on the part of the barons misplaced. When Sibylla crowned her husband king, and all the barons (except Ramla and Tripoli) grudgingly accepted him, he led them to the avoidable disaster at Hattin. In short, Agnes de Courtenay's interference in the affairs of Jerusalem led directly to the loss of the entire kingdom.

In retrospect, Agnes de Courtenay was an ambitious woman who clawed her way from comparative helplessness and impoverishment to become the effective 'power behind the throne' of her son. She suffered setbacks in her life, most notably the High Court's refusal to recognise her as queen. She allegedly hated bitterly the woman who was crowned queen in her place, Amalric's second wife, Maria Comnena. The extent to which her subsequent actions were motivated by a consuming thirst for revenge should, therefore, not be underestimated. Whether she was motivated by a conscious desire to debase those she blamed for her own humiliation or simply lacked intelligence commensurate with her ambition, her overall impact on the history of the crusader states was tragically negative.

Alice of Antioch, Princess of Jerusalem and Antioch (b. 1110–d. 1151)

Alice of Antioch was another ambitious woman who was highly controversial in her time. Again, contemporaries are quick to speak about her in pejorative terms. However, it is harder for historians to find convincing evidence of ineptitude or malice, much less wrongdoing. Furthermore, her legacy is considerably more ambiguous than that of Agnes of Courtenay.

Alice was the second daughter of Baldwin II and his wife, Morphia. She was probably born in or about 1110, and in 1126, aged 16, she married the Prince of Antioch, Bohemond II. She was given the coastal lordships of Latakia and Jabala as her dowry, which were, in turn, bestowed back on her as her dower. Only four years later, when Alice was roughly 20 years old, Bohemond II was killed, leaving her a widow with a 2-year-old infant daughter, Constance. Since Constance was the heiress to the principality, Alice was free from the duty to remarry. Since Constance was so young, however, the ever-vulnerable principality needed a regent until Constance came of age or married.

Despite Alice's youth, as a princess of Jerusalem and mother of the heiress, there was nothing inherently illogical about Alice assuming the regency of Antioch for Constance until her marriage. However, Alice was shunted aside with surprising rapidity, first by her father, Baldwin II, and then by her brother-in-law, Fulk d'Anjou. The conventional explanation is that Alice, unlike her elder sister Queen Melisende, had a bad and untrustworthy character. For example, Steve Tibble dismisses Alice as follows:

> [Fulk's] sister-in-law, Princess Alice, spent most of the period 1130–
> 1136 trying to take control of the Principality of Antioch in the most
> divisive fashion, and launched no fewer than three attempted coups, in
> the course of which she incited some of Fulk's leading vassals to revolt
> and, possibly, entered into secret alliances with the main Muslim enemies
> of the crusader states.[99]

Although greatly oversimplified, this negative interpretation of Alice's actions is based on William of Tyre's history. Given Tyre's fulsome praise of Melisende and his concern for the rights of Alice's infant daughter, Tyre cannot be dismissed as a misogynous cleric. Yet Tyre makes no bones about his opinion of Alice. He writes of her being led 'by an evil spirit' and hoping to 'acquire Antioch for herself in perpetuity'.[100] In another passage, he claims:

> The widow of the late prince, a daughter of King Baldwin and sister of
> Queen Melisende, was an extremely malicious and wily woman. With
> the help of certain accomplices in her designs, she was intriguing ... to
> disinherit the daughter whom she had borne to her husband and thus
> secure for herself the entire kingdom. Then after obtaining possession of
> the principality, she intended to marry again according to her pleasure.[101]

Particularly damning is Tyre's allegation that Alice, 'In order to make her position more secure ... sent messengers to a certain powerful Turkish chief [Zangi]. By his aid she hoped to acquire Antioch for herself in perpetuity, despite the opposition of her chief men and the entire people'.[102] While alliances between the kings of Jerusalem and Muslim powers were routine throughout the history of the crusader states, attempts by Frankish lords to exploit alliances with Saracens to shore up their positions in domestic disputes consistently provoked outrage and condemnation. This had been true when Hugh of Jaffa tried to oppose Fulk d'Anjou with Muslim help and would again be true when Raymond of Tripoli concluded a defensive alliance with Saladin. In short, what ignited Tyre's condemnation was not Alice's sex but her politics.

Yet Thomas Asbridge has convincingly challenged Tyre's narrative and, with it, the prevailing view.[103] Asbridge suggests that at the time of Bohemond's death, the High Court of Antioch was not as united in its opposition to Alice as is usually assumed. He notes that several key figures, such as the patriarch and the constable of the kingdom, appear to have sided with Alice. The majority, however, were less interested in legal technicalities and more concerned about effective government and defence. The 20-year-old Alice might have been the logical and legal regent, but she could not lead armies.

Asbridge further challenges Tyre's tale of Alice sending a messenger to Zengi that 'by chance' fell into the hands of her father, the king. He notes the allegations appear nowhere except in Tyre's account and are not corroborated by Arab sources. The latter is significant as it would be strange if such an important development as a chance to seize control of Antioch with the aid and assistance of its regent went unreported – if it had happened. Asbridge points out that since the prince of Antioch was either a vassal of the Byzantine Emperor or an independent ruler – but on no account a vassal of Jerusalem – concluding a defensive alliance with a Muslim power would not have been treason (as it was in the case of Hugh of Jaffa or Raymond of Tripoli), but foreign policy. Indeed, it would have been in the best traditions of the crusader states.

Nothing, however, could alter the fact that a 20-year-old widow could not lead the Antiochene feudal host. For the majority of Antioch's feudal elite, trusting in a truce with a notoriously treacherous enemy appeared a risky option compared to rule by a strong military leader such as King Baldwin II. This majority faction favouring a strong military leader, sent to Baldwin II requesting he resume the regency that he had ably held during the minority and absence of the late Bohemond II.

Baldwin II responded promptly to the appeal of the Antiochene nobility, riding north to see to affairs in the principality personally. Although Alice initially ordered the city gates closed against him, she did not resort to force. When supporters of the king inside the city opened the gates to him, she was persuaded to submit to him peacefully. According to Tyre, Baldwin II was initially 'indignant' with his daughter, yet he does not appear to have been outraged. He advised her to retire to her generous and prosperous dower lands, the coastal lordships of Latakia and Jabala, which does not suggest he viewed his second daughter as fundamentally evil, irresponsible or dangerous.

Two years later, however, Baldwin II died and was succeeded by Fulk d'Anjou. Asbridge suggests this opened a welcome opportunity for the Counts of Tripoli and Edessa to assert greater autonomy. The two counts, however, wanted support from Antioch, which geographically separated them and formed the largest of the three crusader states outside the Kingdom of Jerusalem. United, the three northern crusader states stood a fair chance of ending their de facto – albeit not de jure – subservience to the kings of Jerusalem.

Alice evidently joined forces with Tripoli and Edessa, and Tyre acknowledges that she gained the support of many Antiochene nobles in doing so. Other historians suggest that growing dissatisfaction with Fulk's rule enabled Alice to become a focal point for disaffected subjects of the Angevin king. Thus, Alice's court in Latakia attracted, in addition to Tripoli and Edessa, the rebels Hugh of Jaffa and Ralph of Fantanelle from Jerusalem. There is no evidence, however, that she was the ringleader or that she induced rebellion against their better judgement. On the contrary, the disaffected lords and autonomous counts may have exploited Alice's youth and inexperience for their purposes. Certainly, her actions at this point are in no way indicative of plans to disinherit her daughter. The most that can be said with certainty is that the 22-year-old princess appeared eager to take control of her destiny.

Unfortunately for Alice, Tripoli was defeated in the field by Fulk, seriously weakening her coalition. Furthermore, Fulk, with the help of the feudal army of Antioch, defeated a Muslim threat led by the sultan of Aleppo. This later event swayed public opinion in Antioch back in Fulk's favour. Yet, Alice continued to build up her power base on the coast. Here she established a princely administration complete with chanceries, constables and other household officials – and steadfastly styled herself as Princess of Antioch.

In the autumn of 1135, five years after the death of her husband, she rode back into Antioch and assumed the role of regent without protest on the part of the High Court, the Church or the population. Significantly, this occurred after King Fulk's attempt to sideline Queen Melisende had failed. It appears that Melisende, now firmly back in the saddle, told her husband not to interfere in her sister's affairs, and Fulk obeyed. It is hard to imagine that Alice's move in 1135 was not coordinated and approved by Melisende in advance.

Yet envoys had already been sent to Poitiers to seek a consort for Alice's daughter, Constance, the young heiress of Antioch. In 1136, Raymond of Poitiers arrived in Antioch. As before, Alice could not compete with a vigorous and militarily competent alternative to her rule; the nobles and commons preferred a prince who could actively fight for them to a woman who could not. The fact that in the six years since Bohemond II's death, Antioch had suffered several military setbacks at the hands of their neighbours weighed heavily against Alice. Losses included the cities of Tausus, Adana and Mamistra to Armenia and four other cities to Zengi. Thus, although Constance was only 8 years old – below the age of consent – she was married to Raymond of Poitiers, and he assumed the title and duties of Prince of Antioch (by right of his wife), thereby ending Alice's last attempt to rule Antioch.

Stripped of Tyre's pejorative assessment, Alice's actions hardly seem particularly ill-advised or selfish, much less evil. That she failed had less to do with her sex than her refusal to remarry. Had she married a man capable of leading Antioch's feudal host, she could almost certainly have replicated her sister Melisende's successful model of corporate rule. Her husband could have fulfilled the military duties of the regency while she held power internally until Constance came of age and married. Alice's regency was always bound to be temporary, but she might have enjoyed power longer had she been willing to share it with a fighting man who satisfied the demands of the Antiochene feudal elite for a militarily capable leader.

Alice de Champagne, Princess of Jerusalem, Queen Consort of Cyprus, and Regent of Cyprus and Jerusalem (b. 1193–d. 1246)

Alice de Champagne stands out as Outremer's most dynamic and powerful royal woman of the thirteenth century. She was recognised as regent twice, first by the barons of Cyprus and then of Jerusalem. However, she singularly failed to exploit her position successfully and ended up more of a pawn than a powerbroker.

Alice, the daughter of Isabella I of Jerusalem and Henri de Champagne, was born in or about 1193. She was only a little girl at the time of her father's tragic death in 1197 and probably no more than 11 at the time of her mother's death in early 1205. Thereafter, she fell under the guardianship of her maternal grandmother, the dowager queen of Jerusalem, Maria Comnena. Professor Bernard Hamilton credits the formidable Comnena dowager with arranging the dynastically astute marriage between Alice, titular heiress to Jerusalem after her elder sister Maria de Montferrat, and the future King Hugh of Cyprus. However, it is recorded that the fathers of both children (Aimery de Lusignan and Henri de Champagne) had expressed an interest in such an alliance before their deaths.

In 1210, Alice was escorted to Cyprus by her uncles John and Philip d'Ibelin. In the Cypriot capital Nicosia she formally married Hugh de Lusignan and was crowned queen of Cyprus. She would have been roughly 17 years old while her husband was just 14. Shortly afterwards, Hugh assumed his majority – with a vengeance. He immediately accused his regent and brother-in-law of embezzlement and either exiled him outright or forced him to flee. In either case, Walter de Montbéliard quit the kingdom and went to the court of his cousin John de Brienne in Acre.

In 1217, aged 22, Hugh joined what we know as the Fifth Crusade and led a contingent of Cypriot crusaders to the mainland, where they made some incursions into Saracen territory preliminary to the start of the main crusade against Egypt. During the winter lull in fighting, Hugh travelled north to attend the wedding of his and his wife's half-sister Melisende de Lusignan to Bohemond IV of Antioch. (Melisende was the daughter of Aimery de Lusignan, Hugh's father, by Isabella of Jerusalem, Alice's mother. She was, thus, Hugh's paternal half-sister and Alice's maternal half-sister.) During the festivities, Hugh became ill, and on 10 January 1218, he died.

Hugh left behind two small daughters and a son, Henry, only 8 months old. His queen, Alice de Champagne, was now a 25-year-old widow. The sudden death of her young husband, especially when he was not actively campaigning, must have been a shock. By all accounts, however, Alice was immediately recognised by her vassals as the regent for her infant son. Yet, either at the advice of the High Court or following the dying king's wishes or, possibly, of her own accord, Alice publicly appointed her uncle Philip d'Ibelin as her 'baillie' or ruling deputy. Significantly and unusually, after all the liegemen had done homage to Queen Alice as regent, the barons allegedly at Alice's request swore to obey Philip d'Ibelin 'until her son Henry came of age'.[104]

According to the chronicles, the kingdom's revenues largely went to Alice, who therefore controlled patronage, while the day-to-day business of administration and the critical task of leading the armies of Cyprus devolved upon her appointed baillie, Philip d'Ibelin. By no means was Alice's role passive or nominal. In 1220, Alice was actively involved in mediating a dispute between the Latin and Orthodox churches in Cyprus. The pope had designated Cardinal Pelagius, the leader of the Fifth Crusade, to resolve the issue; he wanted the Orthodox bishops removed and the land turned over to the Latin Church. Queen Alice actively supported the interests of the Orthodox Church, enabling a compromise that allowed most Orthodox bishops to remain in place, albeit as nominal suffragans of their Latin colleagues. She also insisted that the Orthodox clergy be excused from paying taxes or performing labour services. Unfortunately, the pope was displeased with the agreement, and negotiations were reopened in 1222, leading to renewed frictions.

Meanwhile, Alice's baillie, Philip d'Ibelin, rebuffed efforts by the Duke of Austria to disinherit the Lusignan kings altogether. The Austrian duke spuriously alleged that Cyprus was a part of the ransom Richard the Lionheart agreed to pay his family. In addition, Ibelin repelled an Ayyubid raid on Cyprus' principal southern port of Limassol, during which ships were burnt in the harbour, and as many as 13,000 Cypriots were killed or captured. This was the first Arab attack on Cyprus in roughly 200 years and must have terrified the population and shaken the government under Ibelin, who likely recalled vassals then involved in the crusade in Egypt to defend Cyprus. Two years later, Cyprus was devastated by a severe earthquake that damaged three major cities, Nicosia, Limassol and Paphos. The latter was particularly ravaged, with the castle and much of the city levelled.

Perhaps the costs of rebuilding and repair caused by these calamities strained the Cypriot treasury and put Ibelin on a collision course with Queen Alice. The thirteenth-century historian Philip de Novare, an intimate and supporter of the House of Ibelin, claims that Alice spent money 'freely', implying irresponsibly.[105] Another chronicle is even more specific, saying: 'Queen Alice was very generous and spent the revenues of the kingdom liberally, and disposed of them entirely as seemed good to her'.[106] Ibelin evidently disagreed about how the revenues should be spent and tried to curb the queen. Alice resented his interference, leading to a rupture between them.

The High Court sided decisively with Ibelin. In 1223, Queen Alice abandoned her three children and went into voluntary exile in Tripoli, but not with any intention of giving up the fight. On the contrary, there, she married the eldest son of the Prince of Antioch, Bohemond V, with the apparent aim of returning to Cyprus with Bohemond as her consort in order to dismiss Ibelin.

News of her intentions alarmed the barons of Cyprus. According to Novare, the barons feared that Bohemond, heir to an independent principality, would not be willing to recognise the minor Lusignan king as his sovereign. In short, the barons suspected Antioch was planning to depose Henry de Lusignan in favour of his dynasty. Whether such fears were justified or not is moot. Queen Alice's plans, whatever they were, foundered on a papal dissolution of her marriage to Bohemond based on consanguinity.

Alice next tried to outflank Ibelin by appointing a different baillie, a disaffected Cypriot lord by the name of Aimery Barlais. The High Court of Cyprus rejected Barlais' claim to the regency by citing their oath to obey Ibelin until King Henry came of age. Meanwhile, and ominously, Alice faced opposition from a different and more powerful quarter – namely, the Holy Roman Emperor, Frederick II Hohenstaufen. The emperor rejected Alice's right to be regent, proclaiming his exclusive right to the position. As with his claim to be king of Jerusalem after his wife's death and his attempt to force the prince of Antioch to do homage to him, his presumption of the regency of Cyprus violated the constitution of the kingdom and was vehemently opposed by the High Court of Cyprus.

Indeed, despite Alice's frictions with Ibelin and the High Court of Cyprus, the barons of Cyprus (including Ibelin) remained nominally loyal to her. When Frederick II tried to make them do homage to him, they refused on the grounds that they had already done homage to Alice, and she was the legal regent. Frederick II was not interested in the legality of his claims; he ignored Alice and the High Court and appointed his own baillies for Cyprus

– five men whose rapaciousness soon led to bloodshed and the only instance of violence against Orthodox clergy in the history of Frankish Cyprus.

Just as Frederick II's arrogance and disregard for the law had turned the Ibelins, the Prince of Antioch and the common citizens of Acre against him, his treatment of Alice pushed her into open rebellion as well. As soon as Frederick had sailed away (still drenched in the offal and innards the people of Acre had thrown at him as he walked down to his galley), Alice went before the High Court of Jerusalem to lay claim to the crown of Jerusalem. It was early May 1229.

Her reasoning was cogent and highly sophisticated. Queen Yolanda of Jerusalem died on May 5, 1228. Her infant son, Conrad, was her successor, and it was only as regent to Conrad that the barons of Jerusalem had submitted to Frederick II. However, Alice now pointed out, in accordance with the laws of the kingdom, whoever inherited a fief while not resident in the domain must return to claim their inheritance within one year. A year had now passed since Conrad had inherited his title, and he had not yet come to claim it. In consequence, Alice argued, his claim had lapsed, and the next in line to the throne should be recognised as the rightful ruler of Jerusalem. After Conrad, Alice was the closest blood relative to the last queen, her niece Yolanda.

Alice's legal reasoning was based on the laws of inheritance for fiefs and, up to this time, had not been applied to the crown itself but her arguments could not be dismissed out of hand. The High Court informed Frederick II of the kingdom's customs and demanded he send Conrad east to enforce his claim. Frederick, of course, ignored the High Court as he always did. Yet while the emperor's attitude inflamed anti-imperial sentiment in Outremer, it did nothing to help Alice. Instead, a full-scale civil war exploded in which Alice's abandoned son, King Henry of Cyprus, played a prominent role on the side of the rebellious barons. He and his supporters (headed by the Ibelins) had no desire to complicate things by doing homage to a woman who had tried to push an Ibelin from power – and possibly depose her own son earlier. Alice had made the wrong enemies in 1223–24.

Alice, however, was nothing if not tenacious. Since her regency in Cyprus ended when her son Henry came of age in May 1232, she decided it was time to press her claims to the Counties of Champagne and Brie in France. Her claims were based on the fact that when her father, Henri de Champagne, had set out on crusade in 1190, he had been a bachelor without children. Fearing he might die on the dangerous crusade, Henri had designated his brother Theobald as his heir in the event he never returned and died without heirs. As it turned out, Henri never returned from his crusade, but not because he died. Instead, he had been persuaded to marry Isabella of Jerusalem and remain in

Outremer. Although he died young and unexpectedly in 1197, he was not without heirs. On the contrary, he had three daughters by Isabella, the eldest of whom was Alice.

When word reached France of the Count of Champagne's death, the king of France ignored Henri's three daughters (we will never know whether it was because they were so far away or because they were girls) and invested Henri's brother Theobald III with the County of Champagne. By 1233, when Alice decided to go to France and demand her father's county, it was thirty-six years since her father had fallen to his death. His brother, too, was long since dead and buried, and Alice's cousin, Theobald IV, was a grown man who had held the county nearly all his life. Yet he was aware of Alice's claims.

Many years earlier, Alice's younger sister Philippa and her husband Erard de Brienne had laid claim to Champagne. At the time, Theobald IV was still a minor, and his mother Blanche had been his regent. To protect her son's inheritance, Blanche alleged that both Alice and Philippa were illegitimate because their mother (Isabella I of Jerusalem) was still legally married to Humphrey de Toron at their birth. This made her marriage to Champagne bigamous and, thus, null and void, and all issue from it illegitimate. Blanche trotted out French crusaders and clerics who all swore profusely to the perfidy of Conrad the Montferrat, all the barons of Jerusalem and, especially, Maria Comnena, whose 'Greek filth' corrupted everything under the sun. These 'witnesses' were produced for one purpose only: to ensure Blanche's son did not lose his inheritance, Champagne. That they denigrated the leading lords of Outremer and blithely dismissed as bastards all the rulers of Jerusalem since Isabella, including the current king of Cyprus (not to mention confusing and distorting the historical record) was of no account to Blanche or her witnesses.

When Alice returned to France to lay her claim, her cousin trotted out the old arguments and 'testimony'. The pope was asked to rule on the validity of Isabella's marriage to Champagne without access to contemporary documentation or witnesses from the Kingdom of Jerusalem. At this point, Louis IX intervened. Although he had not yet taken the cross, his concern for the Holy Land was sufficient for him to oppose any judgement that might disrupt the ruling dynasties in the remaining crusader states. He persuaded Alice to renounce her claims in exchange for the payment of the considerable sum of 40,000 livres Tours and an annuity from estates yielding 2,000 livres annually. Alice returned to Outremer substantially wealthier than when she had left. She appears to have been content – for the moment.

Nothing more was heard about her until late 1239 when a young nobleman in the entourage of her erstwhile rival, Theobald IV of Champagne (now king of Navarre as well), proposed (or accepted a proposal of) marriage; it is not clear which of the pair took the initiative. By this time Alice was 47 years old, and her bridegroom, Ralph Count of Soissons, is thought to have been roughly half her age. Presumably, he was most attracted by the fact that she was queen-mother of Cyprus and still the heir presumptive to Jerusalem since Conrad Hohenstaufen had no heirs yet.

It is hard to imagine that subsequent events were entirely coincidental. The conflict between Frederick II and the leading rebels of Outremer had been frozen for roughly a decade. The emperor had lost all influence in Cyprus with the victory of King Henry over the Imperial Forces at the Battle of Agridi in 1232. On the mainland, Frederick's baillie Richard de Filangieri held sway only in Tyre, while the rest of the kingdom recognised the baillies appointed by the High Court. In early 1243, the rebel barons were told that there was disaffection in Tyre and elements within the city would welcome them if they could liberate it from imperial control.

Suddenly, the legal advisors to the leading barons of the anti-imperial faction remembered that a minor king had just one year to claim his inheritance after coming of age. If he failed to do so, his right to exercise power lapsed. Since Conrad had come of age in 1242 (some say 1243), his father, Frederick II, could no longer call himself regent and no longer had the right to appoint baillies (e.g., Filangieri). On the other hand, Conrad had no right to appoint baillies either, or at least not until he had come to the kingdom and been properly crowned and anointed. The argument went that instead of the absentee monarch, power in the kingdom should be exercised by the king's closest relative resident in Outremer. In this case, that was Alice de Champagne.

At once a written agreement was drawn up in which the leaders of the baronial faction, Balian d'Ibelin of Beirut (the son of John d'Ibelin, the former regent of the kingdom), and Philip de Montfort, Lord of Toron, agreed to swear homage to Alice as regent of Jerusalem. She promised to invest the named lords with all the fortresses in the kingdom, that is, to delegate the defence of the realm to them. On 5 June, an assembly was summoned and attended by members of the High Court, representatives of the Church, the military orders and the Italian communes. Alice was formally invested as regent, and those present swore homage to her, starting with Balian of Beirut, the foremost baron in the Kingdom of Jerusalem at this time. He was followed by his cousin Philip of Toron, a cousin of the English Earl of Leicester, Simon de Montfort.

A week later, Beirut led a military assault on Tyre, slipping through a postern with a few men and opening the chain to the harbour to admit a fleet loyal to the barons. The Imperial Forces were driven back to the citadel and soon agreed to surrender. They were granted free passage out of the city and returned to

Sicily to face the wrath of the Hohenstaufen. Ralph de Soissons immediately demanded the victors turn Tyre over to him in his capacity as regent-consort.

Beirut and Toron did not share his interpretation of his role as husband to the regent Alice. They could legitimately argue they had been entrusted with the defence of the realm and that task 'naturally' included such a vital and nearly impregnable city as Tyre. Furthermore, as an immature newcomer from France who had not been held hostage and tortured by Frederick II (as Balian of Beirut had), nor fought in the vicious and violent phase of civil war from 1228–1232, Soissons was not taken seriously. Beirut and Toron flatly refused to surrender Tyre to Soissons.

Soisson immediately demonstrated the depth of his feelings for Alice by setting sail for France. There he complained bitterly about his lack of power and the double-dealing and treachery of the barons of Outremer. This narrative reinforced the prejudices of Western chroniclers against the Franks resident in the Holy Land. The natives of Outremer had long been viewed by West Europeans as excessively luxury-loving. They notoriously preferred baths to battles, and were suspected of being soft on the Greeks and Saracens.

Strikingly, Alice did not join her husband. Moreover, she does not even appear to have shared his indignation. She took control of the kingdom's revenues. She actively revoked appointments and grants made by Frederick II, whether at her behest or because it was the will of the High Court is unclear. She effectively regained the position she had held in Cyprus following the death of her first husband, King Hugh. While she enjoyed the status and revenues of regent, the real power in the kingdom lay with an Ibelin baron.

Nevertheless, while Alice never attained absolute power, she was anything but passive or helpless. Alice was bright, ambitious, educated and tenacious. She repeatedly seized the initiative and sought to bend others to her will. She actively impacted the history of her times, albeit not always to her benefit or credit. Yet she was unquestionably taken seriously and accorded respect by the men around her.

It is hard to escape the conclusion that a different woman with, perhaps, less pride and more charm would have been able to convert her acknowledged legal status into a position of yet greater influence. Abandoning her kingdom and her son when she clashed with her baillie and the High Court of Cyprus over finances was an unwise decision. Marrying a young French adventurer who did nothing to improve her legal status and alienated her barons was another ill-advised move. If Alice had allied with the Ibelins during the constitutional crisis of 1229, they might have opted to exploit her undeniable status as the resident heir apparent. They might have proclaimed her regent of Jerusalem immediately. She could have become a vital counterweight and rallying point to Hohenstaufen's power. With a husband chosen from among the local barony, she could have given the kingdom what it needed most: a resident ruler dedicated to the welfare and defence of the Franks in the Near East.

Constance of Antioch, Ruling Princess of Antioch (b. 1128–d. 1163)

Constance was born an heiress and refused to be cowed into marrying a man she did not choose. Yet, while she got her way in marriage, her chosen husband proved the more dominant personality. In short, Constance became a victim of her poor judgement.

Constance, the heiress to the Principality of Antioch, was born in 1128. She was the daughter of Queen Melisende's sister Alice and Alice's husband, Bohemond II of Antioch. Constance's father was killed in 1130, making her heiress to the principality at the age of 2 – long before she could consent to marriage. Although her mother initially acted as her regent, as described above power soon devolved to the kings of Jerusalem acting in consort with the High Court of Antioch.

In 1136, that body selected Raymond de Poitiers, the younger brother of the Duke of Aquitaine, as Constance's husband, and he came out to the Near East armed with a papal dispensation to marry the 8-year-old Constance. The issue of consent was brushed aside for dynastic reasons, and Constance was duly married to the much older Raymond. The marriage lasted thirteen years until 1149, when Raymond de Poitiers died fighting against Nur ad-Din in the Battle of Inab. Constance was left a widow at 21 with four young children, including a 5-year-old son, Bohemond III. The latter succeeded to the principality, but, as a minor, could not yet rule. Constance, unlike her mother, was recognised as regent without dissent and assumed this role.

After her year of mourning, the king of Jerusalem, Constance's cousin Baldwin III, urged her 'repeatedly' (according to William of Tyre) to take a new husband. Tyre goes on to note that 'there were in the land at that time a number of noble and distinguished men … [anyone of whom] seemed with justice quite capable of protecting the region'.[107] He carefully listed three candidates, along with their qualities and bloodlines, to show that they were worthy consorts for the Princess of Antioch. However, as Tyre says: 'The princess … dreaded the yoke of marriage and preferred a free and independent life. She paid little heed to the needs of her people and was far more interested in enjoying the pleasures of life'.[108]

While Tyre's opinion of Constance's motives may be biased, the more important point is that the king singularly failed to convince – or coerce – Constance to take one of his 'suitable' candidates. Indeed, he summoned what

Tyre called a 'General Council' at Tripoli and sent for Constance's aunts, Queen Melisende and Countess Hodierna of Tripoli. Yet, as Tyre laments, 'neither the king nor the count, her kinsmen, neither the queen nor the countess of Tripoli, her two aunts, was able to induce her to yield and thus provide for herself and her land'.[109]

Then, three years later, in 1153, Constance finally married for a second time; a man of her choosing. She chose the soon-to-be notorious adventurer, Reynald de Châtillon. It is hard to imagine this marriage was entirely harmonious as Châtillon notoriously abused his power as Prince Consort of Antioch. In the eight years between his marriage to Constance and his capture by Nur ad-Din's forces in 1161, Châtillon engaged in some of the most nefarious activities recorded in the crusader states. These included the imprisonment and torture of the Patriarch of Antioch and a raid on the Christian island of Cyprus, during which his troops committed many atrocities. His actions were so notorious that King Baldwin III conveyed to Emperor Manuel I Comnenus that he would not stand in the way of a Byzantine expedition of retribution. Recognizing he was trapped, Châtillon submitted to the Byzantine Emperor, as William of Tyre describes it:

He is said to have appeared before the emperor barefooted and clothed in a woollen tunic short to the elbows, with a rope around his neck and a naked sword in his hand. Holding this by the point, he presented the hilt to the emperor. As soon as he had surrendered the sword, he threw himself on the ground at the emperor's feet, where he lay prostrate till all were disgusted and the glory of the Latins was turned to shame; for he was a man of violent impulses, both in sinning and in repenting.[110]

Missing in the descriptions of Châtillon's misdeeds is any mention of his wife. We hear neither that she approved nor disapproved. Tyre, our principal source, may well have felt that having refused to marry more suitable candidates when offered them, she had 'made her bed and must now lie in it'.

Yet no sooner was Châtillon deep in a Saracen dungeon than Constance again tried to take control of her inheritance. Unfortunately for her, her son Bohemond III, was already 15 and deemed of age according to the laws of the crusader states. Bohemond, rather than Constance, was recognised as the legal ruler of Antioch by King Baldwin III. Constance attempted to override this decision by taking her case to the Byzantine Emperor, the acknowledged overlord of Antioch, after Châtillon's submission to him earlier. The emperor sent ambassadors back to Antioch, who appear to have temporarily bolstered Constance's position – at least for as long as they remained in Antioch.

They departed after negotiating a marriage between Constance's daughter (Bohemond's sister) Maria and Emperor Manuel. Shortly afterwards, however, Bohemond III with the backing of his barons compelled Constance to leave the principality. This suggests she had made herself unpopular, most probably by her second marriage and/or her appeal to the ever unpopular Byzantine Emperor. She died of unknown causes soon afterwards and before the release of Châtillon from Saracen captivity.

Like her mother, Alice, Constance was handicapped in her play for power by her sex because the barons of Antioch wanted (and legitimately needed) a fighting man at their head. With the wisdom of hindsight, it is clear that Alice blundered in choosing Châtillon as her consort, but he may well have seemed an ideal candidate at the time. He certainly proved to be a courageous and hard-bitten fighting man, even if his ethics and judgement left much to be desired. The fate of Constance, like that of her mother and Alice de Champagne, demonstrates that legal rights alone did not ensure the exercise of power.

Eschiva d'Ibelin, Lady of Cyprus (b. ca. 1165–d. 1196 or 1197)

Although Eschiva d'Ibelin never wore a crown, she was the founder of a dynasty that ruled Cyprus for roughly 300 years. Eschiva was married to a landless adventurer as a child and ended up married to a king without changing husbands. While we know very little about her, what we do know hints at a vital role during a critical juncture in history.

Eschiva was the daughter of Baldwin d'Ibelin, who held the barony of Ramla and Mirabel by right of his wife, Richildis. Eschiva's birthdate is not recorded, but she must have been born about 1165 and had one sister, Stephanie. The Ibelins' comparatively low rank at this time is illustrated by the fact that Stephanie married Amaury, viscount of Nablus (i.e., a household official, not a lord), while Eschiva was married to a landless adventurer from France, Aimery de Lusignan. Aimery was the third son of the French Lord de la March, and he married Eschiva before his brother Guy came to Jerusalem and seduced his way to a crown.

Eschiva was probably already married when her father distinguished himself at the Battle of Montgisard in 1177, an event which appears to have gone to his head and sparked new ambitions. In that same year but months before the battle, the heiress of Jerusalem, Sibylla, had been widowed, and rumours soon started to circulate that Baldwin of Ramla hoped to marry her. Of course, that was only possible if Baldwin could rid himself of the wife he already had,

Richildis, the mother of his two daughters. This he successfully did, although no grounds for the divorce are given in the surviving records.

Furthermore, the divorce did not bring him the desired results. Princess Sibylla was instead betrothed to the far more powerful and prestigious Duke of Burgundy. Ramla consoled himself with a marriage to the daughter of the Lord of Caesarea, Elizabeth Gotman. Two years later, however, she was dead, and Baldwin's ambitions again turned towards Sibylla. He may have had some form of encouragement from Sibylla herself because when he found himself in Saracen captivity in the summer of 1179, Saladin felt he could ask a king's ransom for Ramla's release. Presumably, the sultan had heard rumours that Ramla was about to marry the heir apparent to Jerusalem's throne and would one day be king consort. Furthermore, the Byzantine Emperor agreed to pay a large portion of that ransom apparently likewise on the assumption that Baldwin of Ramla would become king of Jerusalem in due time.

Instead, Sibylla married Guy de Lusignan in haste and secrecy. This meant that with one stroke, Eschiva's brother-in-law had snatched away from her father the prize he had been pursuing for roughly three years. That act created an irreparable breach between Eschiva's father and husband. Although her father married a third time to Maria of Beirut, Ramla never reconciled with Guy de Lusignan.

Meanwhile, around 1182, Baldwin IV appointed Eschiva's husband, Aimery de Lusignan, constable of the kingdom. While this was a prestigious and important position, Eschiva's joy at seeing her husband raised in status may have been dimmed by rumours that he owed his appointment to an intimate relationship with the Queen Mother Agnes de Courtenay.

At the death of Baldwin IV, Eschiva's father and husband found themselves on a collision course. Aimery backed Sibylla and Guy's usurpation of the throne, while Baldwin of Ramla opposed them and sought to crown Sibylla's half-sister Isabella. Although Sibylla's coup was successful, and she crowned Guy herself, Ramla was one of two barons who flatly refused to accept it. Rather than do homage to his hated rival Guy, Ramla chose exile, abandoning his third wife Maria, his infant son Thomas – and Eschiva, who probably never saw him again.

While we cannot know what Eschiva felt, it is hard to imagine that she was unaffected by such a bitter break between her father and her husband. On the surface, she remained loyal to her husband, but any joy in the triumph of Guy de Lusignan must have rapidly turned sour. Firstly, Aimery benefitted in no way from Guy's crown; Aimery was neither appointed to new offices nor awarded lands and titles. Secondly, within a year, Guy had led the kingdom to disaster at the battle of Hattin, and Aimery was a prisoner of Saladin. Soon

Ramla and Mirabel, along with Acre, Jaffa and Ascalon, had been overrun by Saladin's armies. Eschiva was a refugee with young children. Her father had disappeared, her husband was a prisoner, and she had no means to support herself or her children, let alone raise a ransom for her husband. We have no idea where she found refuge in this period of great uncertainty. The most likely scenario is that she joined the household of her father's younger brother, Balian d'Ibelin, Lord of Nablus.

The Lord of Nablus had fought his way off the field at Hattin and in the immediate aftermath of Hattin was described by contemporary Arab sources as 'like a king' among the Christians. He extracted his family from Jerusalem before the siege began and had them taken to an unspecified place of safety, possibly Tyre or Tripoli. Most likely, his niece Eschiva and her children were welcomed into his household and maintained by Nablus as long as needed.

Meanwhile, after a year in captivity, Aimery was released by Saladin along with his brother Guy. He remained loyal to the latter, joining him at the siege of Acre in 1189. However, Eschiva's whereabouts during this period are unknown. There is no mention of her at the siege camp of Acre. Had she been there, she would have attended her sister-in-law, Queen Sibylla, at the time of her death. It appears she was left somewhere safer. It is also possible that in the wake of Guy's disastrous reign, she and Aimery were estranged at this time.

At the end of the Third Crusade, Richard of England sold the island of Cyprus to Guy de Lusignan, yet Aimery de Lusignan is conspicuously absent from the names of those who went with Guy to Cyprus to establish his rule there. Instead, Aimery remained in the Kingdom of Jerusalem, where he continued to hold the post of constable. However, his position was undermined by Guy's resentment at losing the Kingdom of Jerusalem. Rumours spread that Guy with the support of the Pisans was plotting against Queen Isabella and her husband, Henri de Champagne. When Aimery spoke up in favour of the Pisans, Henri de Champagne concluded that Aimery sided with his brother Guy and ordered Aimery's arrest. The High Court sided with Aimery and pressured Champagne into releasing him. Yet, all trust between the two men was gone. Aimery could ill resume his tenure as constable. Instead, he joined his brother in Cyprus. It is not recorded if Eschiva went with him.

In 1194, Guy de Lusignan died. Despite Aimery's years of loyal support and service to his younger brother, Guy slighted Aimery to bequeath the island to their elder brother Hugh. For Eschiva, Guy's ungratefulness would have been particularly bitter since Aimery's loyalty to Guy had cost her all contact with her father.

Hugh de Lusignan, however, had no interest in abandoning his French lands for distant Cyprus, and the rich island fell to Aimery by default. Aimery seized the opportunity and rapidly proved to be a far more able administrator than Guy had ever been. He pacified Cyprus and opened it to immigration by those made homeless through Saladin's victories in Syria. Yet wisely, he left the Greek civil service largely in control of the administration and made no disruptive changes to the tax structure. Likewise, although he established a Latin church on the island, he left the Greek Church in possession of most of its lands and tithes. Finally, to elevate his own status, he offered to do homage for Cyprus to the Holy Roman Emperor in exchange for a crown. Emperor Henry VI agreed and sent word that he would crown Aimery when he came to the Holy Land on his planned crusade. In the meantime, the emperor sent the archbishops of Brindisi and Trani with a sceptre as a symbol of monarchy. Aimery styled himself 'king of Cyprus' from this time forward.

At some point, Eschiva had joined him in Cyprus. By the time Aimery was recognised as king of Cyprus, she was roughly 30 years of age and had given Aimery six children, three boys and three girls. Two of her sons and a daughter, however, had died young. The surviving children were Burgundia, Helvis and Hugh. Significantly, Hugh was born in 1196, so he was presumably conceived and born in Cyprus after Eschiva had joined her husband there.

That same year, Eschiva took ill from an unknown cause, probably in the aftermath of Hugh's birth. This led to her becoming a victim of her husband's otherwise admirable efforts to curb the rampant piracy in the eastern Mediterranean. What befell her is described in considerable detail in the Lyon Continuation of William of Tyre. The account deserves to be quoted in full.

'[The pirate Canaqui] learned that ... the queen and her children had come to stay near the sea in a village named Paradhisi. The queen had been ill, and ... had come there to rest and recuperate. As soon as Canaqui knew where she was, he landed with some companions. He was familiar with the lie of the land, and he came at dawn to the village where he surprised the people who were with her, captured the queen and her children, and took them off in his galley.[111]

'After he had absconded with the queen, the hue and cry arose in the land and the news came to the king who was greatly angered ... The king and queen's relations and everyone else were very sorrowful at this shameful event that had taken place in the Kingdom of Cyprus ... When Leo of the Mountain, who was lord of Armenia, came to hear of the outrage that had befallen King Aimery and his lady, he was deeply saddened because of the love that he had both for King Aimery who was his friend and for Baldwin of Ibelin whose daughter she had been. He immediately sent messengers to Isaac [the backer of Canaqui] to say that if he valued his life, he would have the lady and her children brought to Gorhigos the moment he read this letter. As soon as Isaac heard this order from the lord of Armenia, he accepted that he would have to do as he was told. He sent [the kidnapped lady and her children] to Gorhigos in fitting style, and when Leo heard of their arrival, he went to meet them and, receiving them with appropriate honour, did much to please them.[112]

'As soon as the lady had arrived in Gorhigos, he sent messengers to King Aimery telling him not to be angry or troubled for he had freed his wife and children from the power of their enemies. When the king heard this news, he was delighted at the great service and act of kindness [Leo] had done them. He had galleys made ready and went to Armenia, accompanied by his best men. There he was received honourably, and he was overjoyed to find his wife and children safe and sound'.[113]

Several points are striking in this account. The reference to Baldwin d'Ibelin being a friend of Leo of the Mountain is intriguing, as it suggests that after leaving the Kingdom of Jerusalem, the former lord of Ramla went to Armenia. More significant for Eschiva herself, however, is that there is no hint of sexual abuse or disgrace. On the contrary, much is made of her being greeted with 'appropriate honour'. Furthermore, Eschiva was clearly welcomed back by Aimery without recriminations or doubts. Was this because the kidnapper was an Orthodox Christian rather than Muslim or because the entire episode was considered political hostage-taking rather than a criminal or military kidnapping?

Even in the absence of sexual abuse, however, the experience of being held hostage by a known pirate must have been traumatic in the extreme for Eschiva, both as a young woman and the mother of two young, possibly nubile, daughters and an infant son. Although Eschiva returned with Aimery to Cyprus, she appears to have never fully recovered from the trauma or the illness that had taken her to Paradhisi in the first place. Although she lived long enough to witness the reconciliation between her husband and Henri de Champagne, who came to Cyprus explicitly for that purpose, she died before she could be crowned. Her husband of more than twenty years was crowned and anointed king of Cyprus in September 1197 without Eschiva at his side. Within weeks, Henri of Champagne fell to his death, and before the end of the year, Aimery had married the widowed Queen Isabella I of Jerusalem.

Eschiva lived in the vortex of Jerusalem politics in the last two decades of the twelfth century. She was an Ibelin by birth and a Lusignan by marriage.

She founded a dynasty that would rule Cyprus for more than 300 years. But we do not know if she was politically active. Did she have a say in affairs of state? Did she whisper advice to her husband? Or did she console and support her sister-in-law Sibylla? Did she advise Sibylla not to renounce Guy, no matter how great the pressure from the High Court was? Or did she see what her father and uncle saw in him, that Guy would make a disastrous king and try to talk Sibylla into abandoning him? Unless new sources come to light, we will never know.

Yet it does not take too much imagination to see Eschiva as the bridge that enabled the Ibelins to become the most powerful supporters of the Lusignan dynasty in Cyprus. Historians puzzle over the fact that the Ibelins, who were inveterate opponents of Guy de Lusignan, could quickly become so entrenched in his brother's Kingdom of Cyprus. Eschiva was likely the key.

Eschiva de Montbéliard, Lady of Beirut (b. ca 1207–1208 – d. after 1250)

The force of Eschiva's personality rather than her rank or titles earned her a mention in two of the most important and lively chronicles of the thirteenth century, those of Philip de Novare and Jean de Joinville. In both instances, Eschiva acted on her own and in material support of military operations. Yet she was also the heroine of a scandalous love match. Due to her secondary status as a non-royal woman, the historical record has left us with only glimpses of what must have been a forceful and highly intelligent woman.

Eschiva was the daughter of one of the many adventurous younger sons of the French nobility who went to the Holy Land to make his fortune, Walter de Montbéliard. Walter was the second son of Amadeus, Count of Montbéliard, and he took the cross in 1199 but, rather than joining the ill-fated Fourth Crusade, struck out on his own, arriving in the Holy Land sometime after 1201. By 1204, he had already won so much favour with Aimery de Lusignan – at that time king of Cyprus and king consort of Jerusalem – that he was appointed constable of Jerusalem (the same position Aimery had himself once held). At the same time, Aimery gave the hand of his eldest daughter Burgundia to Montbéliard in marriage.

Burgundia of Lusignan was probably already 22 or 23 at the time of her marriage. She had been betrothed briefly to Raymond VI of Toulouse between 1193 and 1196, possibly while still very young and certainly before her father had been crowned. Burgundia may also have been one of the children kidnapped along with her mother by the pirate Canaqui in 1196. If her marriage had recently been dissolved and she had returned to Cyprus, then it would have been considered appropriate for her to help her mother with her younger siblings.

In 1205, Aimery de Lusignan died unexpectedly, leaving the thrones of Cyprus and Jerusalem in the hands of minors. In Jerusalem, Aimery was succeeded by Maria de Montferrat, whose maternal uncle, John d'Ibelin, Lord of Beirut, assumed the regency. In Cyprus, however, the crown fell to Aimery's only surviving son, Hugh, his last child by Eschiva d'Ibelin. Hugh was only 9 years old at his father's death, and the High Court of Cyprus chose as regent the husband of Hugh's heir (his sister Burgundia), Walter de Montbéliard.

Eschiva, Walter and Burgundia's daughter, was born on the island shortly after her father became regent in 1206 or 1207. While she would have been far too young to notice, her father pursued a highly controversial and aggressive foreign policy that included an expensive expedition to seize the port of what is now Antalya on the southern coast of modern Turkey. In addition, during Montbéliard's regency, King Hugh's marriage to Alice de Champagne, the heiress of Jerusalem, was celebrated.

In 1210, Hugh I of Cyprus came of age, and no sooner had he taken control of his kingdom than he accused Montbéliard of massive malfeasance. He demanded Montbéliard return the astronomical sum of 240,000 bezants to the Cypriot treasury. Convinced that the king intended him harm, Walter de Montbéliard fled Cyprus overnight with his wife and his household aboard a Templar ship bound for Tripoli. From there, he made his way to Jerusalem, where his cousin John de Brienne had recently been installed as king consort after marrying Maria de Montferrat. Thus, Eschiva would have experienced a headlong flight from danger at a very tender age.

Just two years later, in 1212, Eschiva's father died, possibly fighting the Saracens. She was, at most, 6 years old, and again, it is difficult to know how deeply affected she would have been. Her mother was still the heiress to Cyprus and, with her husband dead, appears to have reconciled with her brother, who restored many, if not all, of the properties once held by Montbéliard. In addition, John de Brienne remained protective of his relatives, and in 1220, he named Eschiva's older brother Odo constable of Jerusalem, the position his father had once held and a lucrative honour. Either Hugh of Cyprus or John de Brienne may have been responsible for arranging a suitable marriage for Eschiva. Sometime between 1220 and 1229, Eschiva was married to Gerard de Montaigu.

Little is known about Gerard beyond the curious fact that he was the nephew of the Master of the Knights Templar, Pedro de Montaigu; the Master of the Knights Hospitaller, Guerin de Montaigu and the nephew of the Archbishop of Nicosia, Eustace de Montaigu. (How three brothers came to hold three such powerful ecclesiastical positions simultaneously is a coincidence unexplained in the source material.) In any case, Gerard died at the Battle of Nicosia on 14 July 1229. He died fighting on the side of the rebel barons led by John d'Ibelin, the Lord of Beirut, against the Holy Roman Emperor's baillies. Eschiva became a widow at the age of 23, at most, and, more likely, 20 or 21.

Eschiva had no children by Montaigu. However, she was evidently an extremely wealthy widow. Furthermore, while her brother spent his entire career in the Kingdom of Jerusalem serving as constable and briefly as deputy regent, Eschiva's inheritance and wealth appears to have come exclusively from properties she held in Cyprus.

Heiresses in the Kingdom of Cyprus, surrounded as it was by water, were not required to marry to ensure sufficient fighting men for the feudal army. No one could have forced Eschiva de Montbéliard to remarry after the death of Gerard de Montaigu, but roughly one year after the Battle of Nicosia, she made a love match that scandalised society.

The man she chose to wed was Balian d'Ibelin, the eldest son of the Lord of Beirut. Balian's appeal to Eschiva is easily imagined. He was roughly her age, or at most a couple years older, but he had already distinguished himself as an audacious knight and effective commander.

His career would have been well known to Eschiva, particularly the fact that in 1228, Balian was one of twenty hostages seized by Emperor Frederick II Hohenstaufen for the good behaviour of his father. Balian and his younger brother Baldwin were 'put in pillories, large and exceedingly cruel; there was a cross of iron to which they were bound so that they were able to move neither their arms nor their legs'.[114] Although Balian's father secured his release from this inhumane detention within several weeks, Balian remained a hostage of the emperor (albeit in better conditions) for the length of the emperor's bogus 'crusade'.

Yet when the emperor's baillies set about despoiling Ibelin properties after the emperor's departure in 1229, Balian was among the small body of troops who accompanied his father to Cyprus to confront the five baillies. He distinguished himself at the battle of Nicosia, rallying dispersed Ibelin troops and leading them back into the thick of the fight after the Lord of Caesarea had been killed and when his father had been unhorsed and was defending himself in a churchyard. That is to say, when the Ibelins were on the brink of a disastrous defeat, Balian turned the battle into a victory. During the siege of St Hilarion that followed, when a sally from the castle overran the Ibelin camp, 'Sir Balian came ... recovered the camp, and, spurring up to the gate of the wall, broke his lance on the iron of the wall gate'.[115] At another point, when the later historian and philosopher Novare was badly wounded before the castle, Balian 'succoured him and rescued him most vigorously'.[116] Even taking into account Novare's bias and affection for his 'compeer' Balian, it is clear that Balian had already established his reputation as a bold knight by the time he married Eschiva.

The couple married clandestinely, evidence there was (or they expected) opposition to the match. Since Eschiva's overlord, King Henry I of Cyprus was a minor, opposition could have come from only one source, the king's regent and the bridegroom's father: the Lord of Beirut. On the surface, it appears surprising that the Lord of Beirut would object to the marriage. Balian and Eschiva were equal in rank (she was the granddaughter of a king, and he was the grandson of a queen). Her father had been regent of Cyprus when Beirut had been regent of Jerusalem. Eschiva brought great wealth into the marriage. She was young and healthy, and there was no reason to presume she could not bear children. Most likely, therefore, Beirut's opposition derived from political considerations. Eschiva's brother Odo was a partisan of the Holy Roman Emperor, Frederick II, while Beirut was the emperor's most bitter and intransigent opponent.

The fact that the couple went ahead with the marriage suggests this was an affair of the heart for both. The problem with this strategy was that they were related within the prohibited degrees and consequently required a papal dispensation to marry. A powerful baron like Beirut might expect to obtain such a dispensation; two young lovers in their 20s did not have the kind of influence necessary to win over the papal curia.

When their marriage became public, the Archbishop of Nicosia (perhaps not incidentally, the uncle of Eschiva's first husband) promptly threatened to excommunicate them. Far from intimidating either of them, Balian organised a show of force that drove the archbishop to flee Cyprus altogether. (Notably, Balian's father was in Palestine at the time and so unable to curb his son's anger or mediate between the parties.) The offended and outraged archbishop appealed directly to the pope, who obligingly issued a ban of excommunication on both parties, which arrived in the Holy Land in March 1232.

Meanwhile, the emperor's forces had retaken control of Cyprus while the Ibelins (including Balian) and their knights and troops were on the mainland. The situation immediately became extremely unpleasant.

[The emperor's men] committed all the abominations and outrages and villainies of which they knew and were capable. They broke into the churches and the Temple and the house of the Hospital and all the religious houses, and they dragged the ladies and the children who clung to the altars and to the priests who chanted Masses.... . They put the ladies and children into carts and on donkeys most shamefully and sent them to [Kyrenia] to prison.[117]

Except for those who had disguised themselves as peasants – and Eschiva. Philip de Novare tells us that Eschiva:

> Dressed in the robes of a minor brother ... mounted a [castle] called Buffavento. Therein was she received by an old knight named Guinart de Coches, who was there on behalf of the king, and she supplied herself so that she provisioned [Buffavento] with food, of which it had none.[118]

This underscores that Eschiva had so much wealth she could provision the garrison of a royal castle at her own expense – and that she was exceptionally courageous.

Yet the excommunication hung over her and her husband. Balian's pious father was so outraged by the excommunication (or perhaps by the disobedience that had led to it) that he publicly refused to allow his heir to command a division of troops in the coming confrontation with the emperor's knights. An eyewitness to the battle describes the situation as follows:

> Sir Balian, his son, had always in this war led the first troop. At this time [Beirut] made [Balian] come before him and demanded that he swear to obey the command of the Holy Church, for he was under sentence of excommunication because of his marriage. [Balian] replied that he could not accede to this request. The noble man [Beirut] ... said: 'Balian, I have more faith in God than in your knighthood, and since you do not wish to grant my request, leave the array for, and it please God, an excommunicated man shall never be a leader of our troop'.[119]

In response to this speech, Sir Balian,

> 'Escaped and went to the first rank where were his brother Sir Hugh and Sir Anceau; he gave them advice and showed them that which he knew to be of advantage, and then he left them and placed himself before them to the side. He had but few men who were with him, for at that time there were only five knights who would speak to him, all the others having sworn to respect the command of Holy Church.'

'When the advance guard of the first company of [imperial knights] approached the division of my lord of Beirut and the king, Sir Balian spurred through a most evil place, over rocks and stones, and went to attack the others above the middle of the pass. So much he delayed them and did such feats of arms that no one was able to enter or leave this pass … Many times was he pressed by so many lances that no one believed that he would ever be able to escape. Those who were below with the king saw him and knew him well by his arms and each of them cried to my lord of Beirut: "Ah, Sir, let us aid Sir Balian, for we see that he will be killed there above". [The Lord of Beirut] said to them: "Leave him alone. Our Lord will aid him, and it please Him, and we shall ride straight forward with all speed, for if we should turn aside, we might lose all".'[120]

Ultimately, the Ibelins routed the emperor's men and drove them back to the north coast, and Balian was still alive. The Lord of Beirut appears to have seen his son's survival against such odds as a sign of God's grace. He abandoned his attempt to force Balian to set Eschiva aside and again placed Balian in command, this time conducting the siege of Kyrenia, the last Cypriot fortress still in imperial hands. Following the surrender of Kyrenia, Balian was rewarded by the (now adult) king of Cyprus with the position of constable of Cyprus. Interestingly, contemporary sources make no further mention of the excommunication. Historians assume that the pope, a political animal in this age, had seen the wisdom of withdrawing his excommunication and issuing the necessary dispensation for the marriage. After all, the pope himself was engaged in a vicious struggle against Frederick II.

In 1236, John d'Ibelin, the 'Old Lord of Beirut' died, and Balian succeeded him. Eschiva moved with him to Beirut as his lady. Indeed, she retained that title until her death and her eldest son John succeeded to the barony at his father's death.

In the decade following his father's death, Balian and Eschiva may have divided their time between Beirut and Cyprus because Balian remained constable of Cyprus, although he also took part in the Baron's Crusade of 1239–1241. In 1241, Balian's signature headed the list of names petitioning Frederick II to appoint Simon de Montfort, the English Earl of Leicester, baillie of Jerusalem, but the suggestion fell on deaf ears. In 1243, Balian headed the faction that persuaded the barons of Jerusalem to swear homage to Alice de Champagne. He personally led the risky attack on Tyre, which drove the emperor's representative into exile and ended the imperial presence in the Kingdom of Jerusalem.

At the death of Alice de Champagne, Henry I of Cyprus became regent of Jerusalem and named Balian of Beirut his deputy, ruling from Acre. Here, as effective king of Jerusalem, Balian died of unknown causes, aged 40, on 4 September 1247. Eschiva was widowed a second time, although she now had at least one son, John of Beirut II, who had already come of age. Eschiva appears to have left her son in Beirut and returned to Cyprus, as it is here that Jean de Joinville, the seneschal of France crusading with St Louis, encountered her.

Joinville calls her his cousin because she was the first cousin to the then Count of Montbéliard, as he was himself. He also tells us that she outfitted a small ship at her own expense to aid the crusaders in their amphibious assault on the Egyptian coast and put it at his disposal. Joinville transported eight of his horses on her ship and, during the landing before Damietta, used Eschiva's boat for his landing.[121] This is the last we hear of Eschiva.

Like so many mediaeval women, Eschiva emerged as an independent actor only after she was widowed. After Gerard de Montaigu had been killed, she took fate into her own hands by marrying the man of her choice without the approval of her overlord, her brother or her new father-in-law. She defied the Church by refusing to separate from Balian despite the ban of excommunication. Although her ability to first provision a garrison under siege and later outfit a galley for an amphibious military operation were a function of her wealth, it is noteworthy that many other women of equal wealth did not take such an active interest in the defence of the realm. Conspicuous for its absence is any mention of Eschiva's beauty. Yet it is the episode in which Eschiva disguises herself as a man and crosses twenty miles of enemy-held territory to reach a castle about to be besieged that gives us the best glimpse of Eschiva. Only a woman of extraordinary courage, cleverness and cool nerves would have successfully evaded the notoriously brutal marauding imperial troops. These are the qualities, I believe, that enabled her to capture the heart of the boldest knight of her age, Balian d'Ibelin of Beirut.

Isabella I, Ruling Queen of Jerusalem (b. 1172 – d. 1205, reigned 1192–1205)

Although she was born a princess and ruled Jerusalem for twelve years, Isabella is usually portrayed as a pawn in history books and literature. While Isabella's life was short, eventful and at times tragic, dismissing her as a puppet does her an injustice. She played a significant role in the history of the Holy Land through her conscious choices as an adult.

Isabella was born in 1172, the daughter of King Amalric of Jerusalem, by his second wife, Maria Comnena, a great-niece of the Byzantine Emperor Manuel I. At the time of her birth, her half-brother Baldwin was already 11 years old and suffering from leprosy. There can be little doubt that her sex was a disappointment to her father, who had undoubtedly hoped for a son to replace the stricken Baldwin as his heir. (It was the custom in the Kingdom of Jerusalem for noblemen suffering from leprosy to abdicate their secular titles and join the religious Order of St Lazarus.) Amalric was still young (in his 30s), and his wife Maria was not yet 20, so he undoubtedly hoped a male heir might yet be born in the future.

Just two years later, however, Amalric fell victim to dysentery and died. Isabella's half-brother Baldwin was recognised as King of Jerusalem and placed under the regency of the Count of Tripoli. Isabella's mother, a 21-year-old widow, retired from court to her dower lands, the wealthy barony of Nablus, taking her 2-year-old daughter with her. Nablus was known for its scents and soaps and its large, cosmopolitan population of Jews, Orthodox, Latin Christians and Muslims. (The latter were specifically granted the right to engage in the hajj to Mecca.) For Isabella, it must have been an exciting place to live.

When Isabella was 5, her mother chose a new husband, Balian d'Ibelin. He was the younger (landless) brother of the wealthy second Baron of Ibelin, Ramla and Mirabel. The king, who explicitly sanctioned the marriage, was probably responsible for persuading the baron of Ramla to transfer the comparatively insignificant barony of Ibelin to his younger brother to ensure he was a more 'suitable' match for the dowager queen of Jerusalem. Balian thus became Isabella's stepfather – and the first and only father she knew ever.

For the next three years, Isabella lived with her mother and stepfather, spending time (one presumes) at both Nablus and Ibelin. She soon had two new half-siblings, a sister Helvis and a brother John, born to her mother and stepfather. Yet, her idyllic childhood abruptly ended at age 8. The king's mother, Agnes de Courtenay, convinced her son that his half-sister was a threat to his throne. To ensure that the threat posed by Isabella was neutralised, she was betrothed at the age of eight to another pawn: the underage nobleman Humphrey de Toron. Humphrey was firmly under the control of his widowed mother and her new and notorious husband, Reynald de Châtillon. Thus, Isabella was taken from the only family she had ever known over the furious objections of her mother and stepfather and imprisoned in one of the most exposed castles of the kingdom: Kerak. Furthermore, possibly on orders from Agnes de Courtenay, Châtillon's lady expressly prohibited the child from visiting her parents for the next three years. In this phase of her life, Isabella was indeed nothing but a pawn.

In late 1183, for reasons lost to history, someone (Châtillon? The king? Agnes de Courtenay?) decided it was time for Isabella and Humphrey to marry. Isabella was only 11 and below the canonical age of consent; she had nothing to say about the matter. Her mother and stepfather were not present and presumably not consulted. Humphrey was, by now, at least 15 and possibly a couple of years older, which may have prompted the marriage as there was the risk that since he could now govern his own affairs, he might choose to break the betrothal; a marriage, on the other hand, could not so easily be reversed. Whatever the reasons, the marriage was planned, and the nobility of Outremer was invited to attend.

The guests had started to gather when Saladin's armies overran the town of Kerak and laid siege to the castle. Coincidentally, a session of the High Court was taking place in Jerusalem. Because most of Jerusalem's barons attended the latter, Saladin's siege trapped the kingdom's leading ladies but not their husbands in the besieged fortress. Among these were Isabella's mother, who was seeing her daughter for the first time in three years, Isabella's half-sister Sibylla (now 23 and married for a second time), and Queen Mother Agnes de Courtenay. Despite the circumstances, the marriage went ahead. Allegedly, Saladin agreed to spare the tower where the nuptials were taking place, even as he continued bombarding the rest of the castle with his siege engines. Before long, food and water rationing came into effect. The sanitary conditions of a castle crowded with townspeople and extra guests must have been unpleasant, but it held for roughly two months before the Army of Jerusalem under Baldwin IV came to its relief. Although no harm came to any of the high-born guests, it was hardly a promising start to Isabella's marriage.

The next phase of Isabella's life is poorly recorded. At the time of his betrothal, Humphrey de Toron's guardian (Châtillon) had agreed to return Humphrey's important barony of Toron to the crown. In exchange, Humphrey received a 'money fief' (a pension). Consequently, Isabella and Humphrey had no castle or fief in which to live and appear to have lived in town houses in either Acre or Jerusalem. For Isabella, the implications of her husband's abdication of effective baronial power may not have been evident (she was only 11, after all), and she probably enjoyed being able to visit with her mother, stepfather and four Ibelin half-siblings at last.

Then in 1186, the boy King Baldwin V, who had succeeded the 'Leper' King Baldwin IV, died without a direct heir. The barons of Jerusalem had earlier sworn to seek the advice of the kings of England and France, the Holy Roman Emperor and the pope regarding a successor, but the Western rulers were far away. Furthermore, Isabella's half-sister, the mother of Baldwin V and sister of Baldwin IV, felt she ought to succeed to the throne. While most acknowledged she had a legitimate claim, the majority of barons and bishops abhorred her husband, Guy de Lusignan, and resisted crowning her. Sibylla consequently organised a coup. Without the consent of the High Court of Jerusalem but with the help of the Templars and Reynald de Châtillon, she contrived to have herself crowned and anointed in the Church of the Holy Sepulchre. After she was anointed, she crowned Guy as her consort over the opposition of the patriarch, who refused to crown him.

Most of the barons and bishops were not in Jerusalem to witness Sibylla's usurpation of the throne; they were meeting in Nablus to discuss options. The news that Sibylla had seized the throne and crowned her detested husband pushed them to act. It was agreed that Isabella, the other surviving child of King Amalric, should be crowned in Bethlehem as the legitimate queen. Isabella offered an ideal alternative to the usurpers because, as the child of Amalric's second marriage, she was not tainted with illegitimacy. Furthermore, she had been born after he was crowned and anointed, an essential point in mediaeval inheritance law. Her husband would, naturally, become king consort at her side.

The barons had not reckoned with Humphrey de Toron. Either from fear or simply because he remained abjectly loyal to his stepfather, Châtillon, Humphrey slipped away during the night to go to Jerusalem where he did homage to Sibylla and Guy. Without an alternative rallying point, the baronial resistance to Sibylla and Guy's coup d'état collapsed.

While these facts are recorded in history, how Isabella felt is not. Did Isabella side with her husband – and the man who had imprisoned her for three years? Or did she side with her mother and stepfather, who both vehemently opposed Sibylla and sought to put her on the throne? Did 14-year-old Isabella *want* to be queen? We have no way of knowing. Yet just because the historical record is silent, we should not assume she did not care. Like most barons, including her stepfather, Isabella accepted what Humphrey had done and made peace with Sibylla and Guy, but she may nevertheless have resented what happened intensely. It might well have created marital tensions.

Less than a year after usurping the crown, Guy de Lusignan led the army of Jerusalem to an unnecessary and devastating defeat. Not only was the battle lost, but thousands of fighting men were slaughtered, and the bulk of the remainder were enslaved. Most of the barons of Jerusalem were taken captive; among them was Isabella's husband, Humphrey.

Saladin offered to release Humphrey in exchange for the surrender of the critically important Frankish border fortresses of Transjordan (which

Humphrey had inherited after Saladin personally decapitated Reynald de Châtillon). According to some (romanticised) versions, Humphrey arrived home, only to have the garrisons refuse to obey his orders, at which point he voluntarily (or at his mother's urgings) returned to Saracen captivity. It is more probable that Humphrey's release was contingent on Kerak and Montreal being handed over to Saladin first. Since this never occurred, there was no chivalrous return to the dungeon from freedom. Both castles, however, were eventually reduced by siege, and, at that point, Saladin agreed to release Humphrey as he served no useful purpose in prison.

Humphrey and Isabella were reunited in early 1189 after roughly eighteen months of separation. Isabella's location between the catastrophe of Hattin and her reunion with Humphrey is unrecorded. Most probably, she was with her mother and stepfather since her stepfather was one of only three barons to have fought his way off the field of Hattin. With King Guy and most of the High Court in captivity, Ibelin was unquestionably one of the most important men in the entire kingdom (Arab chronicles from the period refer to him as 'like a king'). Furthermore, he commanded the respect of those fighting men who escaped capture with him. It would, therefore, have been logical for Isabella to seek his protection in this period.

Ibelin was in Tyre, the only city in the kingdom that did not fall or surrender to Saladin in the wake of Hattin. Also in Tyre at this time was Conrad de Montferrat, the brother of Queen Sibylla's first husband. Conrad was a man of high birth and good connections. More importantly, he had taken command of the defence of Tyre at a critical moment and enjoyed the support of the people, both residents and refugees. If Isabella were in Tyre, she and Conrad would have met and probably known each other well.

When Humphrey returned from captivity, however, he joined not the men who had successfully defended what was left of the kingdom but the architect of the disaster, Guy de Lusignan. Thus, when Guy de Lusignan foolishly decided to besiege Saracen-held Acre, Humphrey went with him. Isabella accompanied him to Acre, but we cannot know if she did so willingly.

A siege camp is not a pleasant place for anyone, much less a high-born lady, which begs the question: why would Isabella choose to expose herself to the filth, privations, confinement and mortal hazards of a siege? Was it love for her husband? The passionate desire not to be separated from him again after eighteen months of forced separation caused by his captivity? Or did she go at the insistence of her half-sister Sibylla, who was also at the siege with her two infant daughters and commanded the attendance of her little sister? Did Humphrey insist on Isabella coming with him because he was jealous of a budding friendship between his wife and Conrad de Montferrat? Any of these motives are plausible, but we will never know the truth.

The only thing that is certain is that Isabella was still there in November of 1190 when her half-sister Sibylla and her two nieces died of fever. In the eyes of the High Court, which had favoured her since the constitutional crisis of 1186, Isabella was the heir presumptive to the crown and, as such, the preferred candidate for the next ruler of Jerusalem.

In the middle of a November night, Isabella was dragged from the tent and bed she shared with Humphrey and taken into the custody of the leading prelates of the Church present at the siege of Acre. Among these were the Papal Legate, the Archbishop of Pisa; Philip, the Bishop of Beauvais; and Baldwin, the Archbishop of Canterbury, along with two other unnamed bishops. She was informed that an ecclesiastic inquiry would be conducted on the validity of her marriage to Humphrey de Toron.

At this point, Isabella had been living under the same roof as Humphrey for fourteen years and had been married to him for eleven. Although she had no children and the marriage had possibly never been consummated, she nevertheless viewed herself as legally married. All accounts agree that she objected to being taken from Humphrey and resisted the efforts to annul her marriage because she loved him.

All accounts also agree that during the proceedings, Isabella's attitude changed. Clerics in the service of the English king and bitterly hostile to her second husband attribute her change of heart to the misogynous thesis that 'a girl can easily be taught to do what is morally wrong' and that 'a woman's opinion changes very easily'.[122] More neutral contemporary accounts attribute her change of heart to her mother's influence.

> [Maria Comnena] remonstrated ... that she [Isabella] could not become the lady of the kingdom unless she left Humphrey. [The queen mother] reminded [her daughter] of the evil deed that [Humphrey] had done, for when the count of Tripoli and the other barons who were at Nablus wanted to crown him king and her queen, he had fled to Jerusalem and, begging forgiveness, had done homage to Queen Sibylla ... So long as Isabella was his wife she could have neither honour nor her father's kingdom, Moreover ... when she [Isabella] married she was still under age and for that reason the validity of her marriage could be challenged.[123]

The dowager queen's arguments are enlightening. The Constitution of Jerusalem required a reigning queen to have a consort, and Isabella was married to a man who had betrayed the High Court of Jerusalem in 1186. The

High Court of Jerusalem was unprepared to do homage to the man who had betrayed them.

Unstated because it was obvious to all involved in this incident: the Kingdom of Jerusalem had been reduced to the single city of Tyre following the disastrous Battle of Hattin, and the desperate bid to recapture the city of Acre had bogged down into a war of attrition with the besiegers surrounded by the army of Saladin. Jerusalem needed a legitimate queen and a king capable of leading the fight to recover the lost kingdom. Isabella's husband, Humphrey de Toron, was patently not that man. Thus, regardless of Isabella's impeccable claim to the throne, the High Court (which consisted of the barons and bishops of the kingdom) was not prepared to recognise her as queen unless and until she set aside Humphrey de Toron and took another husband more suitable to the High Court.

The High Court, it will be remembered, had taken the same stance with both her father and elder sister, compelling her father to set aside his first wife Agnes de Courtenay and demanding that her sister divorce Guy de Lusignan. Her father apparently willingly complied with the demands of the High Court, while Sibylla agreed to divorce Guy only on the condition that she be allowed to choose her next husband. However, after she had been crowned and anointed queen, she had blithely announced that she chose none other than Guy de Lusignan as her new husband. In short, she reneged on her promise to put him aside. This incident was very much on the minds of the barons when they faced a similar situation in 1190. They were determined not to repeat their mistake of four years earlier. Isabella had to be legally separated from Humphrey before the High Court would acknowledge her as queen.

The Catholic Church, on the other hand, upheld the sanctity of marriage. Isabella's marriage to Humphrey could not simply be invalidated. There had to be a reason for annulling it, and this, too, is stated explicitly in the argument put forth by her mother: she had not yet attained the legal age of consent at the time of her marriage. This objective fact was both indisputable and not subject to Isabella's whim. Whether she liked it or not, she was not legally married in the eyes of the Church. Five prelates, including a papal legate, ruled her marriage to Humphrey invalid.

Most accounts of Isabella's divorce in history and literature latch onto the fact that she initially resisted the divorce 'out of love for Humphrey' and that her mother 'remonstrated with' (i.e., bullied) her as evidence that Isabella was again only a pawn in the hands of the powerful people around her. They ignore the fact that Isabella changed her testimony, admitting she had not consented to the marriage with Humphrey. Then, once the marriage to Humphrey was dissolved, she married Conrad Marquis of Montferrat within a week. In short, she did not follow her sister's example of remarrying her first husband. This is an important point. Although her marriage to Humphrey as a child was not valid because she had been below the canonical age of consent, she *could* have married Humphrey as a consenting adult in 1190 had she wanted to. That she did not says one thing: Isabella preferred to wear the (at that point almost worthless) crown of Jerusalem over marriage to the man she reputedly loved.

So maybe she did not love Humphrey all that much? Or maybe she was more ambitious than people give her credit for? Either way, she made a choice.

Her second husband, Conrad de Montferrat, was a man with a formidable reputation at arms. He had almost single-handedly saved Tyre from surrender to Saladin in July 1187 and defended it a second time in December of that same year. Before that, he had charmed the court in Constantinople with his good looks, manners and education. He was twice Isabella's age at the time of their marriage.

Isabella would have had no illusions about why Conrad was marrying her – it was for the throne of Jerusalem. As a royal princess, that would neither have surprised nor offended her. Isabella and Conrad, one can argue, chose one another because together they offered the Kingdom of Jerusalem the best means of avoiding obliteration. The legitimacy of Isabella and the military prowess of Conrad gave the barons and people of Jerusalem a rallying point around which to build a comeback. Notably, Isabella called on her barons to do homage to her immediately after her marriage to Montferrat; that is the act of a woman determined to establish her position and remind her vassals of it.

Unfortunately for both Isabella and Conrad, the king of England, either out of feudal loyalty or sheer petulant hostility to his rival, the king of France (who was related to and backed Conrad), chose to uphold the claim of Sibylla's widowed husband Guy de Lusignan to the throne of Jerusalem. What this meant for Isabella was that, despite her marriage to the man preferred by the High Court, she was not recognised or afforded the dignities of a queen because the powerful king of England (who rapidly seized command of what we know as the Third Crusade) opposed her husband. Conrad responded by refusing to support Richard and by seeking a separate peace with Saladin. This can only have been an incredibly frustrating experience for Isabella, but she would have been cheered when she, at last, became pregnant in early 1192.

In April 1192, the English king finally relented, and word reached Tyre that he was prepared to recognise Isabella and Conrad as queen and king consort of Jerusalem. The people of Tyre, fiercely loyal to Conrad since he'd saved them from Saladin, rejoiced rapturously. In a dramatic gesture, Conrad asked God to strike him down if he did not deserve the honour of the crown of the Holy City. He then walked out into the streets to be stabbed by two assassins.

Mortally wounded, he was carried to his residence, where he died in agony in Isabella's arms. She was not yet 20 years old.

Isabella was, however, still the last surviving direct descendent of the kings of Jerusalem, and her kingdom had never needed her more. The king of England had already received news of his brother's rebellion and was anxious to return to the West. The precarious gains of the Third Crusade needed defending. Isabella had to remarry, and she had to remarry a man acceptable to the High Court and the king of England. But Isabella was an adult and a widow to whom the barons had already sworn homage. They could not force her into a new marriage. That Isabella remarried within eight days is not evidence of her powerlessness but demonstrates her sense of responsibility to her kingdom.

Furthermore, her choice shows exceptional intelligence and an understanding of the precarious balance of power among the crusaders fighting to restore her kingdom. She chose the nephew of the kings of England and France, a grandson of Eleanor of Aquitaine, Henri, Count of Champagne. The count had been one of the first to take the cross and come out to Outremer to fight for the recovery of Isabella's kingdom. He was only 26 years old and known as gallant and courteous. According to *Itinerarium*, far from being greedy for a crown, he was a reluctant candidate who was distressed by Isabella's situation and only persuaded to consent when she assured him that it was indeed her wish. Certainly, he never styled himself as king of Jerusalem, preferring the title to which he had been born.

In the five years of her marriage to Champagne, Isabella gave birth to a posthumous daughter by Montferrat, Maria, and three daughters by Champagne, Marguerite, Alice and Philippa. During this marriage, a degree of stability descended over her kingdom with a three-year, eight-month truce with the Saracens signed 2–3 September 1192. Then on 10 September 1197, Henri fell backwards from a window to his death. The circumstances remain obscure. A balcony or window frame possibly gave way, or he simply lost his balance in a sudden turn.

Isabella was again a widow, and the truce with Saladin had expired. The kingdom was again in need of a king capable of leading armies in its defence. As in 1192, Isabella was an adult ruling queen who no one could force to remarry. Her barons had sworn homage to her five years earlier. She was in control of her fate, but also accepted her duty to her kingdom. Four months after Champagne's death, Isabella married a fourth time, and again, her choice reflects her astute judge of character and uncanny understanding of power politics. She married a man with years of experience fighting in the Holy Land, strong credentials as a good administrator and popular with his peers. She chose her former brother-in-law, Aimery de Lusignan. They were crowned jointly as king and queen of Jerusalem in Acre in January 1198.

Their first child, Sibylla, was born the same year as their marriage (1198) and a second daughter, Melisende, followed two years later. Their son, named Aimery for his father, was born last but died first, in February 1205. Two months later, on 1 April 1205, King Aimery died of food poisoning; he would have been between 55 and 60 years of age. Isabella died shortly afterwards, likely shattered by the loss of her only son and her fourth husband in such quick succession. She was 33 years old.

Four of her daughters survived her. The eldest, Maria de Montferrat, the posthumous daughter of Conrad de Montferrat, was 13 years old and succeeded to the crown of Jerusalem. Isabella's eldest surviving daughter by Champagne, Alice, married Aimery de Lusignan's eldest son by his first marriage, Hugh I, king of Cyprus. Her eldest daughter by Aimery de Lusignan married Leo I, king of Armenia. Her youngest daughter Melisende married Bohemund IV, Prince of Antioch.

Isabella's life was short by modern standards and filled with drama: forced separation from her family at age 8, her dramatic divorce in the siege camp of Acre, the assassination of one husband, and the death of two more. Yet, there is no available evidence that she saw herself as a victim or pawn. Instead, she rose to her destiny and fulfilled it as best she could – every inch a queen.

Isabella II (Yolanda), Ruling Queen of Jerusalem (b. 1212 – d. 1228, reigned (legally, if not in fact) 1212–1228)

If any queen of Jerusalem was powerless, it was Isabella II, more commonly known as Yolanda. She was a queen almost from birth, yet never exercised the power of a monarch. Not only was she a pawn of emperors, kings and popes engaged in struggles beyond the scope of her kingdom, but she was also largely neglected as a child and abused as a bride. Her fate stands out as the exception to the rule of empowered women in Outremer.

Yolanda became queen of Jerusalem within days of her birth in November 1212. Her mother, Maria de Montferrat, through whom she derived her title, had died at the age of 20 from complications stemming from Yolanda's birth.

Yolanda was, thus, a half-orphan from birth, and her father, John de Brienne, was a parvenu newcomer to her kingdom. Immediately, voices were raised questioning her father's right to remain king. Powerful voices argued that her closest adult relative on her mother's side – the side from which she derived her title – should exercise the regency during her minority. John de Brienne rallied sufficient support for his claim to be regent for his infant daughter to retain his crown, but his position was precarious.

Less than two years after the death of Yolanda's mother, John de Brienne married a second time, this time the Armenian Princess Stephanie. Yolanda would still have been a toddler, mainly in the care of nannies, and Stephanie might well have acted as a surrogate mother to her. Perhaps for the next six years, Yolanda had what we would consider security and happiness surrounded by her father, stepmother and soon, a baby half-brother.

If it ever existed, that idyll was shattered when Stephanie and her son died in early 1220. Furthermore, they died at a time when the bulk of the fighting men were away in Egypt, taking part in the Fifth Crusade, and the Kingdom of Jerusalem was under attack by the sultan of Damascus. Caesarea had been captured and sacked, and other cities seemed likely to succumb to the same fate. Yolanda's father John de Brienne abandoned the Fifth Crusade and rushed home to defend the Kingdom of Jerusalem with the bulk of the Syrian barons and the Knights Templar. Yolanda would have been 7 years old – old enough to feel the pain of losing the only mother she had ever known and her little brother and old enough to sense the fear and alarm that had brought her father back from campaigning in Egypt.

Any joy she felt at seeing her father again was short-lived. John returned to Egypt and the Fifth Crusade, where his advice to trade Damietta (held by the crusaders) for Jerusalem (held by the Ayyubids) was ignored. Instead, the crusade made the fatal mistake of trying to march on Cairo and ended in a debacle. John himself had to stand hostage for the implementation of the negotiated settlement.

Eventually, John returned home to his now 8-year-old daughter, but not for long. In early 1221, he set off on a grand tour of the West, intended to raise money and troops for a new crusade. He would never again set foot in the Kingdom of Jerusalem. Instead, he traversed Europe, traveling as far north as England and Cologne but spending more time in Italy and Spain. During these travels, he secured his third wife, Berengaria of Castile, and negotiated the fateful marriage of Yolanda to the Holy Roman Emperor.

And Yolanda? Just 9 years old when her father departed, she was not yet 13 when she married Frederick II by proxy in Acre. The historical record tells us nothing about her activities during this time; we can only assume she was undergoing the kind of education thought suitable for queens in this period. Most likely, that education was entrusted to one of the convents that traditionally took daughters of the higher nobility into their ranks as pupils, nuns and abbesses.

The quality of such an education should not be underestimated. Convents had a long tradition of being centres of learning and, in the early thirteenth century, were still home to intellectual inquiry and debate. At a minimum, Yolanda learned to read and write in French and Latin. She may also have studied Greek, given how widespread the language was in the Holy Land and the existence of many religious texts still available in the original Greek. She would have been expected to know Christian dogma and theology, which entailed reading the Bible and other religious texts. She would have had a command of arithmetic, though not necessarily geometry or algebra. Yolanda would also have studied the history of her kingdom and its most important supporters, such as the Holy Roman Empire, France and England. She would probably have been educated about the kingdom's enemies, possibly including some knowledge of Arabic. (Many of Jerusalem's nobles were fluent in Arabic, and it was the native tongue of a substantial minority of the population, both Christian and Muslim.) Some knowledge of the natural sciences, particularly human biology and fundamental methods for treating common illnesses and injuries, might also have been included in the curricula. Mandatory studies would have included etiquette, protocol, spinning and needlework.

Yolanda's education would hardly have been considered complete, however, when envoys from the Holy Roman Emperor arrived in Acre with the news that her father had negotiated her marriage to the most powerful monarch on earth, a man already calling himself 'the Wonder of the World'. The wedding followed almost immediately. Still only 12 years old, Yolanda was married by proxy to Frederick in Acre and crowned queen in Tyre before setting sail with a large escort of prelates and noblemen for Apulia. She arrived at Brindisi and married Frederick II on 9 November 1225; it was just days before or after her thirteenth birthday. Her bridegroom was a 30-year-old widower who maintained a harem in the Sicilian tradition.

The marriage got off to a terrible start. John de Brienne had negotiated the marriage with either implicit or explicit assurances from the emperor that John would remain king of Jerusalem until his death. He saw the marriage of his daughter to the Holy Roman Emperor as a means of securing aid in the form of cash and troops to defend his kingdom. Frederick Hohenstaufen, however, declared himself king of Jerusalem the day after the wedding and insisted the barons who had escorted Yolanda to Italy swear fealty to him at once.

John de Brienne was outraged, and so was the Master of the Teutonic Knights, Herman von Salza, who had been instrumental in the negotiations. The latter's indignation strongly suggests that Brienne had not simply been deluding himself. It appears that Frederick had intentionally misled Brienne about his intentions or had lied outright. In any case, Frederick instantly made an enemy of his father-in-law, and the breach ensured that Yolanda never saw her father again.

Perhaps, given how often he had been away during her short life, Yolanda did not miss him, but she found no comfort or companionship from her husband either. Although it is hard to distinguish facts from propaganda, the tales of Yolanda's marriage are unremittingly negative. The horror stories start with one contemporary chronicle that claims Frederick scorned his bride on the wedding night to seduce one of her ladies instead. Several sources agree that 'soon after the marriage, Frederick imprisoned, or otherwise maltreated, his wife'.[124]

Within six months, Yolanda's father was openly at war with her husband by supporting the ever-rebellious Lombard League. Allegedly, the frustrated emperor took out his rage on his 13-year-old bride, beating her so brutally that she miscarried the child she was carrying, according to the *Chronicle of Ernoul*. Whether her husband's abuse was the cause, Yolanda miscarried a child at about this time; she would have been at most 14 years of age.

Meanwhile, Frederick was under increasing pressure to fulfil his repeated promises to go to the aid of the Holy Land. He had first taken crusading vows in 1215 and eleven years later had nothing but excuses to show for it. During the negotiations for his marriage to Yolanda, he had promised to set out on crusade no later than August 1227 or face excommunication. In the summer of 1227, a great army was assembled in Apulia with the goal of liberating Jerusalem from Muslim control, but before the crusaders could embark, they were devastated by a contagious disease that killed thousands. Frederick boarded a vessel but was so ill that his companions urged him to turn back. Frederick put about and landed not in the Holy Land but in Sicily. The pope promptly excommunicated him.

And Yolanda? She remained imprisoned in Frederick's harem. He had not even thought to take her with him when he set off for her kingdom. She was also soon pregnant again.

On 5 May 1228, ten days after delivering a son, Yolanda of Jerusalem died. She was not yet 16. Although she had been a queen almost from the day of her birth, not once had she exercised the authority to which she had been born.

Frederick hardly took any notice of her demise. He continued to claim her kingdom as his own, despite denying his father-in-law the same dignity. Because of his disregard for the laws and customs of Yolanda's kingdom, he soon found himself at loggerheads with the barons of Jerusalem. In the end, Yolanda's subjects defeated her husband, but only decades after she had been sacrificed on the altar of her father and husband's ambitions.

The extent to which Yolanda was a helpless pawn in this game of kings, popes and barons is striking. It is particularly noteworthy when one considers how powerful her predecessors had been. Queen Melisende commanded the support of barons and bishops to such an extent that her husband was forced to submit to her will. Sibylla refused to cave into pressure from her brother King Baldwin IV and foisted her (utterly unsuitable) candidate for king upon the entire kingdom. Isabella I went through four husbands but was never pushed off the stage, imprisoned, neglected or ignored. She remained queen of Jerusalem after her fourth husband's death. Was it just circumstances, particularly Yolanda's youth, that condemned her to a life little better than a slave's? Or was it the interplay of personalities? Emperor Frederick was certainly full of pompous pride and arrogance, but could a different girl have confronted him more forcefully or defended her undeniable rights more effectively? We will never know.

Iveta, Princess of Jerusalem, Abbess of St Lazarus at Bethany (b. 1120 – d. 1178)

Iveta is too readily dismissed as insignificant because modern readers underestimate the independence and influence of women in the Church in this period. Iveta was an abbess at a time when the power of women in such a position was at its height, as the examples of Hildegard von Bingen, Mathilda of Fontevrault and Herrad of Landsberg illustrate. There is no evidence to support the thesis that Iveta was forced to take the veil against her will. Iveta's biography is a reminder that women in the clerical sphere enjoyed a high degree of independence and power.

Iveta was the youngest of the four daughters born to King Baldwin II of Jerusalem by his Queen, Morphia. Born in 1120, she was the only one of his children born after Baldwin II was crowned king. Furthermore, her older sisters were substantially older, Melisende by fifteen years, Alice by ten, and Hodierna by nine. Therefore, it is unlikely she had a close relationship with any of them.

Furthermore, Iveta was just 3 years old when her father was taken captive by the Saracens, and 4 or 5 when she was sent into Saracen captivity as a hostage for the payment of her father's ransom. Although, as discussed above, there is no evidence that Iveta was mistreated, much less sexually abused, it would surely have been a traumatic experience for a 5-year-old to leave her home and family. At least one nurse probably accompanied her, perhaps a nurse known for her piety whose mandate was to protect Iveta from attempts to convert her to Islam. Certainly, she would have been aware that she was in the hands of 'the enemy' and among people speaking a different language and following a different faith.

Iveta spent roughly eighteen months in Saracen hands until her father had paid off his ransom; she was returned to Jerusalem in 1125. One presumes she was relieved to be reunited with her mother and sisters. But that joy was tragically short-lived. Her mother died within a year in 1126, and the marriages of her sisters Alice and Hodierna to the Prince of Antioch and the Count of Tripoli respectively, followed shortly afterwards. It is not unreasonable to suppose that Iveta felt lonely, possibly even out of place or unwanted. Yet her eldest sister Melisende was still in Jerusalem and, at 21, may well have become a surrogate mother to her. Undoubtedly, the sisters remained close all their lives.

In 1134, at the age of 14 and an adult under mediaeval law, Iveta entered the Benedictine convent of St Anne in Jerusalem, as a novice. There is no reason to believe she was forced into the convent against her will, much less to suppose she was sequestered there following a scandal of some kind. Four years later, she entered the newly founded nunnery at St Lazarus in Bethany, which had been lavishly endowed by her sister Melisende, now the ruling queen. Indeed, Melisende's patronage continued throughout her reign, and Bethany prospered both from royal gifts and the considerable pilgrimage traffic to the site of St Lazarus' tomb and the home of Mary and Martha, beside which the convent was located.

Iveta was elected abbess by the convent chapter in 1144 at age 24. In this capacity, she took charge of the substantial financial resources, management of the various estates, upkeep of the buildings and pilgrimage sites and administration of the convent itself with its population of nuns and lay sisters. Iveta was, in short, an independent and wealthy landlord with her own seal, household and staff. She is credited with influencing ecclesiastical appointments due to her position and royal blood. She nursed her sister Melisende at the end of the latter's life and was likely with the queen when she died in 1161.

Two years later, after her nephew Amalric had set aside his wife Agnes de Courtenay in order to wear the crown of Jerusalem, Iveta was entrusted with rearing King Amalric's daughter by Agnes, Princess Sibylla. Sibylla was 4 years old, close to the same age Iveta had been when she was a hostage of the Saracens. Sibylla remained under Iveta's care for thirteen years, receiving a rigorous education until her marriage to William of Montferrat in 1176 at the age of 17.

Iveta, never subject to a husband or brought to childbirth, lived to the comparatively old age of 56 or 57, dying sometime between 1176 and 1178.

Maria Comnena, Princess of Constantinople, Queen Consort of Jerusalem and Lady of Ibelin (b. ca 1154 – d. 1217)

Ever since Richard I's chronicler depicted her as 'godless' and 'fraudulent', novelists and historians alike have vilified the Greek wife of King Amalric, Maria Comnena. These portrayals of her, which include one novelist depicting her as a witch poisoning her own daughter, are based on the slander spread by opponents of Conrad de Montferrat and Alice de Champagne respectively. Reliable contemporaries such as William of Tyre have only good to say about her. It's time to set the slander aside.

Maria Comnena was probably born in 1154 or 1155. She was the great-niece of the ruling Byzantine Emperor, Manuel I, and, as a member of the Byzantine imperial family enjoyed the famously luxurious lifestyle of Byzantine royalty in her youth. More importantly, she undoubtedly also benefited from the high level of education typical of the women of her family. The Comnenas were literate in Greek classics, well-versed in theology and history and wrote the latter.

When Amalric I of Jerusalem decided to seek a second wife, he turned to the Byzantine Emperor and sent an embassy to Constantinople in 1165. Although we do not know why, Emperor Manuel and Amalric's ambassadors settled on Maria as the most suitable candidate. Two years later, Maria Comnena landed at Tyre. She was, at most, 12 or 13, while her bridegroom, King Amalric, was already 30.

While Maria's young age precluded a major role in politics, she may have had a guiding or oversight role in the magnificent renovation of the Church of the Nativity. This work, which included beautiful mosaics with a heavy Byzantine influence, was initiated after her arrival in the Kingdom of Jerusalem and employed many Byzantine master craftsmen. It is also notable that four years after his marriage to Maria, Amalric undertook a state visit to Constantinople. Amalric was the first Latin king to do so as a reigning monarch. Furthermore, Byzantine sources suggest he acknowledged Manuel I as his overlord during this trip.

In 1172, Maria gave birth to a daughter, Isabella. Since Maria was, at most, 18 at the time, expectations for further children would have been high. Instead, two years later, King Amalric was dead, succumbing to dysentery following a short military campaign. As the crowned queen of Jerusalem, Maria would have taken part in the sessions of the High Court of Jerusalem that followed, including the one that elected the next king. Without serious dissent, the choice fell on Amalric's only son, Baldwin, a son from his first marriage. Baldwin was crowned King Baldwin IV. Tragically, he was already suffering from leprosy.

Maria, now the dowager queen, retired from court and did not attempt to interfere in the government of the realm. She withdrew to her dower lands, the barony of Nablus. This wealthy and important lordship, directly north of the royal domain of Jerusalem, owed eighty-five knights to the feudal levee, making it militarily one of the strongest baronies in the kingdom. It was home to a diverse population of Samaritans, Jews and Muslims, in addition to Latin settlers. Thus, at the age of 20, Maria Comnena was an independently wealthy and powerful widow. Furthermore, the laws of the Kingdom of Jerusalem ensured that she could not be forced into a second marriage by her stepson or great-uncle.

Notably, rather than scheming, as historians and novelists would have you believe, Maria had so little involvement in the politics of the realm that she did not appear in the historical record again until mid-1177. Philip II, Count of Flanders, had come to the Holy Land with a small army of crusaders and sought Maria out in Nablus. Flanders was at loggerheads with Baldwin IV and the High Court of Jerusalem about a proposed campaign against Egypt. The Byzantines and Latins were undertaking this campaign jointly, and Manuel I had sent a fleet of seventy warships. That Flanders sought out Maria in Nablus suggests he saw her as a woman who could advise him on the likely reaction of the Byzantine Emperor to his actions and demands. Even more noteworthy, as a result of his meetings with Maria, he had a change of heart. From Nablus, he sent messengers to Jerusalem, declaring his acceptance of the High Court's plans for the campaign in Egypt. Maria Comnena, at 23, was obviously a woman who could talk politics with the savviest of Western noblemen and be persuasive without the slightest personal interest in the outcome.

In late 1177, Maria Comnena made a surprise second marriage, selecting as her husband the landless younger brother of the Baron of Ibelin, Ramla and Mirabel, Balian d'Ibelin. Although it is recorded that Maria had the explicit consent of the king for this marriage, there is no reason to suppose the marriage was imposed on her. The fact that the candidate was the younger brother of a local baron from a parvenu family makes it all but certain he was her choice; otherwise, she could have rejected him as beneath the dignity of a Comnena. No one, much less the weakened Baldwin, would have risked a break with the Byzantine Emperor over a marriage that brought no apparent advantages to the crown. In short, we can assume that Maria's marriage to Balian d'Ibelin was a love match, at least on her side.

Shortly thereafter, Maria faced the first serious crisis of her life. Her daughter by Amalric, 8-year-old Isabella, was taken from her against her will in 1180. The king, allegedly on his mother's advice, had betrothed his half-sister Isabella to Humphrey de Toron, and Isabella was sent to live with her future husband. Humphrey, still a minor, was living with his mother and her third husband, the infamous Reynald de Chatillon. The timing of the marriage is significant. Agnes had just engineered (or at least secured her son's consent to) the marriage of her daughter Sibylla to Guy de Lusignan. She thereby earned the enduring enmity of Baldwin d'Ibelin, Baron of Ramla and Mirabel, who had harboured hopes of marrying Sibylla. Due to this ill-advised marriage, the Ibelins (and other barons of Jerusalem) became bitter opponents of Guy de Lusignan. Under the circumstances, King Baldwin ostensibly felt it was advisable to remove his half-sister Isabella from Ibelin control.

The historical record demonstrates that King Baldwin was unjustified in imputing treasonous intentions to the Ibelins; both brothers remained staunchly loyal to Baldwin and his nephew and heir. Furthermore, there is no objective way to portray the removal of a small child from her mother's care to place her in the hands of a notoriously brutal and unscrupulous man as benign. It was a cruel, vindictive act that undoubtedly acerbated the hostility between Maria and Agnes – and between the Ibelins and Lusignans – to the detriment of the kingdom.

For three years, Isabella was denied the right to visit her mother in Nablus. It was not until 1183 that Maria saw her daughter again when Isabella married Humphrey at the age of 11. No sooner had Maria, Agnes and other wedding guests arrived at the bleak castle of Kerak set atop a mountain overlooking the desert than Saladin laid siege to the castle. Maria was trapped inside with her daughter, her new son-in-law and hundreds of wedding guests.

Meanwhile, the bulk of the barons of Jerusalem, including her husband, were gathered in Jerusalem at a meeting of the High Court. It was a stormy session in which the barons unanimously refused to accept Guy de Lusignan as regent or go to the relief of Kerak (and incidentally both princesses of Jerusalem). That is quite a resounding vote of "no-confidence" in Guy de Lusignan. Baldwin IV, now completely lame and going blind because of his leprosy, had to take up the reins of government and personally lead the royal army to the relief of Kerak. Saladin retreated.

One year later, Maria found herself under siege a second time, this time in her barony of Nablus. After a second siege of Kerak had been thwarted by the timely arrival of the feudal host of Jerusalem, Saladin withdrew, plundering and burning his way north to Damascus. Nablus, an unwalled town, was in his path. Since Ibelin was with the feudal army summoned by the king, Maria commanded at Nablus. Remarkably, there were no Frankish casualties because Maria provided refuge for the entire civilian population inside the citadel, in marked contrast to neighbouring towns and cities.

The next time Saracen forces threatened to overrun Nablus, such a response was unthinkable. In July 1187, Saladin obliterated the Christian army, killing or enslaving roughly 17,000 men and taking the king of Jerusalem, most of his barons, and the grand masters of both the Templars and Hospitallers captive. In short, like every other city and castle in the crusader kingdom, Nablus had no hope of relief because there was no longer an army capable of coming to its aid. Maria was a realist. She abandoned Nablus and fled to Jerusalem with her children, household, and probably most of the other inhabitants of her barony.

Jerusalem was flooded with refugees from the surrounding countryside. Most were women, children, churchmen and elders because able-bodied men had been called up to the army and were now dead or enslaved. The leaders selected (by what means we do not know) to represent the city refused Saladin's generous terms for surrender. They answered Saladin by saying they preferred martyrdom to shame.

Maria Comnena was not part of the delegation, but as dowager queen, she had probably been involved in selecting both the spokesman and the answer. Yet it is hard to imagine she was not relieved when – against all odds – her husband appeared in Jerusalem to escort her and her four young children (all under the age of 10) to safety.

The arrival of Balian d'Ibelin in Jerusalem sometime after the fall of Hattin struck the Christians in Jerusalem as miraculous. He had escaped from the debacle at Hattin and gained the safety Tyre or Tripoli, yet he returned unarmed to bring his wife and children to freedom. This act, more than any other, suggests the depth of feeling Balian had for his wife. Other lords, notably Raymond of Tripoli, abandoned their wives to their fate, trusting Saladin's sense of honour not to harm them. Ibelin, in contrast, took the unprecedented – and risky – step of seeking a safe conduct from the victorious sultan. He also gave his word to go to the city unarmed and remain only a single night.

The arrival of a respected and experienced battle commander in the militarily leaderless city sparked widespread jubilation until the people learned Ibelin intended to rescue his family and withdraw. They begged him to remain and take command of the city's defences and resistance. The patriarch graciously absolved the Christian baron of his oath to the Muslim Saladin. Ibelin decided it was his duty to remain.

Did he decide alone? That is hardly conceivable. He had been married to Maria Comnena for almost ten years, yet she remained his social superior by many orders of magnitude. Ibelin would not have been in the habit of dictating to his wealthier, better-connected and higher-born wife. Maria Comnena must have shared his decision and very likely contributed to it – without knowing that Saladin had another surprise for them.

When Ibelin sent word to the sultan that he was compelled by the appeals of his compatriots to remain in Jerusalem, the sultan showed understanding and respect for the baron's decision. He sent fifty of his personal guard to Jerusalem to escort Maria Comnena and her children to safety. Why? The romantic answer is that he was chivalrous. The more realistic answer is that Maria Comnena was the first cousin of the Byzantine Emperor, and Saladin had signed a truce with the Byzantines. He had no desire to muddy the waters by having a Byzantine princess caught in a city he had vowed to take by storm. The risk of something happening to her, resulting in a diplomatic incident, was too high.

Maria must have been relieved for the sake of her children to get that escort to safety. She was probably equally distressed to leave her husband behind to almost certain death. She could not have known as she rode out of Jerusalem sometime in early September 1187 that Ibelin would pull off yet another miracle: the ransom of tens of thousands of Christian lives after the walls of the Holy City had been breached.

After the fall of Jerusalem, Maria was reunited with Ibelin, but they had lost their estates, castles and income. Yet although the Kingdom of Jerusalem had been reduced to the city of Tyre – a city under siege and frequent attack, Maria did not choose to return to Constantinople. Her decision to remain in the pitiful remnants of the crusader state was unquestionably a tribute and sign of her loyalty to her second husband.

Ibelin, probably with considerable misgivings and inner revulsion, joined the army that Guy de Lusignan had raised after his release in 1188 and took part in the Christian siege of Muslim Acre. Many women were in the Christian camp, including Queen Sibylla and her two daughters by Guy, and Maria's daughter Isabella, but Maria remained in Tyre. In November 1190, Sibylla of Jerusalem and her two daughters died of fever in the siege camp at Acre. With her death, Guy de Lusignan's right to the throne of Jerusalem was extinguished.

The next in line to the throne was Maria's daughter, Isabella. Isabella was 18 years old and still married to Humphrey de Toron, the man imposed on her as a child of 8 by her half-brother, Baldwin IV. The problem with Humphrey in the eyes of most of the surviving barons, knights and burghers of Jerusalem was that he was weak (some say effeminate). He was not credited with the ability to play a constructive role in regaining the lost territories of the kingdom. Perhaps more significantly, he had betrayed the barons once before. Following Guy de Lusignan's usurpation of the throne, most of the barons in the High Court wanted to crown Isabella, but Humphrey had slipped away in the dark to do homage to Guy and Sibylla. As a result, several barons refused to recognise Isabella as queen unless she first divorced Toron and married the candidate of their choice, Conrad de Montferrat.

Since Isabella had been married to Toron at age 11 (before the legal age of consent for girls in the twelfth century), there were legal grounds for the annulment of her marriage. However, Isabella had grown attached to Humphrey, and the chronicles agree that her mother had to 'browbeat' her into accepting a divorce. This is the source – the *only* source – for all the negative commentary about Maria Comnena's character.

The image of an unscrupulous and ambitious woman heartlessly pressuring a sweet young girl into betraying the man she loved has captured the imagination of chroniclers, historians and novelists alike. Yet it is a gross distortion of the facts. First, the sources are hostile to Conrad de Montferrat and/or Alice de Champagne should, therefore, be treated with caution. Second, the divorce was undoubtedly in the best interests of the Kingdom of Jerusalem, and Maria should be given credit rather than blame for putting the interests of the kingdom ahead of the affections of her teenage daughter. Third, there is no indication whatsoever that Maria profited from her daughter's marriage to Montferrat, as would have been the case had she acted from base motives. Finally, when Conrad de Montferrat was murdered, Isabella did not seek to marry Humphrey de Toron and make him king, although as an anointed queen, she was free to choose her husband. This makes clear that her attachment to him was less than critics of Maria would have us believe. Nor should this single incident outweigh Maria's demonstrated lack of meddling, grasping and self-aggrandisement throughout the rest of her life as queen, dowager and queen mother.

Isabella's elevation to the throne opened the gates for Maria to play a similarly sinister and interfering role in the politics of the kingdom as Agnes de Courtenay had done; she did not. Instead, she appears to have retired with Ibelin and their children to the much-reduced estates at their disposal. (Although the truce between Richard of England and Saladin did not restore either Nablus or any of the Ibelin lordships to Christian control, Ibelin was explicitly granted the smaller lordship of Caymont, northeast of Caesarea.) Ibelin, as the queen's stepfather, initially took precedence over all other lords in the kingdom, but he disappeared from the historical record after 1193. It is usually assumed that he became ill or died around this time, although he may have been active in Cyprus instead.

Maria Comnena is credited with helping reconcile Aimery de Lusignan with her son-in-law Henri de Champagne. She may also have acted as a go-between in the negotiations between Walter de Montbéliard, regent for Hugh I of Cyprus, and her son John of Beirut, regent for her granddaughter Maria de

Montferrat, concerning the marriage between Hugh and her granddaughter Alice de Champagne. As the unquestioned 'dowager par excellence' of the family, she would have played an influential role in the education of all of her grandchildren.

Maria Comnena died in 1217 when her 5-year-old great-granddaughter Yolanda was queen of Jerusalem. Her descendents dominated the history of the Latin East for the next century; the progeny from her first marriage ruled as queens of Jerusalem and Cyprus, while the offspring of her second marriage became the powerful, semi-royal Ibelin family that brought forth regents, constables, and seneschals for both kingdoms and multiple queen-consorts for Cyprus.

In the first two decades of her life, Maria was no less a pawn than any other princess sent to a foreign court to fulfil the diplomatic objectives of her family. Yet, from the day she became the dowager queen of Jerusalem, she took control of her fate. She married wisely and exercised influence prudently. In all recorded instances of her doings – whether advising Flanders to tone down his demands, defending Nablus from Saladin's troops, convincing her daughter to put the interests of her kingdom first, or reconciling her son-in-law with the king of Cyprus – her actions and intentions are characterised by selflessness and intelligence. Rarely, has a woman with such an unblemished record of wise behaviour suffered from such a baseless reputation for evil and intrigue. Few women are more deserving a revisionist reappraisal than Maria Comnena.

Maria de Montferrat, Ruling Queen of Jerusalem (b. 1192 – d. 1212, reigned 1210–1212)

Maria did not live long enough to leave much of an imprint on the historical record, much less a legacy, but as a ruling queen, she deserves a short biography.

Maria de Montferrat was the first and eldest child of Isabella I of Jerusalem. She was born to the uncrowned but acknowledged queen of a kingdom that had almost ceased to exist five years earlier. At the time of her birth, Maria's future kingdom clung to existence by its bare fingernails only after a massive intervention from the West known in history as the Third Crusade. She arrived in a world exhausted by warfare and entering a fragile three-year truce. Furthermore, her father, Conrad Marquis de Montferrat, was already dead, the victim of an assassin only months earlier.

As the ruling queen's firstborn, Maria was heir apparent from the day of her birth, but she would have grown up knowing that the birth of a brother would instantly displace her in the succession. That probably meant less to her as a child than the fact that she was raised by parents who were fond of one another. She soon had three half-sisters, Marguerite, Alice and Philippa, the daughters of her stepfather, Henri de Champagne.

When she was five, however, tragedy struck. The only father she had ever known fell to his death from a window in a bizarre accident. Such a loss would have been bad enough, but it occurred when the Saracens were threatening Acre. Maria would surely have been acutely aware of the alarm and distress of those around her.

Her mother rapidly married again, and Maria had a new stepfather, Aimery de Lusignan. He was substantially older than Henri de Champagne, having been born in 1153, so he was 44 at the time of his marriage to Isabella I. He already had several children by his first marriage. Although we cannot know for sure, it seems unlikely that Maria would have formed strong bonds with him.

She soon had two more half-sisters, Sibylla and Melisende, and in November 1204, a brother Amalric was born, displacing her as heir apparent. Her brother lived less than six months, however, dying in February 1205. Two months later, her stepfather died of food poisoning, and shortly after that, her mother also died. At 13 years of age, Maria de Montferrat was the queen of Jerusalem. It is hard to imagine that she rejoiced at her sudden elevation. No matter how ambivalent her feelings for her stepfather and infant brother may have been, the loss of her mother must have been devastating.

At 13, Maria was not of age to rule, so the control of her kingdom was put into the hands of her nearest male relative until she married. Her regent was her mother's half-brother, John d'Ibelin, Lord of Beirut. The Lord of Beirut would have been a frequent visitor at court and was unlikely to have been a stranger to her. Yet there is no reason to believe they were particularly close before he was appointed regent. Aside from keeping the Saracens at bay, his primary job was to find a suitable consort for Maria in cooperation with the High Court. The court initially pursued a possible marriage with the king of Aragon, but when this fell through, they sent to the king of France requesting him to suggest a candidate. King Louis' choice fell on John de Brienne. Maria had no say in the matter.

John de Brienne may not have come from the highest nobility, but by 1208, when he was selected as Maria's husband by the High Court of Jerusalem, he had already established a fine reputation as a tournament champion and dabbled in poetry and music. He came from Champagne, the heart of chivalry, and (probably not incidentally) was the first cousin of the then regent of Cyprus, Walter de Montbéliard. It took him two years to raise money and an entourage of 300 knights before arriving in 1210 to marry Maria. On his arrival, he was in his mid-30s; Maria was 18.

There is no reason to believe that Maria was displeased with her husband, but their reign did not get off to a good start. While the couple was being crowned jointly in Tyre, the Saracens attacked Acre. The attack was beaten off, and the newly crowned King John boldly retaliated with raids into Syria and Egypt. Yet while these yielded substantial plunder, they failed to secure territorial acquisitions. In retaliation, the Saracens seized control of Mont Tabor, a significant strategic position threatening Nazareth. Meanwhile, the knights that came to the Levant with Brienne had fulfilled their contracts and returned to France, leaving King John with insufficient troops to retake Mont Tabor or any other strategic objective. He was forced to seek another six-year truce with the Saracens.

This might have suited Maria well, as she was now pregnant. In November 1212, Maria gave birth to a daughter, who was named after the queen's mother, Isabella. Maria, however, survived the ordeal by only a few days.

Despite her short reign and tragic death at so young an age, there is no reason to assume that Maria would have been a powerless pawn as her daughter Yolanda became. She had been prepared to rule by her Comnena grandmother and one of the most celebrated legal scholars of the age, John d'Ibelin of Beirut. Consequently, she would have known her rights – and the traditions of her house – very well. Her consort, on the other hand, was disadvantaged in any power struggle with her by being an outsider and coming from a decidedly lower status. Had she lived, Maria would most likely have followed the traditions of Queen Melisende and might well have replicated Melisende's successful corporate monarchy model. Unfortunately, we will never know.

Melisende, Ruling Queen of Jerusalem (b. 1105 – d. 1161, reigned 1131–1161)

Melisende, born in 1105 and queen from 1131 until she died in 1161, was the first and unquestionably the most forceful of Jerusalem's queens. She was the hereditary heir to the kingdom and tenaciously defended her right to rule against her husband and son, weathering two attempts to sideline her. She was praised for her wisdom and administrative effectiveness, as well as for being a patron of the arts and the Church. Although largely forgotten, she ought to be remembered alongside her contemporaries, Empress Mathilda and Eleanor of Aquitaine, as one of the powerful women rulers of the twelfth century.

Melisende of Jerusalem was born in 1105, the first of four daughters born to King Baldwin II and his Armenian wife, Morphia of Melitene. At the time of her birth in Edessa, her father was Count of Edessa, but thirteen years later, in 1118, her father was elected by the High Court of Jerusalem to succeed Baldwin I. Some sources claim her father was urged at this time to set aside his Armenian wife and seek a new and better-connected bride who might bear him sons as Morphia had failed to do. Baldwin refused. Furthermore, he designated his eldest daughter his heir, and she was given precedence in the charters of the kingdom ahead of all other lords, both sacred and secular.

In 1128, when Melisende was already 23 years old, her father sent to the king of France, requesting a worthy husband for her. This appeal was sanctioned by the High Court, as all subsequent searches for consorts of Jerusalem's queens would be in the coming years. The French king proposed Fulk d'Anjou.

Although Anjou is a small county, in the twelfth century, it was a pivotal and powerful lordship in the heart of France. Fulk's mother had married Philip I of France, and Fulk's daughter had been engaged to William, the heir to Henry I of England. When William died in a shipwreck, the agreement was modified, so King Henry's daughter Mathilda married Fulk's eldest son and heir, Geoffrey. It was from the marriage of Mathilda and Geoffrey d'Anjou that the Angevin kings of England sprang.

Meanwhile, Fulk had travelled to the Holy Land and served with the Knights Templar. Now widowed, he responded positively to the proposed marriage to Melisende, although some sources contend he insisted on being named king, not merely consort. In fact, the terms may have been ambiguous or at least open to alternative interpretations. Certainly, Fulk had a reputation for centralising power and ruling unruly vassals with an iron fist. He was undoubtedly an able military leader, a vital qualification for ruling the ever-vulnerable Kingdom of Jerusalem.

In 1129, Fulk returned to the Kingdom of Jerusalem and married Melisende, now 24. He was, at once, associated with his father-in-law in the government of the kingdom. Nevertheless, when Melisende gave birth to a son the following year, the proud grandfather took the precaution of publicly investing his kingdom to his daughter, son-in-law and grandson, who had been named Baldwin after him. This was not a partitioning of the kingdom but a means of binding his vassals to his heirs. Furthermore, when he fell ill the following year, the king reaffirmed on his deathbed that his daughter Melisende, her husband Fulk and their joint son, Baldwin, were his successors. The year was 1131 and Melisende and Fulk were crowned jointly in the Church of the Holy Sepulchre after his death.

Despite this, Fulk evidently wanted to be the *sole* ruler of Jerusalem. Melisende was abruptly excluded from the charters of the kingdom, suggesting she was barred from power. The contemporary chronicle of Orderic Vitalis provides this revealing description of what happened next:

> To begin with [Fulk] acted without the foresight and shrewdness he should have shown and changed governors and other dignitaries too quickly and thoughtlessly. As a new ruler he banished from his counsels the leading magnates who from the first had fought resolutely against the Turks and helped Godfrey and the two Baldwins to bring towns and fortresses under their rule and replaced them by Angevin strangers and other raw newcomers ... turning out the veteran defenders, he gave the chief places in the counsels of the realm and the castellanships of castles to new flatterers.[125]

While this was bad enough, he also appeared to seek the removal of his wife, Melisende. The suspicion was that he wanted to push aside the legitimate heirs of Jerusalem and replace them with his younger son by his first wife, Elias. His weapon was a not-so-subtle attempt to sully his wife's reputation with an accusation of adultery. In 1134, Melisende was (conveniently) accused of a liaison with the most powerful of the local barons, Hugh, Count of Jaffa.

While all chronicles agree that the charges were trumped up, the very fact that King Fulk was presumed to be behind them induced Jaffa to refuse to face a trial by combat, apparently fearing foul play. The failure to show up for a trial by combat, however, gave the king the right to declare him (and, with him, the queen) guilty. This also gave Fulk justification for declaring Jaffa's fief forfeit. (Which some historians suggest may have been Fulk's primary motive in the first place.) What is notable about this incident is that the bulk of the High Court – and most significantly, the Church – sided with Jaffa rather than Fulk. This underlines the degree to which Melisende was viewed as innocent of wrongdoing and the degree to which the local nobility resented the Angevin influence.

When the royal army moved against Jaffa, the southern lords, many of them Jaffa's vassals, initially held firm for Jaffa. Then Jaffa made a severe tactical error: he sought military support from the Muslim garrison at Ascalon. The latter was delighted to see the Franks fighting among themselves and Jaffa beat off the royal army. However, the price was the loss of support among his men. Many of his vassals (and, incidentally, his constable, Barisan d'Ibelin) deserted his cause and reconciled with the king.

Yet, just when Fulk seemed on the brink of complete victory, the Church intervened to end the self-destructive civil war and forced Fulk to offer astonishingly mild terms to the rebels. Hugh of Jaffa and those men who had remained loyal to him were induced to surrender Jaffa and accept exile for a mere three years rather than the permanent loss of their fiefs, much less their lives. Although not explicit, subsequent events suggest that Melisende was behind this agreement, and Fulk was anything but happy with it. Before Hugh could leave the kingdom to begin his exile, however, he was stabbed in the streets of Acre by a knight widely believed to be fulfilling Fulk's wishes, if not his orders.

Hugh survived the attack and went into exile to die before the terms expired, but meanwhile, sympathy for the injured Hugh was so high that the Angevins found themselves in fear for their lives. Indeed, no one was more outraged than Queen Melisende. Contemporary historian, William of Tyre, reported that Fulk feared for his life in the company of the queen's men. Fulk had won the battle but lost the war. He had discovered he could not rule Jerusalem as he had ruled Anjou. He could not impose his counsellors and ignore the men (and their sons) who had conquered his kingdom for him one bloody mile at a time. Most importantly, he could not replace his wife at whim but must instead recognise her as her father had intended, as his co-regent and equal in power.

William of Tyre reports that after Jaffa's exile, Fulk 'did not attempt to take the initiative, even in trivial matters, without [Melisende's] knowledge'.[126] This assessment is underscored by the subsequent documentary evidence that shows Melisende again signing charters and otherwise actively engaged in the administration of the kingdom. She made some spectacular grants at this time (one presumes to her supporters), especially to the Church. The reconciliation was satisfactory enough to bring forth a second son, Amalric, born in 1136.

In 1138, when Fulk and Melisende's son Baldwin turned 8, he too was included in the charters of the kingdom. This reaffirmed his investiture along with his parents as a ruler of Jerusalem and restored the situation to what it had been at the time of Baldwin II's death. This troika of rulers continued until 1143, when Fulk died suddenly in a hunting accident at the age of 53.

At Fulk's death, there was no need for the High Court to convene and elect a new ruler because Melisende was already crowned, anointed and recognised, not merely as regent for her 13-year-old son but as queen in her own right. Therefore, Melisende continued to rule without debate or contradiction. Her son Baldwin III was crowned and anointed (and Melisende crowned a second time) on Christmas Day 1143. Since Baldwin was only 13, he was still a minor and not entrusted with an active role in governing.

During her son's minority, Melisende moved rapidly and vigorously to fill all critical crown appointments with men loyal to her. She deftly promoted her husband's chancellor to bishop, thereby eliminating his influence at the core of the kingdom with a 'golden handshake' that would offend no one. For the crucial position of constable, the effective commander-in-chief in the absence of a king, she appointed a relative and recent newcomer, Manassas of Hierges, a man dependent on her favour.

She could not stop the clock, however. In 1145, Baldwin III turned 15, the age at which heirs reached maturity in the Kingdom of Jerusalem. Baldwin and some members of the nobility expected he would now be permitted to rule. He was wrong, and Melisende had the law (and evidently the Church) on her side. She was an anointed queen, the hereditary heir, and had demonstrated her ability over the previous fourteen years. Because her husband had tried to sideline her, she was alert to the threat and determined to prevent her son from doing the same thing.

Although there is evidence that Baldwin made sporadic attempts to defy his mother, he failed, mainly because she had surrounded herself with (and evidently obtained the loyalty of) some of the most powerful men in the country. These included Rohard, Viscount of Jerusalem; Elinard, Lord of Tiberias and Prince of Galilee; Philip of Nablus and, through the latter, the lords of Ramla, Mirabel and Ibelin. These lords, combined with the royal domain in Hebron and around Jerusalem, gave Melisende solid control of Samaria and Judea – the heartland of the kingdom.

Yet Melisende could not undertake military action, so it was perhaps not surprising that it was in this field of endeavour that Baldwin sought to distinguish himself. In 1147 at 17 years of age, Baldwin blundered into a campaign against Damascus, issuing the arrière ban (which only he could do) and calling up all able-bodied men to defend the realm. It is unclear to what extent his mother had approved of the campaign, but when the military operation ended badly, despite the king's courage, Melisende could blame her son.

After this incident Melisende started including her second son, Amalric, on royal charters. This is significant and suggests that she saw him as a future co-ruler – or possibly a replacement – to Baldwin. Amalric, who was not born until 1136, had not known his father well and proved consistently loyal to his mother.

But Baldwin soon had another opportunity to shine militarily: the Second Crusade. In 1148, large forces had arrived in the Holy Land from the West. In a council meeting prior to the public council in Acre, the decision to attack Damascus (long an ally of Jerusalem) was taken by King Conrad III of Germany, the Knights Templar and Baldwin III – without his mother present. Baldwin III was also entrusted with the vanguard of the armies, following the kingdom's tradition that the frontline be led by the lord in whose territory the fighting would occur; only the king could lay claim to territory not yet conquered. Unfortunately, this campaign was another miserable failure, damaging the reputation of all participants (although the 18-year-old Baldwin III suffered less than Conrad III and Louis VII). In contrast, Melisende's reputation remained untarnished.

Yet Melisende's inability to physically defend the kingdom remained a handicap. In June 1149, the defeat of Raymond of Antioch by Nur ad-Din at the disastrous battle of Inab left the Principality of Antioch virtually defenceless. The surviving lords of Antioch called on the king of Jerusalem to come to their aid. Baldwin (now 19 years old) responded immediately and effectively. Naturally, the lords of Antioch had not called for the help of a woman. Yet just as significantly, Baldwin assumed political control of the principality – without any concessions to joint rule with his mother.

Melisende took note and started to reduce her son's role inside Jerusalem by issuing charters in her name alone. Tensions were undoubtedly rising between Melisende and her firstborn. Indeed, the conflict between them was beginning to affect the functionality of the kingdom. Around this time, Melisende appears to have forced the chancellor out of office without replacing him. The appointment of a chancellor required the consent of the High Court in which Melisende and Baldwin *jointly* presided. They were likely at loggerheads. Therefore, Melisende tried to replace the chancellery altogether, issuing charters under her privy seal. This forced Baldwin to do the same. The two monarchs were no longer ruling jointly but separately. It was a dangerous situation for a kingdom that was always vulnerable to outside attack.

While Melisende was effectively fighting a rearguard action to retain her hold on power, Baldwin, now 20, was on the ascent. He continued to increase his following and support in the north and along the coast in the economically vital coastal cities of Acre and Tyre. He won to his side the important and capable Humphrey of Toron II and Guy of Beirut. More significantly, he rebuilt the castle at Gaza, far to the south, thereby cutting off Ascalon, still in Egyptian hands. Rather than installing one of his supporters, he wisely handed the castle over to the Knights Templar, evidently a (not entirely successful) attempt at gaining their goodwill.

Baldwin was gaining power, but many lords remained loyal to Melisende. So much so that when Count Jocelyn of Edessa was captured in May 1150 and Baldwin wanted to lead a relief expedition, half his barons failed to follow his summons. This was a serious – and dangerous – breach of a vassal's feudal obligation and can only be explained if those barons did not recognise Baldwin's authority to issue a summons without his mother's consent. This indicates the degree to which Melisende's right to joint rule was still viewed as legitimate and the degree to which men respected her ability to exercise that right.

But with Edessa and Antioch (indirectly) at severe risk, this refusal to engage in a military relief operation did more to discredit Melisende and her supporters than strengthen them. Despite having a small following, Baldwin III went north and ably negotiated with the Muslims and Byzantines. Again in 1151, Baldwin successfully campaigned against Nur ad-Din in the northeast and fought off the Egyptian Fleet's naval attack against the coast. Baldwin III's stature and position vis-à-vis his mother increased with each diplomatic and military victory.

Meanwhile, the queen made a grave tactical error in advocating the marriage of her constable Manassas to the heiress of Ramla and Mirabel, the widow of Barisan d'Ibelin. The marriage rewarded her loyal and landless relative but alienated Barisan's three sons, causing them to change sides in the struggle with her son. To counter this loss, Melisende made a fatal mistake: she unilaterally created the County of Jaffa and named her favourite son Amalric count. Amalric was just 15 and, like her Constable Manassas, already a supporter. In short, it gained her little, but provoked Baldwin, who could no longer afford to let his mother ignore him. Furthermore, the elevation of his brother may have made Baldwin fear that his mother intended to replace him altogether.

At Easter 1152, Baldwin III demanded a coronation in the Church of the Holy Sepulchre without his mother. In mediaeval parlance, this was a clear bid for exclusive power. The Patriarch of Jerusalem, a staunch supporter of Melisende, begged Baldwin to include his mother. When Baldwin refused, the Patriarch refused to carry out a coronation. Baldwin countered by conducting a public crown-wearing ceremony, sparking a debate in the High Court. Here Baldwin upped the stakes by demanding that the kingdom be divided territorially between himself and his mother. Surprisingly, the High Court agreed, although it was clear that such a division would weaken an already vulnerable kingdom.

Almost immediately, however, Baldwin appointed Humphrey de Toron his constable and initiated military action against his mother. He captured Mirabel, held by the queen's loyal constable Manassas, and forced him into exile. He then occupied the unfortified city and barony of Nablus, his mother's principal power base. With men rapidly going over to Baldwin, Queen Melisende retreated to the Tower of David with just a handful of loyal followers: her younger son Amalric, Philip of Nablus and Rohard, Viscount of Jerusalem.

Although the patriarch met Baldwin before the gates of Jerusalem and urged him to withdraw, Baldwin sensing victory refused.

The citizens of Jerusalem, long loyal to Melisende, could tell which way the wind was blowing and opened the gates to Baldwin III. Not satisfied with taking the city, Baldwin laid siege to the Tower of David, only to meet spirited resistance. The unseemly fight continued for several days, but eventually, the spectacle of the king of Jerusalem attacking the Tower of David held by his mother, the queen, was too much. Negotiations were resumed, and Melisende admitted defeat at last. She surrendered the Tower of David and withdrew to Nablus but did not abdicate.

Furthermore, and astonishingly, there was no permanent breach between the co-monarchs. As she had done with her husband before, Melisende managed a rapprochement with her son now. Thus far from disappearing into a convent or obscurity, Melisende remained active in the Kingdom of Jerusalem. As with Fulk, the more Baldwin III became engaged in military affairs, the more Melisende exerted a leading role in internal policy. This included important negotiations with the Pisans concerning their rights in Tyre, issuing charters, settling disputes, dispensing patronage, conducting marriage negotiations (notably with the Byzantine Emperor) and most strikingly, dispatching royal troops to attack a Muslim-controlled fortress on the Jordon River. Melisende accomplished all of this after her short but forceful clash with Baldwin III. Furthermore, these are not nominal acts; they represent the very essence of royal power.

Early in 1160, Melisende was incapacitated by an unknown illness. She lingered until September 11, 1161, when she died. According to her will, she was buried beside her mother in the shrine of our Lady of Jehoshaphat.

Melisende's life contradicts modern commentary that dismisses mediaeval women as chattels or pawns. Melisende's right to inherit not just the title but the power of a monarch was not only recognised by the High Court (i.e., her vassals) but defended by her barons and the Church. Melisende wielded real power and won the respect of her contemporaries.

Yet, the woman herself, her feelings, temperament, motives, fears and dreams are largely lost to us. A few things are clear, however. Melisende was not passive, submissive or docile. She was strong-willed, determined and tenacious, particularly when exercising the power that was her hereditary right. While we can assume she was never overly fond of her much older and domineering husband, it is harder to know what she felt towards her eldest son. That she consistently tried to exclude him from the reins of government might suggest that she did not entirely trust him. Had she loved and trusted him the way Eleanor of Aquitaine loved her son Richard, she would surely have worked with rather than against him. Yet it is just as possible that they were simply different in temperament and clashed with one another as parents and children often do. The fact that she could concede defeat and then play a constructive role in the last decade of her life suggests that whatever divided them was not fatal. In the end, they were able to work together. It is probably best to leave judgement to those who had known her personally. Here are the words William, Archbishop of Tyre, used to describe her after her death:

> Queen Melisende, a woman of unusual wisdom and discretion, fell ill of an incurable disease for which there was no help except death. ... For thirty years and more, during the lifetime of her husband as well as afterwards in the reign of her son, Melisende had governed the kingdom with strength surpassing that of most women. Her rule had been wise and judicious.[127]

Sibylla, Ruling Queen of Jerusalem (b. 1160 – d. 1190, reigned 1186–1190)

Sibylla of Jerusalem was undoubtedly a tragic figure, but not because she was a pawn or a victim. On the contrary, she masterminded a coup d'état by outwitting her supporters as well as her opponents. Yet, Sibylla was the antithesis of a power-hungry woman. Her scheming was not for herself but for her husband. Ultimately, she put her affection for her second husband above the well-being of her kingdom – and doomed her kingdom to humiliation, defeat and almost complete annihilation.

Sibylla was born in 1160, the daughter of Amalric of Jerusalem, the younger brother of King Baldwin III and his wife, Agnes de Courtenay. At the time of her birth, her father was Count of Jaffa and Ascalon, while her mother was landless since the entire County of Edessa had been lost to the Saracens. Shortly after her birth in 1163, King Baldwin III died without issue. The High Court of Jerusalem agreed to recognise Amalric as his heir – on the condition he set aside Agnes de Courtenay. The official grounds for the annulment were that Amalric and Agnes were related within the prohibited degrees of kinship, something the Church had allegedly only discovered after six years of marriage. The real reasons likely lay elsewhere, but it is not possible to know from this distance if it was Agnes' alleged immorality (as the *Chronicle of Ernoul* imputes) or fear that the Courtenays would try to muscle themselves into positions of power in Jerusalem (as Malcolm Barber suggests in *The Crusader States*) or other considerations lost to the historical record. For Sibylla, however, the implications were severe. Her mother was discarded by her father and then banished from court, leaving her and her younger brother Baldwin under their father's exclusive control.

While her brother remained at court to be raised near their father and learn his future role as king of Jerusalem, Sibylla was sent to the convent at Bethany near Jerusalem to be raised by her father's aunt, the Abbess Iveta. Henceforth, although she may have seen her father or brother on special occasions, she would have seen almost nothing of her mother, who promptly remarried.

By 1170, it was apparent that her brother Baldwin was suffering from leprosy. This meant he might not live to adulthood and, even if he did, was unlikely to have heirs of his body. Therefore, finding a husband for the 11-year-old Sibylla became a matter of paramount importance to the kingdom. Friedrich, Archbishop of Tyre, was dispatched to the West to find a suitable husband, who when the time came, would be able to rule the kingdom effectively as her consort. A year later, Friedrich of Tyre returned with Stephen of Sancerre of the House of Blois.

Stephen was clearly of sufficient rank; his sister was married to Louis VII of France, and his brothers were married to Eleanor of Aquitaine's daughters by Louis VII. But Stephen unexpectedly refused to marry Sibylla and returned to France, squandering his chance to be king of Jerusalem. It is hard to imagine that anything about a young girl living in a convent could have offended an ambitious nobleman; his decision almost certainly had nothing to do with Sibylla. Perhaps he disliked the climate, food, exceptional power of the High Court of Jerusalem, or the military situation in light of Saladin's increasing power. Whatever his motives for rejecting the crown, Sibylla was probably offended or hurt by the public rejection.

In 1174, Sibylla's father died unexpectedly, and her younger brother ascended the throne as Baldwin IV. He was only 13 at the time, and so placed under a regent, Raymond, Count of Tripoli. It now became Tripoli's duty to find a husband for Sibylla in consultation with the High Court. This time, the High Court selected William, the eldest son of the Marquis de Montferrat. William was first cousin to Louis VII of France and the Holy Roman Emperor Friedrich I. Furthermore, his family had a long tradition of crusading.

William of Montferrat arrived in the Holy Land escorted by a Genoese fleet in October 1176 and, within six weeks, he had married the then 16-year-old Sibylla. He was invested with the title of Count of Jaffa and Ascalon, the now traditional title for the heir apparent to the throne. The contemporary chronicler and then Chancellor of the Kingdom of Jerusalem, William of Tyre, describes William of Montferrat as follows:

The marquis was a rather tall, good-looking young man with blond hair. He was exceedingly irascible but very generous and of an open disposition and manly courage. He never concealed any purpose but showed frankly just what he thought in his own mind. He was fond of eating and altogether too devoted to drinking, although not to such an extent as to injure his mind. He had been trained in arms from his earliest youth and had the reputation of being experienced in the art of war.[128]

There is no reason to think that Sibylla was ill-pleased with the High Court's choice or he with her. He accepted her, and she became pregnant shortly after the marriage. Unfortunately, William de Montferrat became ill within six months, and in June 1177, he died. Sibylla gave birth to a posthumous son in August and named him Baldwin after her brother.

At once, the search for a new husband for Sibylla commenced. Philip II, Count of Flanders, arrived with a large force even before Sibylla gave birth to her son, and as a close kinsman (his mother was Baldwin and Sibylla's aunt), he felt entitled to choose Sibylla's next husband. The High Court of Jerusalem disagreed. Worse, the name he put forward was a comparatively obscure Flemish nobleman viewed by the High Court as an insult to the crown of Jerusalem. Furthermore, he wanted to marry this man's younger brother to Sibylla's half-sister, thereby binding both princesses to his vassals – a crude means of making himself master of the kingdom without doing the hard work of fighting for it or ruling it. Understandably, the High Court of Jerusalem rejected the suggestions, and the Count of Flanders returned to Europe. Sibylla was still without a new husband.

According to the Chronicles of Ernoul, it was now, after Sibylla had been widowed, that the Baron of Ramla and Mirabel showed an interest in marrying her. While Ernoul is considered a biased and unreliable source, it is evident from other sources that Ramla had designs on Sibylla three years later. Therefore, it is not unreasonable to hypothesize that the High Court's rejection of Flander's unsuitable suggestions triggered Ramla's hopes that a powerful local baron might be favoured over an unknown and unbefitting nobleman from the West.

Meanwhile, Baldwin IV took the step of associating his sister with him in some public acts to reinforce her status as his heir. (His great-grandfather, Baldwin II, had done the same towards the end of his reign to stress that his daughter Melisende would succeed him.) Baldwin IV also wrote to King Louis VII of France (perhaps convinced that the king of England, as represented by Philip of Flanders, did not have the best interests of his kingdom at heart) and begged him to choose a man from among his barons who could take up the burden of ruling the Holy Kingdom (i.e., the Kingdom of Jerusalem). Louis chose Hugh, Duke of Burgundy, a very high-ranking nobleman. He was expected to arrive in the spring of 1180.

In the summer of 1179, Baldwin of Ramla was taken captive at a skirmish on the Litani. For his release, Sultan Saladin demanded the outrageous ransom of 200,000 bezants, a price higher than the ransom demanded for Baldwin II and more than twice the ransom paid for the Count of Tripoli just five years before. Such a sum was far beyond what Ramla's modest baronies pay; it was quite clearly 'a king's ransom'. The demand suggests that Saladin thought (or had intelligence suggesting) that Ramla was destined to be Sibylla's next husband. Saladin assumed that as the future king of Jerusalem, Ramla could command the resources of the entire kingdom. Even more significantly, the Byzantine Emperor paid a significant portion of Ramla's ransom. Again, there is hardly any other plausible explanation of such generosity except that the Byzantine Emperor believed Ramla would become the next king of Jerusalem by marrying Sibylla.

This scenario appeared more plausible than ever when, for a second time, Sibylla (and, with her, Jerusalem) was rejected. The Duke of Burgundy's excuse was that the king of France had died, leaving the kingdom to his young son Philip II. Since the Plantagenets were predatory, Burgundy felt it was his duty (or in his best interests) to remain in France.

Sibylla was approaching 20 years of age and had been a widow for three years. Two noblemen from Europe had jilted her, and one had been rejected on her behalf by the High Court of Jerusalem. Her name was probably associated with the Baron of Ramla, who had set aside his first wife (according to Ernoul) to marry her, but there had been no official announcement of a betrothal. Then, abruptly at Easter 1180, only weeks after Burgundy's decision could have been made known, she married the landless, fourth son of the French Lord de la March, Guy de Lusignan.

Guy de Lusignan had only recently come to the Holy Land, probably landing in the kingdom around the same time as the news arrived that Burgundy was not coming. At this point in time, Ramla was in Constantinople trying to raise his ransom. According to William of Tyre, shortly before Easter and after the news of Burgundy's default on his promise, King Baldwin learned that Prince Bohemond of Antioch and the Count of Tripoli had entered the kingdom with an army. According to Tyre, Baldwin became so terrified that they had come to lay claim to his kingdom that he 'hastened his sister's marriage' to a man Tyre patently describes as unworthy (Guy de Lusignan), adding, 'acting on impulse causes harm to everything'.

While the Archbishop of Tyre, Baldwin's tutor and now his chancellor, can be counted as an insider, his explanation of Sybilla's marriage to Guy is illogical. Antioch and Tripoli were Baldwin's closest relatives on his father's side. They had been bulwarks of his reign until now. Tripoli had served as his regent and could have deposed him then if he had wanted. Furthermore, Tripoli continued to support him to his death. Baldwin himself chose Tripoli to act as regent for his nephew. Except for Tyre's speculation, there is no evidence of treason on Tripoli's part at any time during Baldwin IV's life. Even Tyre admits that Tripoli and Antioch 'completed their religious devotions in the normal way' and returned home without fuss upon learning that Sibylla was already married. That's hardly the reaction of men unexpectedly thwarted in a coup attempt. In short, Tripoli and Antioch probably came to Jerusalem for Easter and, despite having large entourages with them (as nobles of the period were wont to have), they never posed any threat to the king.

The much-maligned Ernoul offers a far better explanation of what happened. He claims Guy de Lusignan seduced Sibylla, causing Baldwin to threaten to hang the Frenchman for debauching a princess of Jerusalem. Baldwin was dissuaded from this by his mother (the highly influential but self-serving Agnes de Courtenay) and his sister's tears. He then allowed Sibylla to marry her lover in haste and secrecy. This explanation of events makes perfect sense and appears borne out by Sibylla's subsequent behaviour.

Sibylla had just been jilted for a second time. She probably felt very sorry for herself and may even have wondered if something was wrong with her. Ramla may have been his choice for her husband rather than hers – or he might have been too far away at a critical moment. Suddenly, a dashing, handsome young nobleman was paying court to her, flattering and making love to her. Sibylla fell for him. Such behaviour is not unusual for a 20-year-old girl.

The evidence that Guy was Sibylla's choice is provided by her subsequent actions. Within three years, Baldwin IV was desperately trying to find a way to annul his sister's marriage to Guy, and she was doing everything in her power to prevent it. Had Sibylla been forced into a dynastic marriage by her brother in 1180, she would have willingly accepted a dynastic divorce in 1183–1184. She did not.

Furthermore, by the time her brother and young son by Montferrat were dead, it was obvious that nearly the entire High Court, secular and sacred, mistrusted Guy de Lusignan and did not want to see him crowned king beside her. Bernard Hamilton, in his excellent history of Baldwin's reign, *The Leper King and his Heirs*, admits that even sources *favourable* to Guy de Lusignan acknowledge that Sibylla's *supporters* 'required her to divorce Guy before they would recognise her as queen'.[129] Sibylla reportedly agreed to divorce Guy but asked that she be allowed to choose her next husband. Once this concession was made, she then proceeded to select Guy as her next husband. By clinging to Guy as her husband and consort, she alienated not only the barons and bishops already opposed to her but also those who had loyally supported her on the condition she divorce Guy. Again, these are hardly the actions of a woman in a dynastic marriage but very much the actions of a woman deeply in love with her husband.

Typically, it is admirable for a wife to be devoted to her husband, as Church chroniclers quickly pointed out. For a queen, however, clinging to an unpopular man at the price of alienating the men she depended upon to defend her kingdom is neither intelligent nor prudent.

Furthermore, it is rare for a man to provoke so much unanimous opposition and animosity as Guy de Lusignan. Even if we cannot fully fathom it today, there is no reason to think the hostility was baseless. On the contrary, Guy proved all his opponents right when, within a year of usurping the throne, he had lost roughly 17,000 Christian fighting men at an avoidable defeat at the battle of Hattin, with the consequence that nearly the entire kingdom fell to the Saracens within three months. Moreover, as a captive of Saladin, Guy ordered Ascalon to surrender to Saladin when it might well have resisted successfully.

In September of 1187, Sibylla found herself trapped in Jerusalem along with tens of thousands of other refugees as her kingdom crumbled before Saladin's onslaught. Her husband's incompetence had ensured that the men who might otherwise have defended the cities and castles had been killed or enslaved.

Sibylla was still the crowned and anointed ruling queen. Yet unlike Beatrice of Edessa, who worked day and night to restore the defences of her endangered cities, unlike Eschiva of Tiberias or Maria Comnena, who took command of the garrisons of the cities they held, and unlike Eschiva de Montbéliard who organised provisions to withstand a siege, Queen Sibylla did nothing. Nothing that is, except beg the destroyer of her kingdom to allow her to join her husband in captivity. In short, she begged to put the ruling queen of Jerusalem in the hands of the kingdom's worst enemy. This is more than a gesture of love; it is evidence of Sibylla's stupidity and lack of elementary common sense.

Saladin naturally granted Sibylla's wish – what better way to ensure that his enemies were entirely in his hands? Meanwhile, the defence of the last remnants of her kingdom fell in Tyre to Conrad de Montferrat, the younger brother of her first husband, and in Jerusalem to Balian d'Ibelin, the second husband of her mother's hated rival Maria Comnena.

Still, Sibylla's devotion to Guy was unbroken. After Guy de Lusignan promised Saladin he would never take up arms against Muslims again, the sultan released him. Lusignan immediately broke his word by laying siege to Muslim-held Acre. This siege, militarily dubious from the start, turned into a drawn-out debacle, voraciously consuming Christian lives. Deplorable conditions reigned, including acute hunger and, eventually, disease. Yet Sibylla, the crowned queen of Jerusalem, preferred to be with her beloved husband, Guy, than to act the part of queen. Not only did Sibylla join her husband in the unsanitary siege camp, but she brought her only children and heirs, two small daughters, with her. They all paid the price. Sibylla and her two little girls died of a fever in November 1190. Sibylla was 30 years old.

Queen Sibylla shares the blame with Guy de Lusignan for losing the Kingdom of Jerusalem in 1187. Her stupidity and stubbornness left the kingdom in the hands of an incompetent and despised man. At no time in her life did she show even a flicker of responsibility for the hundreds of thousands of Christians entrusted to her or demonstrate a shred of royal dignity. Had she been a baker's daughter and a butcher's wife, her devotion to her husband might have been admirable; as a princess, she was tragic. Yet, at no time was she a mere chattel or pawn. Sibylla's tragedy is not that she had too little power but that she had too much – and did not know how to use it.

Notes

1. Bernard Hamilton, 'Women in the Crusader States: The Queens of Jerusalem', in *Medieval Women*, ed. Derek Baker (Oxford: Basil Blackwell, 1978), 143.
2. Sue Blundell, *Women in Ancient Greece*, (London: British Museum Press, 1995), 131.
3. The situation of women in the Mycenaean age and women in Doric societies such as Sparta and Gortyn were markedly better. There is extensive literature on these societies and comparisons of them to classical Athens.
4. An excellent source on women in the mediaeval church is Regine Pernoud, *Women in the Days of the Cathedrals* (San Francisco: Ignatius, 1989); and *Medieval Women*, ed. Derek Baker (Oxford: Basil Blackwell, 1978) contains biographies of female mediaeval religious women and others.
5. Pernoud, *Women in the Days of the Cathedrals*, 180.
6. Ibid.
7. Fatima Mernissi, *Beyond the Veil: Male-Female Dynamics in Modern Muslim Society*, (Indianapolis: University of Indiana Press, 1975), 45.
8. Nabih Amin Faris, 'Arab Culture in the Twelfth Century', in *The Crusades: The Impact of the Crusades on the Near East*, eds. Kenneth M. Setton, Norman Zacour, and Harry Hazard (Madison: University of Wisconsin Press, 1985).
9. Mernissi, *Beyond the Veil*, 48.
10. Julie Scott Meisami, *The Sea of Precious Virtues (Bahr al-Fava'id): A Medieval Islamic Mirror for Princes* (Salt Lake City: University of Utah Press, 1990), 232; quoted in Niall Christie, *Muslims and Crusaders: Christianity's Wars in the Middle East, 1095–1382, From the Islamic Sources*, (London: Routledge, 2014), 77–78.
11. Niall Christie, 'An Illusion of Ignorance? The Muslims of the Middle East and the Franks before the Crusades', in *The Crusader World*, ed. Adrian Boas (London: Routledge, 2016), 312.
12. Sylvia Schein, 'Women in Medieval Colonial Society: The Latin Kingdom of Jerusalem in the Twelfth Century,' in *Gendering the Crusades*, eds. Susan B. Edgington and Sarah Lambert (Cardiff: University of Wales Press, 2001), 140.
13. Sarah Lambert, 'Crusading or Spinning', in *Gendering the Crusades*, eds. Susan B. Edgington and Sarah Lambert (Cardiff: University of Wales Press, 2001), 11.
14. The myth of Muslim tolerance is so widespread and popular that rebutting it requires explanations and documentation that exceed the parameters of this book. For a comprehensive overview of the status and conditions for Jews and Christians under Islamic rule in the Holy Land and recommendations for further reading, see Helena P. Schrader, *The Holy Land in the Era of the Crusades: Kingdoms at the Crossroads of Civilizations* (Barnsley, UK: Pen & Sword, 2022). Another excellent book based on Arab, Syriac, Coptic, Turkish and Armenian sources is Bat Ye'or, *The Decline of Eastern Christianity under Islam: From Jihad to Dhimmitude* (Madison: Fairleigh Dickinson University Press, 1996). For the situation in Spain, see Dario

Fernandez-Morera, *The Myth of the Andalusian Paradise: Muslims, Christians, and Jews under Islamic Rule in Medieval Spain* (Wilmington: ISI Books, 2017).

15. Thomas F. Madden, *The Concise History of the Crusades*, (Washington, DC: Rowman and Littlefield, 2014), 10.

16. Sabine Geldsetzer, *Frauen auf Kreuzzuegen, 1096–1291*, (Darmstadt: Wissenschaftliche Buchgesellschaft, 2003), 12–13.

17. The large pockets of Muslim settlers that later made up a sizable minority population in the Kingdom of Jerusalem were located along the coast and around Nablus, which did not come under crusader control for several years.

18. Byzantine princess, Anna Comnena, noted in her twelfth-century history that much of the region had been reduced to uninhabited desert. For more details on depopulation under Arab rule, see Ye'or, *The Decline of Eastern Christianity under Islam*.

19. See note 1, Hamilton, 'Women in the Crusader States', 150.

20. William of Tyre, *A History of Deeds Done Beyond the Sea, Volume 2*, trans. Emily Atwater Babcock and A.C. Krey (London: Octagon Books: 1976), 76.

21. Hamilton, 'Women in the Crusader States', 161

22. Amalaric's Egyptian policy is described in considerable depth in Helena P. Schrader, *The Holy Land in the Era of the Crusades*.

23. Baldwin d'Ibelin had inherited the Barony of Ramla and Mirabel through his mother and the Barony of Ibelin from his elder brother Hugh, the husband of Agnes de Courtenay, who had died childless. About the same time as his younger brother's marriage to the Dowager Queen Maria Comnena, Baldwin appears to have given the smaller and less important paternal barony to his younger brother, Balian. The details are unknown, but Baldwin is consistently referred to as 'Ramla' and Balian as 'Ibelin' or 'Nablus'.

24. John France, 'Crusading Warfare in the Twelfth Century', in *The Crusader World*, edited by Adrian Boas (London: Routledge: 2016), 77.

25. *Itinerarium Peregrinorum et Gesta Regis Ricardi*, trans. Helen Nicholson (Farnham: Ashgate: 1997), 123.

26. *Itinerarium*, 124.

27. *The Conquest of Jerusalem and the Third Crusade*, trans. Peter Edbury (Farnham: Ashgate, 1998), 95–96.

28. *The Conquest of Jerusalem and the Third Crusade*, 115.

29. *Itinerarium*, 312.

30. *Itinerarium*, 313.

31. Angel Nicolaou-Konnari, Angel and Chris Schabel, eds. 'Economy,' in *Cyprus: Society and Culture 1191–1374* (London: Brill, 2005), 113.

32. Bernard Hamilton, 'Queen Alice of Cyprus', in *The Crusader World*, ed. Adrian Boas (London: Routledge: 2016), 229.

33. Philip de Novare, *The Wars of Frederick II against the Ibelins in Syria and Cyprus*, trans. John La Monte (New York: Columbia University Press: 1936), 63.

34. Chronique de Terre Sainte quoted by Hamilton, 'Queen Alice of Cyprus', in *The Crusader World*, 231.

35. Christopher Tyerman, *The World of the Crusades: An Illustrated History*, (New Haven: Yale University Press: 2019), 238.

36. *Itinerarium Peregrinorum et Gesta Regis Ricardi*, trans. Helen Nicholson (Farnham: Ashgate, 1997), 48.

37. Constance Rousseau, 'Home Front and Battlefield: The Gendering of Papal Crusading Policy (1095–1221)', in *Gendering the Crusades*, eds. Susan B. Edgington and Sarah Lambert (Cardiff, University of Wales, 2001), 39.

38. Michael the Great or Michael the Syrian, Patriarch of the Syriac or Jacobite Church 1166–1199, quoted in Christopher MacEvitt, *The Crusades and the Christian World of the East: Rough Tolerance*, (Philadelphia: University of Pennsylvania Press, 2008), 25.

39. Fulcher of Chartres, *A History of the Expedition to Jerusalem, 1095–1127*, trans. F.R. Ryan (Knoxville: University of Tennessee Press, 1969), 238.

40. Fulcher of Chartres, *A History of the Expedition to Jerusalem*, 238.

41. Fulcher of Chartres, *A History of the Expedition to Jerusalem*, 239.

42. Ibid.

43. Peter W. Edbury. *Law and History in the Latin East*, (Farnham: Ashgate, 2014), V, 285.

44. Natasha R. Hodgson, *Women, Crusading and the Holy Land in Historical Narrative*, (Woodbridge, UK: Boydell & Brewer, 2007), 723. Hodgson cites Philip de Novare as her source.

45. William Miller, *The Latins in the Levant: A History of Frankish Greece (1204–1566)* (Boston: Dutton and Company, 1908), 116.

46. Tyre, *A History of Deeds Done Beyond the Sea*, Volume 2, 401.

47. Edbury, *Law and History in the Latin East*, V,287.

48. Tyre, *A History of Deeds Done Beyond the Sea*, Volume 2, 213.

49. Ibid.

50. The Magna Carta quoted in Schein, 142.

51. Tyre, *A History of Deeds Done Beyond the Sea*, Volume 2, 425.

52. Edbury, *Law and History in the Latin East*, V, 292.

53. Erin Jordan, 'Corporate Monarchy in the Twelfth-Century Kingdom of Jerusalem', *Royal Studies Journal* 6, no. 1 (Winchester, UK: Winchester University Press, 2019): 4.

54. Bernard de Clairvaux, quoted in Malcolm Barber, *The Crusader States*, (New Haven: Yale University Press: 2012), 175.

55. Tyre, *A History of Deeds Done Beyond the Sea*, Volume 2, 140.

56. Tyre, *A History of Deeds Done Beyond the Sea*, Volume 2, 283.

57. Thomas Asbridge, 'Alice of Antioch: a case study of female power in the twelfth century', in *The Experience of Crusading: Defining the crusader kingdom*, eds. Jonathan P. Phillips and Peter W. Edbury (Cambridge: Cambridge University Press, 2003), 29–47.

58. Tyre, *A History of Deeds Done Beyond the Sea*, Volume 2, 201–202.

59. Tyre, *A History of Deeds Done Beyond the Sea*, Volume 2, 209.

60. *The Lyon Continuation of William of Tyre*, trans. Peter Edbury (Farnham: Ashgate, 1998).

61. *Itinerarium Peregrinorum et Gesta Regis Ricardi*. Chpt. 63, p.122.

62. Tyre, *A History of Deeds Done Beyond the Sea*, Volume 2, 133.

63. Gordon M. Reynolds, 'Opportunism & Duty: Gendered Perceptions of Women's Involvement in Crusade Negotiation and Mediation (1147–1254)', *Medieval Feminist Forum*, Vol. 54, No.2 (April 2019): 5–6.

64. Jaroslav Folda, *Crusader Art: The Art of the Crusaders in the Holy Land, 1099–1291*, (London: Lund Humphries, 2008), 127.

65. Helen Nicholson, 'Women and the Crusades', Remarks before the Hereford Historical Association (22 February 2008): 15.

66. Helen Nicholson, 'Woman on the Third Crusade', *Journal of Medieval History*, Vol. 23, No 4 (1997): 342.
67. Nicholson, 'Women and the Crusades', 17.
68. Anonymous, *Itinerarium Peregrinorum et Gesta Regis Ricardi*, 106.
69. *The Lyon Continuation of William of Tyre*, 55
70. *The Lyon Continuation of William of Tyre*, 58.
71. Ibid.
72. Nicholson, 'Women and the Crusades', 18.
73. Tyre, *A History of Deeds Done Beyond the Sea*, Volume 2, 202.
74. *The Lyon Continuation of William of Tyre*, 77.
75. *The Lyon Continuation of William of Tyre*, 78.
76. Philip de Novare, *The Wars of Frederick II against the Ibelins in Syria and Cyprus*, 142–143.
77. Jean de Joinville, *The Life of St. Louis*, trans. M.R.B. Shaw (London: Penguin Classics, 1963), 202.
78. Nicholson, 'Women and the Crusades', 10.
79. Ibn al-Athir, XI, in *Arab Historians of the Crusades*, trans. Francesco Gabrieli (Oakland: University of California Press, 1957), 142.
80. Tyre, *A History of Deeds Done Beyond the Sea*, Volume 2, 31–32.
81. Yvonne Friedman, 'Captivity and Ransom', in *Gendering the Crusades*, eds. Susan B. Edgington and Sarah Lambert (Cardiff: University of Wales Press, 2001), 121.
82. Albert of Aachen, quoted in Yvonne Friedman, 'Captivity and Ransom', *Gendering the Crusades*, 125.
83. Albert of Aachen, quoted in Natasha Hodgson, *Women, Crusading, and the Holy Land in Historical Narrative* (Woodbridge, UK: Boydell & Brewer, 2007), 97–98.
84. Albert of Aachen, quoted Natasha Hodgson, 97–98.
85. Albert of Aachen, quoted in Friedman, 125.
86. Yvonne Friedman, *Encounter between Enemies: Captivity and Ransom in the Latin Kingdom of Jerusalem* (Leiden, Netherlands: Brill, 2002), 170.
87. Imad ad-Din, quoted in *Arab Historians of the Crusades*, trans. Francesco Gabrieli (Oakland: University of California Press, 1957), 163.
88. Fulcher of Chartes, quoted in Friedman, 171.
89. Friedman, *Encounter between Enemies*, 172.
90. Albert of Aachen, quoted in Hodgson, 148.
91. Ibn al-Athir, quoted in John Gillingham, 'Crusading Warfare, Chivalry and the Enslavement of Women and Children', in *The Medieval Way of War*, ed. Gregory Halfond (London: Routledge, 2019), 10.
92. Ibn al-Athir, quoted in Malcolm Barber, *The Crusader States* (New Haven: Yale University Press, 2012), 308.
93. Friedman, *Encounter between Enemies*, 179.
94. Ibn al-Athir quoted in P.M. Holt, *The Crusader States and their Neighbours* (London: Pearson Longman, 2004), 61.
95. Friedman, 'Captivity and Ransom', 130.
96. Pernoud, *Women in the Days of the Cathedrals*, 7.
97. Both Arab sources are cited in Nial Christie's *Muslims and Crusaders: Christianity's Wars in the Middle East, 1095–1382, From the Islamic Sources* (London: Routledge, 2014), 83.
98. James M. Powell, 'Preface', in *Gendering the Crusades*, eds., Susan B. Edgington and Sarah Lambert (Cardiff: University of Wales Press, 2001), vii.

99. Steve Tibble, *The Crusader Armies* (New Haven: Yale University Press, 2018), 185.

100. Tyre, *A History of Deeds Done Beyond the Sea*, Volume 2, 44.

101. Tyre, *A History of Deeds Done Beyond the Sea*, Volume 2, 53.

102. Tyre, *A History of Deeds Done Beyond the Sea*, Volume 2, 44.

103. Thomas Asbridge, 'Alice of Antioch: a case study of female power in the twelfth century', in *The Experience of Crusading: Defining the Crusader Kingdom* (Cambridge University Press, 2003), 29–47.

104. Hamilton, 'Queen Alice of Cyprus', 229.

105. Novare, *The Wars of Frederick II against the Ibelins in Syria and Cyprus*, 63.

106. Chronique de Terre Sainte quoted by Hamilton, *Queen Alice of Cyprus*, 231.

107. Tyre, *A History of Deeds Done Beyond the Sea*, Volume 2, 213.

108. Ibid.

109. Ibid.

110. Tyre, *A History of Deeds Done Beyond the Sea*, Volume 2, 277.

111. *The Lyon Continuation of William of Tyre*, 127, paragraph 149.

112. *The Lyon Continuation of William of Tyre*, 127, paragraph 150.

113. *The Lyon Continuation of William of Tyre*, 128, paragraph 152.

114. Novare, *The Wars of Frederick II against the Ibelins in Syria and Cyprus*, 77.

115. Novare, *The Wars of Frederick II against the Ibelins in Syria and Cyprus*, 106.

116. Novare, *The Wars of Frederick II against the Ibelins in Syria and Cyprus*, 106.

117. Novare, *The Wars of Frederick II against the Ibelins in Syria and Cyprus*, 143.

118. Novare, *The Wars of Frederick II against the Ibelins in Syria and Cyprus*, 142–143.

119. Novare, *The Wars of Frederick II against the Ibelins in Syria and Cyprus*, 151.

120. Novare, *The Wars of Frederick II against the Ibelins in Syria and Cyprus*, 152.

121. Jean de Joinville, 202.

122. *Itinerarium Peregrinorum et Gesta Regis Ricardi*. Chpt. 63, p.124.

123. *The Lyon Continuation of William of Tyre*, 95–96, paragraph 104.

124. Guy Perry, *John of Brienne: King of Jerusalem, Emperor of Constantinople, c. 1175–1237*, (Cambridge University Press, 2013), 135.

125. Orderic Vitalis, quoted in trans. Hans Eberhard Mayer, 'Angevins versus Normans: The New Men of King Fulques of Jerusalem', in *Kings and Lords in the Latin Kingdom of Jerusalem*, (Farnham: Ashgate Publishing, 1994), IV, 3.

126. William of Tyre, quoted in translation by Bernard Hamilton; and 'Women in the Crusader States: The Queens of Jerusalem (1100–1190)', in *Medieval Women*, ed. Derek Baker (Oxford: Basil Blackwell, 1978), 150.

127. Tyre, *A History of Deeds Done Beyond the Sea*, Volume 2, 283.

128. Tyre, *A History of Deeds Done Beyond the Sea*, Volume 2, 416.

129. Bernard Hamilton, *The Leper King and His Heirs: Baldwin IV and the Crusader Kingdom of Jerusalem*, (Cambridge University Press, 2000), 218.

Bibliography

Primary Sources

Anonymous, *Chronicle of the Third Crusade: A Translation of the Itinerarium Peregrinorum et Gesta Regis Ricardi. Crusade Texts in Translation.* Translated by Helen Nicholson (Ashgate Publishing Ltd, 1997).

Anonymous, *The Conquest of Jerusalem and the Third Crusade. Crusade Texts in Translation.* Translated by Peter W. Edbury (Ashgate Publishing Ltd, 1998).

Anonymous, *Crusader Syria in the Thirteenth Century: The Rothelin Continuation of the History of William of Tyre with part of the Eracles or Acre Text. Crusades Texts in Translation.* Translated by Janet Shirley (Ashgate Publishing Ltd, 1999).

Ibn Shaddad, Baha al-Din, *The Rare and Excellent History of Saladin.* Translated by D.S. Richards (Ashgate Publishing Ltd, 2002).

Gabrieli, Francesco, *Arab Historians of the Crusades.* (University of California Press, 1969).

Letters from the East: Crusaders, Pilgrims, and Settlers in the 12th and 13th Centuries. Crusade Texts in Translation. Translated by Malcolm Barber and Keith Bate (Ashgate Publishing Ltd, 2013).

Novare, Philip de, *The Wars of Frederick II Against the Ibelins in Syria and Cyprus.* Translated by John La Monte (Morningside Heights Columbia University Press, 1936).

Pilgrimage to Jerusalem and the Holy Land, 1187–1291. Crusades Texts in Translation. Translated by Denys Pringle (Ashgate Publishing Ltd, 2012).

Tyre, William Archbishop of, *A History of Deeds Done Beyond the Sea.* (Morningside Heights Columbia University Press, 1943).

Secondary Sources

Abulafia, David, *Frederick II: A Medieval Emperor.* (Oxford University Press, 1988).

Allen, S.J. and Amt, Emilie, *The Crusades: A Reader.* (University of Toronto Press, 2014).

Andrea, Alfred J., & Holt, Andrew (eds.), *Seven Myths of the Crusades* (Hackett Publishing Company, 2015).

Asbridge, Thomas, 'Alice of Antioch: a case study of female power in the twelfth century', in *The Experience of Crusading: Defining the Crusader Kingdom.* Edited by Jonathan P. Phillips, and Peter W. Edbury. (Cambridge University Press, Cambridge, 2003).

Bale, Anthony (ed.), *The Cambridge Companion to the Literature of the Crusades.* (Cambridge University Press, 2019).

Barber, Malcolm, *The Crusader States*. (Yale University Press, 2012).

Barber, Malcolm, 'The Career of Philip of Nablus in the Kingdom of Jerusalem', in *The Experience of Crusading: Defining the Crusader Kingdom*. Edited by Peter W. Edbury and Jonathan P. Phillips. (Cambridge University Press, 2003).

Barber, Malcolm, *New Knighthood: A History of the Order of the Temple*. (Cambridge University Press, 1994).

Barber, Richard, *The Knight and Chivalry*. (Boydell Press, 1970).

Bartlett, W.B., *Downfall of the Crusader Kingdom*. (The History Press Ltd, 2010).

Baumgaertner, Ingrid and Panse, Melanie, 'Kreuzzuege aus der Perspektive der Genderforschung, Zielsetzung und Forschungsansaetze' in *Das Mittelalter*, Vol. 21(1) (2016).

Brand, Charles M., *Byzantium Confronts the West*. (ACLS Humanities E-Book, 2012.)

Boas, Adrian J., *Crusader Archaeology: The Material Culture of the Latin East*. (Routledge, 1999).

Boas, Adrian J., *Domestic Settings: Sources on Domestic Architecture and Day-to-Day Activities in the Crusader States*. (Brill, 2010).

Boas, Andrian J. (ed.), *The Crusader World*. (Routledge, 2016).

Boulle, Pierre, *Der Denkwuerdige Kreuzzug Kaiser Friedrich II. von Hohenstaufen*. (Christian Wegner Verlag, 1970*)*.

Bromiley, Geoffrey N., 'Philip of Novara's account of the war between Frederick II of Hohenstaufen and the Ibelins', in *Journal of Medieval History* 3 (1977).

Bromiley, Geoffrey N., 'Philippe de Novare: Another Epic Historian?', in *Neophilologus* 82 (1998).

Christie, Niall, *Muslims and Crusaders: Christianity's Wars in the Middle East, 1095–1382, from the Islamic Sources*. (Routledge, 2014).

Cleve, Thomas Curtis Van, *The Emperor Frederick II of Hohenstaufen: Immutator Mundi*. (Oxford University Press, 1972).

Conder, Claude Reignier, *The Latin Kingdom of Jerusalem 1099 to 1291 AD*. (Committee of the Palestine Exploration Fund, 1897).

Donvito, Filippo, 'Hangman or Gentleman: Saladin's Christian Hostages and Prisoners', in *Medieval Warfare IV-1* (2014).

Edbury, Peter W., *John of Ibelin and the Kingdom of Jerusalem*. (The Boydell Press, 1997).

Edbury, Peter W., *The Kingdom of Cyprus and the Crusades, 1191 – 1374*. (Cambridge University Press, 1991).

Edbury, Peter W., *Law and History in the Latin East*. (Ashgate Publishing Ltd, 2014).

Edbury, Peter W., *The Lusignan Kingdom of Cyprus and its Muslim Neighbours*. (Bank of Cyprus Foundation, 1993).

Edbury, Peter W., and Phillips, Jonathan (eds.), *The Experience of Crusading: Defining the Crusader Kingdom*. (Cambridge University Press, Cambridge, 2003).

Edbury, Peter W., and Rowe, John, *William of Tyre: Historian of the Latin East*. (Cambridge University Press, 1988).

Edge, David, and Paddock, John Miles, *Arms and Armour of the Medieval Knight*. (Saturn Books, 1996).

Edgington, Susan B., and Lambert, Susan (eds.), *Gendering the Crusades*. (University of Wales Press, Cardiff, 2001).

Edgington, Susan B., and Nicholson, Helen (eds), *Deeds Done Beyond the Sea: Essays on William of Tyre, Cyprus and the Military Orders Presented to Peter Edbury*. (Routledge, 2014).

Ellenblum, Ronnie, *Frankish Rural Settlement in the Latin Kingdom of Jerusalem*. (Cambridge University Press, 1998).

Ellenblum, Ronnie, *Crusader Castles and Modern Histories*. (Cambridge University Press, 2007).

Ennen, Edith, *Frauen im Mittelalter*. (C.H. Beck, Munich, 1985).

Ehrenkreutz, Andrew S., *Saladin*. (State University of New York Press, 1972).

Evans, Michael R., 'Unfit to Bear Arms: The Gendering of Arms and Armour in Accounts of on Crusade', in *Gendering the Crusades*. Edited by Susan Edgington and Sarah Lambert. (University of Wales Press, Cardiff, 2001).

Folda, Jaroslav, *Crusader Art: The Art of the Crusaders in the Holy Land, 1099–1291*. (Ashgate Publishing Ltd, 2008).

France, John, *Hattin*. (Oxford University Press, 2015).

Friedman, Yvonne, *Encounter between Enemies: Captivity and Ransom in the Latin Kingdom of Jerusalem*. (Brill, 2002).

Galatariotou, Catia, *The Making of a Saint: The Life, Times and Sanctification of Neophytos the Recluse*. (Cambridge University Press, 1991).

Gardiner, Robert (ed.), *Cogs, Caravels and Galleons: The Sailing Ship 1000–1650*. (Conway Maritime Press, 1994).

Geldsetzer, Sabine, *Frauen auf Kreuzzuegen 1096–1291*. (Wissenschaftliche Buchgesellschaft, Darmstadt, 2003).

Gillingham, John, 'Crusading Warfare, Chivalry and the Enslavement of Women and Children', in *The Medieval Way of War*. Edited by Gregory Halfond. (Routledge, 2019).

Gillingham, John, *Richard I*. (Yale University Press, 1999).

Goldman, Brendan, *Arabic-Speaking Jews in Crusader Syria: Conquest, Continuity and Adaptation in the Medieval Mediterranean*. (Unpublished dissertation, Baltimore, 2018).

Goldstone, Nancy, *Four Queens: The Provencal Sisters who Ruled Europe*. (Penguin Books, New York, 2007).

Hamilton, Bernard, *The Latin Church and the Crusader States*. (Routledge, 1980).

Hamilton, Bernard, *The Leper King and His Heirs: Baldwin IV and the Crusader Kingdom of Jerusalem*. (Cambridge University Press, 2000).

Hamilton, Bernard, 'Women in the Crusader States: The Queens of Jerusalem 1100 – 90', in *Medieval Women*. Edited by Baker (Basil Blackwell, 1978).

Harari, Yuval, 'The Military Role of the Frankish Turcopoles: A Reassessment', in *Mediterranean Historical Review*, 12:1 (1997).

Hazard, Harry W. (ed.), *A History of the Crusades, Vol. IV: The Art and Architecture of the Crusader States*. (University of Wisconsin Press, 1977).

Herzog, Annie, *Die Frauen auf den Fuerstenthronen der Kreuzfahrerstaaten.* (Emil Ebering, 1919).

Hill, George, *A History of Cyprus, Vol. 2: The Frankish Period.* (Cambridge University Press, 1948).

Hodgson, Natasha R, *Women, Crusading and the Holy Land in Historical Narrative.* (Boydell Press, Woodbridge, 2007).

Holt, P.M., *The Crusader States and their Neighbours.* (Pearson Education, 2004).

Hopkins, Andrea, *Knights: The Complete Story of the Age of Chivalry: From Historical Fact to Tales of Romance and Poetry.* (Collins and Brown Ltd, 1990).

Jacoby, David, 'Byzantine Culture and the Crusader States' in *Byzantine Culture: Papers from the Conference 'Byzantine Days of Istanbul'* (2010).

Jacoby, David, 'The Kingdom of Jerusalem and the Collapse of Hohenstaufen Power in the Levant', in *Dumbarton Oaks Papers, Vol. 40* (1986).

Jacoby, David (ed.), *Medieval Trade in the Eastern Mediterranean and Beyond.* (Routledge, 2018).

Jacoby, David (ed.), *Studies on the Crusader States and on Venetian Expansion.* (Routledge, 2018).

Jordan, Erin, 'Corporate Monarchy in the Twelfth-Century Kingdom of Jerusalem', in *Royal Studies Journal (RSJ)*, 6, no.1 (2019).

Jordan, Erin, 'Hostage, Sister, Abbess: The Life of Iveta of Jerusalem', in *Medieval Prosopography: History and Collective Biography,* Vol. 32, (2017).

Jotischky, Andrew, *Crusading and the Crusader States.* (Pearson Longman, 2004).

Kedar, Benjamin Z., *Franks, Muslims and Oriental Christians in the Latin Levant.* (Ashgate Publishing Ltd, 2006).

Kostick, Conor (ed.), *The Crusades and the Near East.* (Routledge, 2011).

Laiou, Ageliki, 'Byzantine Trade with Christians and Muslims and the Crusades', in *The Crusades from the Perspective of Byzantium and the Muslim World.* Edited by Angeliki Laiou and Roy Parvis Mottahedeh. (Washington: Dumbarton Oaks Research Library and Collection, 2001).

La Monte, John L., *Feudal Monarchy in the Latin Kingdom of Jerusalem, 1100 to 1291.* (Medieval Academy of America, 1932).

La Monte, John L., 'John d'Ibelin': The Old Lord of Beirut, 1177–1236, in *Byzantion*, Vol. 1/2 (1937).

Lotan, Shlomo, 'The Battle of La Forbie (1244) and its Aftermath – Re-Examination of the Military Orders' Involvement in the Latin Kingdom of Jerusalem in the Mid-Thirteenth Century', in *Ordines Militares*, Vol. XVII. (2012).

Maalouf, Amin, *The Crusades through Arab Eyes.* (Schocken Books, 1984).

MacEvitt, Christopher, *The Crusades and the Christian World of the East: Rough Tolerance.* (University of Pennsylvania Press, 2008).

Madden, Thomas, *The Concise History of the Crusades.* (Rowman & Littlefield, 2014).

Marshall, Christopher, *Warfare in the Latin East 1192–1291.* (Cambridge University Press, 1992).

Mayer, Hans Eberhard, *Kings and Lords in the Latin Kingdom of Jerusalem.* (Ashgate Publishing Ltd, 1994).

Mayer, Hans Eberhard, *Probleme des lateinischen Koenigreichs Jerusalem*. (Variorum Reprints, 1983).

Miller, Peter, *Die Kreuzzuege: Krieg im Namen Gottes*. (Bertelsmann, 1988).

Miller, David, *Richard the Lionheart: The Mighty Crusader*. (Phoenix, 2013).

Miller, Timothy S., and Nesbitt, John W., *Walking Corpses: Leprosy in Byzantium and the Medieval West*. (Cornell University Press, 2014).

Mitchell, Piers D., *Medicine in the Crusades: Warfare, Wounds and the Medieval Surgeon*. (Cambridge University Press, 2004).

Mitchell, Piers D., 'The Spread of Disease with the Crusades', in *Between Text and Patient: The Medical Enterprise in Medieval and Early Modern Europe*. Edited by B. Nance, B and E.F. Glaze. (Florence: Sismel, 2011).

Morgan, M.R., *The Chronicle of Ernoul and the Continuations of William of Tyre*. (Oxford Historical Monographs, Oxford University Press, 1973).

Morton, Nicholas, *The Teutonic Knights in the Holy Land, 1190–1291*. (Boydell, 2009).

Morton, Nicholas, 'Weapons of War: Turkish Archers vs. Frankish Heavy Cavalry', in *History Today*, May 2018.

Mount, Toni, *Medieval Medicine*. (Amberley, 2015).

Mount, Toni, *The Medieval Housewife & Other Women of the Middle Ages*. (Amberley, 2014).

Mourad, Suleiman, 'Jerusalem in Early Islam: The Making of the Muslims' Holy City', in Routledge *Handbook on Jerusalem*. (Routledge, 2019).

Nicholson, Helen, *The Knights Templar: A New History*. (Sutton Publishing, 2001).

Nicholson, Helen, 'Charity and Hospitality in Military Orders', in Isabel Cristina Ferreira Fernandes (coord.). *As Ordens Militares. Freires, Guerreiros, Cavaleiros. Actas do VI Encontro sobre Ordens Militares*, Vol. 1, Portugal: Palmela, (2012).

Nicholson, Helen, 'The Role of Women in the Military Orders', in *Militiae Christi: Handelingen van de Vereniging voor de Studie over de Tempeliers en de Hospitaalridders vzw*, Year 1 (2010).

Nicholson, Helen, 'Women and the Crusades', in *Remarks before the Hereford Historical Association*, (22 February 2008).

Nicholson, Helen, 'Woman on the Third Crusade', in *Journal of Medieval History*, Vol. 23, No 4, (1997).

Nicolaou-Konnari, Angel, and Schabel, Chris, *Cyprus: Society and Culture 1191–1374*. (Brill, 2005).

Nicolle, David, *Hattin 1187: Saladin's Greatest Victory*. (Osprey Military Campaign Series, 1993).

Pernoud, Regine, *Women in the Days of the Cathedrals*. (Ignatius, San Francisco, 1998).

Perry, Guy, *John of Brienne: King of Jerusalem, Emperor of Constantinople, c. 1175–1237*. (Cambridge University Press, 2013).

Phillips, Jonathan, *Defenders of the Holy Land: Relations between the Latin East and West, 1119–1187*. (Oxford University Press, 1996).

Phillips, Jonathan, *The Life and Legend of the Sultan Saladin*. (Yale University Press, 2019).

Pringle, Denys, *Secular Buildings in the Crusader Kingdom of Jerusalem: An Archaeological Gazetteer*. (Cambridge University Press, 1997).

Reynolds, Gordon M., 'Opportunism & Duty: Gendered Perceptions of Women's Involvement in Crusade Negotiation and Mediation (1147–1254)', in *Medieval Feminist Forum*, Vol. 5, # 2, (April 2019).

Robinson, John and Dungeon, J., *Fire and Sword: The Knights Templar in the Crusades*. (Michael O'Mara Books, 1991).

Roehricht, Reinhold, *Die Geschichte des Koenigreichs Jerusalem (1100–1291)*. (Cambridge University Press, 2004).

Riley-Smith, Jonathan, *The Crusades: A History*. (Bloomsbury Academic, 2014).

Riley-Smith, Jonathan, *The Feudal Nobility and the Kingdom of Jerusalem, 1174–1277*. (Macmillan, 1973).

Riley-Smith, Jonathan, *Hospitallers: The History of the Order of St. John*. (Hambledon Press, 1999).

Riley-Smith, Jonathan (ed.), *The Atlas of the Crusades*. (Facts on File, 1991).

Runciman, Sir Steven, *The Families of Outremer: The Feudal Nobility of the Crusader Kingdom of Jerusalem, 1099–1291*. (The Athlone Press, 1960).

Smail, R.C., *Crusading Warfare 1097–1193*. (Cambridge University Press, 1956).

Stark, Rodney, *God's Battalions: The Case for the Crusades*. (HarperCollins, 2010).

Suhr, Heiko, *Friedrich II von Hohenstaufen: Seine politischen und kulturellen Verbindungen zum Islam*. (Grin Verlag, 2008).

Tibble, Steve, *The Crusader Armies*. (Yale University Press, 2018).

Tyerman, Christopher, *How to Plan a Crusade: Reason and Religious War in the Middle Ages*. (Allen Lane, 2015).

Tyerman, Christopher, *The World of the Crusades: An Illustrated History*. (Yale University Press, 2019).

Ward, Jennifer C., *English Noblewomen in the Later Middle Ages*. (Longman, London, 1992).

Ye'or, Bat, *The Decline of Eastern Christianity under Islam: From Jihad to Dhimmitude*. (Fairleigh Dickinson University Press, 1996).

Van Cleve, Thomas Curtis, *The Emperor Frederick II of Hohenstaufen: Immutator Mundi*. (Oxford University Press, 1972).

Zacour, Norman P., and Hazard, Harry W.) *A History of the Crusades Volume Five: The Impact of the Crusades on the Near East*. (Wisconsin University Press, 1985).

Index

144, 148, 165, 168–69, 182–185, 187,
196–97, 199–200, 210, 212, 227–30
Guy, Duke of Athens 106

Hattin, Battle of 132, 139, 144–45, 148–49,
183, 199, 229
Heiresses 9, 34, 54, 65–66, 95–96, 98, 102,
104–11, 115, 119, 121, 127, 133, 148–49,
162, 169, 172–73, 180, 182, 188–89, 222
Helena, St and Roman Empress 16–17
Henri de Champagne, Consort of Isabella I
59, 60–62, 74, 84, 97, 101, 131, 163, 173,
176–177, 184, 186, 201–202, 213, 215
Henry I, King of Cyprus 74–77, 95, 174–176,
178, 190, 193
Henry II, King of Cyprus 71–72, 95
Henry II, King of England 9, 130
Henry VI, Holy Roman Emperor 60, 185
High Court 32, 34, 37, 39–40, 42, 44–48,
53–56, 62–65, 68–70, 74–77, 96–97,
99–100, 102, 104–09, 111–16, 118–21,
123–25, 127–28, 161, 167–70, 172,
174–76, 178–80, 184, 187–88, 195–201,
208–10, 212, 215, 217–19, 221–28
Hodierna, Countess Consort of Raymond II
of Tripoli 109, 128–129, 181, 206–207
Homage 42, 48–49, 53, 55–57, 59, 61, 69, 74,
76–77, 95, 103–04, 108, 119, 131, 174–6,
178, 183, 185, 192, 196, 198–201, 212
Hospitallers 49, 57, 66, 84, 87, 130, 148, 157,
159, 211
Hostages 33, 78, 106, 113–14, 127, 129,
151–52, 163, 179, 186, 189, 203, 206–07
Household 21–22, 92, 102, 105, 122, 125,
130, 133–34, 145, 155, 166, 172, 182, 184,
188, 207, 211
Hugh d'Ibelin, Husband of Agnes de
Courtenay 39, 40, 44, 125, 167–168
Hugh, Duke of Burgundy 96, 97, 183, 227
Hugh I, King of Cyprus 63, 73, 95, 173–174,
179, 185, 188, 202, 213
Hugh II, King of Cyprus 109, 119
Hugh III, King of Cyprus 71, 95, 109, 120
Hugh of Jaffa 34–35, 115–116, 122, 166,
170–172, 218–219
Humphrey of Toron II, Lord of Toron
126, 221–222
Humphrey of Toron III, Lord of Toron 107
Humphrey of Toron IV, First Husband of
Isabella I 54–57, 100, 126–127, 149, 163,
168, 177, 194–200, 209, 212–213

Icons x, 73, 137–38,
Illumination and Illustration 135,
137–38, 164
Imad al-Din 36

Inheritance Laws 103, 196
Innocent III, Pope 65, 82
Isabella d'Ibelin, Lady of Beirut 109–110,
119–121, 131
Isabella I, Queen of Jerusalem 42, 44, 47–48,
53–62, 97–98, 100–101, 107–108, 119,
126–128, 142, 163, 168, 173–174, 176–
177, 183, 186, 193–202, 206, 208–210,
213–215
Isabella II, Queen of Jerusalem see Yolanda of
Jerusalem
Islam ix, 12–13, 17–19, 21, 36, 41, 112, 126,
151, 156, 158, 206
*Itinerarium Peregrinorum et Gesta Regis
Ricardi* 53, 54, 55, 56, 60, 83, 143
Iveta, Abbess of St Lazarus 33, 113, 128–29,
130, 206–08, 225

Jaffa, City of 25, 27, 29, 59–61, 71, 110, 143,
145, 155, 184
Jaffa, Counts of see Amalric I; Guy de
Lusignan; Hugh of Jaffa; John d'Ibelin;
and William de Montferrat respectively
Jerusalem: City of 129;
Kingdom of 14, 32, 36, 38, 41–42, 44, 46,
48, 51–52, 54, 59–60, 62–63, 65–66,
68–70, 72–73, 78, 92, 96–97, 99–100,
104, 108, 112–13, 118–19, 122, 127,
130, 165, 168, 171, 177–78, 184, 186,
189, 192, 194, 199–200, 203, 208–09,
212–13, 217, 220, 223, 225–27, 230;
Kings of 30–31, 42, 49, 57, 65–66, 69–70,
72, 74, 76, 94–95, 97, 99, 109, 114, 119,
124, 167, 175, 180, 183, 193–94, 201,
204, 211, 221, 223, 225, 227;
Queens of 41, 43, 50, 55–56, 59, 61, 67,
71–72, 78, 95, 115, 128, 168, 173,
193–94, 202, 206–08, 214–16, 224, 229;
Siege (1099) ix, xiii, 18, 25–29, 88, 142;
Siege (1187) ix, 49–51, 63, 70, 95, 143–44,
146–48, 153, 165, 200, 211–12, 229–30;
Siege (1244) 70–71
Jewish Law 157
Jews ix, 14, 16, 21, 25, 72, 106, 129, 138, 154,
194, 209
Jihad 18, 44, 71
Joanna Plantagenet, Dowager Queen of
Sicily 84–87
John d'Ibelin I, Lord of Beirut 62, 63, 65,
67–68, 74, 77, 100, 173, 178, 188–89, 192,
194, 213, 215–16
John d'Ibelin II, Lord of Beirut 109,
119–120, 193
John d'Ibelin, Count of Jaffa 98, 113
John d'Ibelin, the "old lord of Beirut" see John
d'Ibelin I